Entrepreneur
MAGAZINE'S

# ULTIMATE

## GUIDE TO

## WORKERS' COMPENSATION INSURANCE

*Secrets for Reducing Workers'*
*Compensation Costs*

## EDWARD J. PRIZ

EP Entrepreneur Press

Editorial Director: Jere Calmes
Cover Design: Beth Hansen-Winter
Composition: CWL Publishing Enterprises, Inc., Madison, Wisconsin, www.cwlpub.com

© 2005 by Entrepreneur Media, Inc.

All rights reserved.
Reproduction of any part of this work beyond that permitted by Section 107 or 108 of the 1976 United States Copyright Act without the express permission of the copyright owner is unlawful. Requests for permission or further information should be addressed to the Business Products Division, Entrepreneur Media, Inc.

This publication is designed to provide accurate and authoritative information in regard to the subject matter covered. It is sold with the understanding that the publisher is not engaged in rendering legal, accounting, or other professional services. If legal advice or other expert assistance is required, the services of a competent professional person should be sought.

> —From a Declaration of Principles jointly adopted by a
> Committee of the American Bar Association and
> a Committee of Publishers and Associations

This Book contains copyrighted material owend by the National Council on Compensation Insurance, Inc. ("NCCI"), which is used with NCCI's permission. NCCI's material may not be reproduced, in whole or in part, without NCCI's express written consent.

ISBN 1-932531-50-5


**Library of Congress Cataloging-in-Publication Data**

Priz, Edward J., 1952-
  Entrepreneur magazine's ultimate guide to workers' compensation insurance / by Edward J. Priz.
    p. cm.
  ISBN 1-932531-50-5 (alk. paper)
  1. Workers' compensation--United States. I. Title.
HD7103.65.U6P753 2005
368.4'1--dc22

                                                              2005008977

10 09 08 07 06 05                 Printed in Canada          10 9 8 7 6 5 4 3 2 1

# Contents

Dedicated to

**Howard Alper**

**with thanks for showing the way**

# Preface

COMMERCIAL INSURANCE (WHICH VERY MUCH includes workers' compensation) has been much in the news over the past year, what with New York State Attorney General Elliot Spitzer uncovering serious abuses on the part of major insurance brokers and insurance companies on a fairly regular basis. Well-known and respected insurance firms have suffered unflattering revelations in the press (along with costly settlements) that would have been unthinkable not very long ago.

Yet as a long-time observer of the field, I have to admit I haven't been completely surprised by these recent news stories. It's long been my contention that the American insurance industry is fairly under-regulated, given the financial impact it has on industry. We see and hear news reports on a daily basis about the gyrations of the stock market, or the latest pronouncements from the Federal Reserve, but rarely do the workings of the insurance industry break through in the non-trade news media. Perhaps the scandals uncovered by Mr. Spitzer will change that. Or perhaps things will return to the status quo when Mr. Spitzer runs for governor. But I believe that all business owners and managers should remember these matters for years to come, because otherwise the mistakes and abuses will resume. And it is employers who will ultimately foot the bill.

I've worked as a consultant on workers' compensation cost since the early 1980's, and in that time I've been unpleasantly surprised at how often mistakes occur that overcharge employers. These overcharges are often far from trivial, and yet are accepted as just the way the system operates. Employers need to exercise greater vigilance to catch these inadvertent overcharges, yet they are at a distinct disadvantage. Workers' compensation insurance is a complicated and technical field, and so employers often have to rely on the expertise and advice of the very people who are selling the product. The intent of this book is to remedy that situation a bit.

*Entrepreneur Magazine's Ultimate Guide to Workers' Compensation Insurance* can't turn every reader into an insurance expert, of course. Even employers who study this guide voraciously will still need to rely on insurance agents, brokers, consultants, and insurance companies, to properly take care of their workers' compensation needs. But I've tried to level the playing field a bit, by explaining these technical matters in a way that (I hope) the non-professional will find enlightening.

I often like to suggest to employers that they adopt an attitude once quoted by President Ronald Reagan. When talking about arms treaties with the Soviet Union, he cited a Russian proverb that he translated as "Trust, but verify". I believe this should also be the approach of employers who purchase workers' compensation insurance and want to make they aren't overcharged or shortchanged on coverage. Of course a qualified insurance agent or broker should be of great assistance in these matters, but I don't believe that a prudent employer can leave it all to the professionals. Mr. Spitzer has documented the folly of that approach.

Every employer needs to understand that even with the assistance of competent insurance agents and brokers, workers' compensation overcharges can and do occur. This is not to suggest some vast conspiracy within the insurance industry. It's been my experience that most insurance professionals are ethical and conscien-

tious. It's just that with inadequate regulation and oversight, even ethical and conscientious people can develop tunnel vision.

The insurance industry is very vigilant about catching those who would defraud them by falsifying claims or by trying to improperly reduce premiums by means of trickery and deceit. And certainly every ethical employer should applaud those efforts, as every instance of successful insurance fraud means that higher costs need to be born by those who play by the rules. But over the decades I've observed that the insurance industry just doesn't devote anywhere near the same level of vigilance to making sure that premium overcharges get caught and corrected. If they did, I wouldn't be able to make a living by catching and correcting them.

But that means that it's up to employers to try to protect themselves from these overcharges. And it doesn't matter if your company is large or small—I've observed overcharges victimizing large national corporations, as well as small machine shops. I've seen overcharges occur to employers who worked with small local insurance agencies, as well as to employers utilizing the services of large national brokers. The problem is endemic and largely overlooked.

But with the information contained in *Entrepreneur Magazine's Ultimate Guide to Workers' Compensation Insurance*, I believe employers can go a long way towards protecting themselves from the most common causes of premium overcharges. And along the way, they can learn more about how to select an insurance agent or broker, what kinds of policies might best suit their needs, and how to tell fact from fiction about how Workers' Compensation insurance is priced, sold, and serviced.

I'd like to also thank a couple of folks who assisted my in putting this book together—my assistants Scott Priz, who helped with research, and Apatcha Chong, who helped organize and layout some of the graphics in the book. And of course, my thanks to John Woods of CWL Publshing, the production manager of *Entrepreneur Magazine's Ultimate Guide to* *Workers' Compensation Insurance,* for his invaluable assistance and patience with me as this work was shaped into its final form.

Workers' Compensation is a vital concern for almost every employer in the U.S. I hope this book helps them better understand how to wisely work with the insurance system to insure their needs at a fair and proper cost.

# CHAPTER 1

# The Big Picture

ALMOST EVERY BUSINESS IN THE UNITED States that has employees has to handle the problem of workers' compensation. Most states (with a few important exceptions) essentially require employers to purchase an insurance policy to handle their statutory obligations to workers who are injured or made ill due to a workplace exposure. Whether your business is small or large, handling the expense and effort of meeting those statutory obligations is an ever-present challenge.

As a consultant to employers on their workers' compensation cost and coverage, I've seen firsthand that the cost of workers' compensation is virtually a universal concern of business owners and managers, no matter the size or type of the enterprise. Whether working with a small machine shop that employs 30 people or a Fortune 100 corporation that employs thousands

across many states, I've found that the details may vary but the concern remains the same: how can the voracious cost of workers' compensation be controlled effectively?

Some researchers have suggested that the earliest roots of workers' compensation can be traced back to the code of Caribbean pirates: those who were injured plying their dangerous trade would be compensated with shares of booty taken by their able-bodied fellow buccaneers. Colorful as that conjecture may be, workers' compensation requirements in the United States began early in the 20th century, back in 1911.

Before then, workers who had been injured or made ill on the job had to take legal action against their employers, resulting in a system that simultaneously made it difficult for workers to obtain compensation for such injuries and yet exposed employers to potentially devastating financial penalties under the tort system. Beginning in 1911, a historic compromise solution was devised by the various states. Wisconsin was the first, but other states quickly followed, enacting a "no fault" system intended to make sure workers received fair and prompt medical treatment and financial compensation for workplace injuries and illness. This compromise system also established limits on the obligations of employers for these workplace exposures, so that the costs could be made more predictable and affordable.

Today, modern workers' compensation laws provide fairly comprehensive and specific benefits to workers who suffer workplace injury or illness. Benefits include medical expenses, death benefits, lost wages, and vocational rehabilitation. Failure to carry workers' compensation insurance or otherwise meet a state's regulations in this regard can leave an employer exposed not only to paying these benefits out of pocket, but also to paying penalties levied by the states.

But our federal system in the United States means that workers' compensation regulations, for the most part, are the jurisdiction of the individual states. There are some federal workers' compensation statutes, such as for longshoremen and harbor workers, but for most employers the system of workers' compensation rules and regulations they usually deal with is enacted by the states (along with Washington D.C. and Puerto Rico). This means that workers' compensation in the United States has something of a patchwork quality to it. There are great similarities among the workers' compensation systems enacted by the various jurisdictions, but also important differences.

## HOW STATES DIFFER

In most jurisdictions, employers can meet their workers' compensation obligations by purchasing an insurance policy from an insurance company. However, five states and two U.S. territories require employers to get coverage exclusively through state-operated funds. If you are an employer doing business in any of these jurisdictions, you need to obtain coverage from the specified government-run fund. These are commonly called *monopoly state funds*. A business cannot meet its workers' compensation obligations in these jurisdictions with private insurance.

### ▼ THE OPTION STATES

Here an employer can use either the state fund or private insurance: Arizona, California, Colorado, Idaho, Maryland, Michigan, Minnesota, Montana, New York, Oklahoma, Oregon, Pennsylvania, or Utah.

Nevada was a monopoly state until recently, but now this state has shifted to a system utilizing private insurance and the former state fund has morphed into a mutual insurance company. Thirteen other states also maintain a state fund,

### ▼ MONOPOLY STATE FUNDS

Your business must use the monopoly state fund for workers' compensation if you have employees in North Dakota, Ohio, Puerto Rico, the U.S. Virgin Islands, Washington, West Virginia, or Wyoming.

but the state funds compete with private insurance. In these states, an employer has an option (at least theoretically) to use either the state fund or private insurance.

## THE STATE-BY-STATE MOSAIC

Since workers' compensation is primarily regulated by the individual states (and territories), there is no one single cohesive set of rules governing benefits, coverage, or premium computation. Even if you have considerable experience in dealing with one state's workers' compensation system, if your business expands to a different state you can easily find yourself dealing with very different rules.

The closest thing there is to a uniform set of rules for premium computation are those established by the National Council on Compensation Insurance (NCCI, www.ncci.com). This organization creates policy forms and writes the rules for premium computation in a bare majority of states.

NCCI is what used to be called a "rating bureau." Nowadays the organization tends to prefer the term "advisory organization," although a lot of folks still use the older term. NCCI performs a number of important tasks for the workers' compensation system in the states that use NCCI. It gathers the statistical data from insurance companies that is used to develop rates, for instance. It also creates the standardized policy forms that are approved by state insurance regulators. Perhaps most importantly, from the standpoint of those who buy workers' compensation insurance, NCCI writes the manuals that govern how workers' compensation insurance premiums are calculated.

If you have a high tolerance for technical and obtuse language, try reading the fine print of your workers' compensation insurance policy. If you stick with it, you may notice something interesting: the policy itself doesn't really spell out how the premiums for the insurance are calculated. Instead, the policy states that premiums on the policy are just an estimate and that the final actual premiums for the coverage will be calculated in accordance with the insurance company's manuals of rules.

But in practice, insurance companies don't write their own manuals of rules. Instead, they find it more practical to use the manuals developed by rating bureaus like NCCI. (Remember: NCCI isn't the rating bureau in all states. Some states maintain their own independent rating bureaus. These other bureaus also develop manuals that govern premium computation in their particular states.)

Also, even among the various NCCI states there can be important differences. Some states tinker with NCCI rules in various ways, so that in some fundamental rules there can be very important differences even among NCCI states.

So to figure out what rules govern the computation of your workers' compensation insurance premiums, you have to first identify the states and then figure out which rating bureau (and thus which manual of rules) has jurisdiction in those particular states.

Here's a state-by-state listing of the workers' compensation jurisdictions and which rating bureau each uses.

### Alabama

Alabama is an NCCI state, which means that workers' compensation insurance premiums in the state are calculated in accordance with manual rules of classification, premium development, and experience rating developed by the National Council on Compensation Insurance. Employers must either purchase private insurance or be authorized to self-insure (realistic only for larger employers). Insurance is regulated by:

Department of Insurance
201 Monroe Street, Suite 1700
Montgomery, AL 36130
phone: 334 269-3550
web: www.aldoi.gov

Sole proprietors and partners are not required to cover themselves, but can elect to be covered. Corporate officers are covered but may elect to be exempted from coverage (and thus premiums).

Independent contractors with fewer than five employees who work on construction of single-family dwellings can file for an exemption from WC coverage; this holds harmless those contracting with such independent contractors.

The premium portion of overtime pay can be deducted from computation of workers' compensation premiums, in accordance with NCCI rules.

## Alaska

Alaska is an NCCI state, which means that workers' compensation insurance premiums in the state are calculated in accordance with manual rules of classification, premium development, and experience rating developed by the National Council on Compensation Insurance. Employers must either purchase private insurance or be authorized to self-insure (realistic only for larger employers). Insurance is regulated by:

Division of Workers' Compensation
P.O. Box 25512
Juneau, AK 99802-5512
phone: 907 465-2790
web: labor.state.ak.us/wc/home.htm

Sole proprietors and partners are not required to cover themselves, but can elect to be covered. Corporate officers are covered but may elect to be exempted from coverage (and thus premiums).

Employers are liable for and must insure independent contractors and subcontractors unless those contractors have their own WC insurance.

The premium portion of overtime pay can be deducted from computation of workers' compensation premiums, in accordance with NCCI rules.

## Arizona

Arizona is an NCCI state, which means that workers' compensation insurance premiums in the state are calculated in accordance with manual rules of classification, premium development, and experience rating developed by the National Council on Compensation Insurance. Employers must purchase private insurance, use the state WC fund, or be authorized to self-insure (realistic only for larger employers). Insurance is regulated by:

Department of Insurance
Consumer Complaint Department
2910 N. 44th Street, Suite 210
Phoenix, AZ 85018
phone: 602 912-8444
web: www.id.state.az.us

In addition to private insurance, Arizona maintains a state-administered workers' compensation fund (www.statefund.com) that competes with private insurers. In fact, the Arizona WC fund is the largest provider of workers' compensation insurance in Arizona.

Sole proprietors and partners are not required to cover themselves, but can elect to be covered. Corporate officers are covered but may elect to be exempted from coverage (and thus premiums).

Contractors and subcontractors who perform work separate from clients' normal work and who are not supervised by clients during execution of that work are considered independent contractors, not employees for purposes of workers' compensation.

The premium portion of overtime pay can be deducted from computation of workers' compensation premiums, in accordance with NCCI rules.

## Arkansas

Arkansas is an NCCI state, which means that workers' compensation insurance premiums in the state are calculated in accordance with manual rules of classification, premium development, and experience rating developed by the National Council on Compensation Insurance. Employers must either purchase private insurance or be authorized to self-insure (realistic only for larger employers).

Workers' compensation is regulated by:

Workers' Compensation Commission
P.O. Box 950
Little Rock, AR 72203-0950
phone: 800 622-4472
web: www.awcc.state.ar.us/

## California

The largest single market for workers' compensation, this state operates by its own rules, not those of the NCCI. The rules and regulations pertaining to workers' compensation classifications, premium development, and experience rating are created by the Workers' Compensation Insurance Rating Bureau of California.

The mailing address is:

Workers' Compensation Insurance Rating Bureau of California
525 Market Street, Suite 800
San Francisco, CA 94105-2767
phone: 415 777-0777
web: wcirbonline.org

Insurance (including workers' compensation insurance) is regulated by:

Department of Insurance
Consumer Communications Bureau
300 South Spring Street, South Tower
Los Angeles, CA 90013
phone: 213 897-8921 or 800 927-4357
Division of Workers' Compensation
P.O. Box 420603
San Francisco, CA 94142
phone: 415 703-4600
web: www.dir.ca.gov/DWC/dwc_home_page. htm

Employers in California can choose between private insurers or the state-administered WC fund (www.scif.com). They can also elect to self-insure, if they meet the requirements imposed by California, but this is typically feasible only for larger employers.

Sole proprietors and general partners are not

required to cover themselves, but can elect to be covered. Working partners of a partnership are covered. Officers and directors of a corporation who are also its sole shareholders are not covered but may elect coverage. Officers and directors who are not the sole shareholders of the corporation are covered and are included in premium computation.

Contractors and subcontractors who are not supervised by clients during execution of that work are considered independent contractors and not employees for purposes of workers' compensation.

## Colorado

An NCCI state, Colorado also maintained a state WC fund that evolved into a nonprofit insurance company specializing in writing Colorado workers' compensation. This entity competes with other private, for-profit insurance companies.

Insurance (including workers' compensation) is regulated by:

Division of Insurance
Department of Regulatory Agencies
1560 Broadway, Suite 850
Denver, CO 80202
phone: 303 894-7499
web: www.dora.state.co.us/insurance

Division of Workers' Compensation
1515 Arapahoe Street
Tower 2, Suite 500
Denver, CO 80202-2117
phone: 888 390-7936
web: www.coworkforce.com/DWC

Sole proprietors and partners are not required to cover themselves, but can elect to be covered. Corporate officers are covered, but

those who own at least 10 percent of the corporations stock may elect to be exempted from coverage (and thus premium).

Independent contractors and subcontractors are considered employees of their clients unless they meet certain very specific criteria for independence and both parties sign a notarized document that spells out how these criteria are met.

## Connecticut

Connecticut is an NCCI state. Insurance is regulated by:

Insurance Department
P.O. Box 816
Hartford, CT 06142-0816
phone: 860 297-3800 or 800 203-3447
web: www.ct.gov/cid

Workers' Compensation Commission
Capitol Place
21 Oak Street, Fourth Floor
Hartford, CT 06106
phone: 860 493-1500
fax: 860 247-1361
web: wcc.state.ct.us/

## Delaware

Delaware and Pennsylvania share a unique non-NCCI classification system that does not match up one for one with the NCCI classification system. Additionally, unlike most other states, the premium portion of payroll is not deductible for purposes of calculating workers' compensation premiums.

Workers' compensation is regulated by:

Office of Workers' Compensation
State Office Building, Sixth Floor
820 North French Street

Wilmington, DE 19801
phone: 302 761-8200
web: www.delawareworks.com/industrialaf-
fairs/ services/workerscomp.shtml

Other insurance is regulated by:

Office of Insurance Commissioner
841 Silver Lake Boulevard, Rodney Building
Dover, DE 19904
phone: 302 739-4251

Delaware Compensation Rating Bureau, Inc.
1 South Penn Square
Widener Building, 6th Floor
Philadelphia, PA 19107
phone: 302 654-1435
web: www.dcrb.com

## District of Columbia

DC is an NCCI jurisdiction, so workers' compensation is written by private insurers. The
District does not maintain any kind of state
fund. Insurance (including workers' compensation) is regulated by:

Department of Insurance, Securities and
Banking
810 First Street, NE, Suite 701
Washington, DC 20002
phone: 202 727-8000
web: www.disr.washingtondc.gov/disr

## Florida

Florida is an NCCI state. This means that workers' compensation is provided by private insurance companies that follow the rules and
regulations developed by NCCI. Insurance,
including workers' compensation, is regulated by:

Department of Financial Services

200 East Gaines Street
Tallahassee, FL 32399-0300
phone: 800 342-2762
web: www.fldfs.com/

Workers' compensation insurance is handled
by a division of the above department:

Division of Workers' Compensation
200 East Gaines Street
Tallahassee, FL 32399-4228
phone: 800 742-2214 or 850 413-1601
web: www.fldfs.com/WC/index.htm

## Georgia

Georgia is an NCCI state, so workers' compensation is provided by private insurance companies.
Insurance (including workers' compensation) is
regulated by:

Insurance Commissioner
2 Martin Luther King Jr. Drive SE
West Tower, Suite 716
Atlanta, GA 30334
phone: 404 656-2070 or 800 656-2298
web: www.inscomm.state.ga.us/

## Hawaii

Hawaii is an NCCI state. Until a few years ago,
Hawaii operated its own independent rating
bureau. Insurance (including workers' compensation) is regulated by:

Insurance Division
Department of Commerce and Consumer
Affairs
P.O. Box 3614
Honolulu, HI 96811
phone: 808 586-2790
web: www.state.hi.us/dcca/ins/

## Idaho

Idaho is an NCCI state. This means that workers' compensation can be written by private insurance companies, which follow the manual rules developed by NCCI. Insurance (including workers' compensation) is regulated by:

Department of Insurance
P.O. Box 83720
Boise, ID 83720-0043
phone: 208 334-4398
web: www.doi.state.id.us/

However, Idaho also maintains a state insurance fund that competes with private insurance companies to write workers' compensation coverage for employers.

Idaho State Insurance Fund
1215 West State Street
P.O. Box 83720
Boise, ID 83720-0044
phone: 208 332-2100 or 800 334-2370
web: www.state.id.us/isif/index.htm

## Illinois

Illinois is an NCCI state, so that workers' compensation is provided by private insurance companies following NCCI manual rules. Assigned risk coverage is through a pooling mechanism administered by NCCI. Insurance, including workers' compensation, is regulated by:

Department of Financial and Professional
Regulation
Division of Insurance
320 West Washington Street
Springfield, IL 62767-0001
phone: 217 782-4515
web: www.ins.state.il.us/default2.htm

## Indiana

Many people in the insurance business believe that Indiana is an NCCI state. This is not so. Indiana maintains its own independent rating bureau, the Indiana Compensation Rating Bureau. This bureau uses NCCI for ratemaking and uses the NCCI manual, *The Scopes® of Basic Manual Classifications* (the *Scopes® Manual*), but does not always follow NCCI classification interpretations. For some classification codes, the Indiana rules can be significantly different from NCCI guidelines. Furthermore, the state exceptions for Indiana listed in the Scopes® Manual are not complete. For classification decisions in Indiana, it's best to contact the ICRB directly.

Indiana Compensation Rating Bureau
5920 Castleway West Drive
Indianapolis, IN 46250
P.O. Box 50400
phone: 317 842-2800 or 800 622-4208
fax: 317 842-3717
web: www.icrb.net
e-mail: icrb@icrb.net

Indiana also allows independent contractors in the construction trades and owner/operator truckers to file a Certificate of Exemption with the Indiana Department of Revenue. This certificate of exemption qualifies the independent contractor to not carry workers' compensation insurance and establishes that companies that use such independent contractors are also not liable for workers' compensation liabilities or premium charges for those exempt independent contractors or owner/operators.

Insurance, including workers' compensation insurance, is regulated overall by:

Department of Insurance
311 West Washington Street, Suite 300
Indianapolis, IN 46204-2787
phone: 317 232-2385
web: www.state.in.us/idoi/

However, according to a 1998 *Wall Street Journal* article, Indiana's Department of Insurance is kept deliberately powerless to actually do anything about insurance problems and complaints, so the above link is provided with a very large grain of salt. Even if you find a clear overcharge by an insurance company, the Indiana Department of Insurance may well have no authority to require the carrier to correct the mistake.

## Iowa

Iowa is an NCCI state. Coverage is provided by private insurance companies. Insurance is regulated by:

Insurance Department
330 Maple Street
Des Moines, IA 50319-0065
phone: 515 281-5705 or 877 955-1212
web: www.iid.state.ia.us/

Claims and benefits are regulated by:
Division of Workers' Compensation
1000 East Grand Avenue
Des Moines, IA 50319-0209
phone: 515 281-5387 or 800 JOB-IOWA
(562-4692)
fax: 515 281-6501
e-mail: IWD.DWC@iwd.state.ia.us
web: www.iowaworkforce.org/wc

## Kansas

Kansas is an NCCI state. Workers' compensation coverage provided by private insurance.

Insurance is regulated by:

Insurance Department
420 SW Ninth Street
Topeka, KS 66612
phone: 785 296-3071
web: www.ksinsurance.org

Claims and benefits regulated by:

Kansas Workers' Compensation
800 SW Jackson, Suite 600
Topeka, KS 66612-1227
phone: 785 296-3441 or 800 332-0353
web: www.dol.ks.gov/wc/html/wc_ALL.html

## Kentucky

Kentucky is an NCCI state. Workers' compensation is provided by private insurance. Insurance is regulated by:

Office of Insurance
215 West Main Street
Frankfort, KY 40601
phone: 502 564-3630 or 800 595-6053
web: doi.ppr.ky.gov/kentucky

## Louisiana

Louisiana is an NCCI state. Workers' compensation is provided by private insurance companies. Insurance is regulated by:

Department of Insurance
1702 North Third Street
Baton Rouge, LA 70802
phone: 225 342-5900 or 800 259-5300
web: wwwldi.ldi.state.la.us/

Claims and benefits are regulated by:

Office of Workers' Compensation
Administration
P.O. Box 94040

Baton Rouge, LA 70804-9040
phone: 225 342-7555
fax: 225 342-5665
web: www.ldol.state.la.us/bus_owca.asp

## Maine

Maine is an NCCI state. Workers' compensation is provided through private insurance companies. Insurance is regulated by:

Department of Professional and Financial Regulation
Bureau of Insurance
Consumer Services Division
34 State House Station
Augusta, ME 04333-0034
phone: 207 624-8475 or 800 300-5000
fax: 207 624-8599
web: www.state.me.us/pfr/ins/ins_index.htm

## Maryland

Maryland is an NCCI state. Workers' compensation is provided through private insurance companies. Insurance is regulated by:

Insurance Administration
525 St. Paul Place
Baltimore, MD 21202-2272
phone: 410 468-2000 or 800 492-6116
web: www.mdinsurance.state.md.us/

## Massachusetts

Massachusetts maintains its own independent rating bureau, the Workers' Compensation Rating and Inspection Bureau. So, although workers' compensation is provided by private insurance companies, they do not follow the manual rules of NCCI, but rather the manual rules of the WCRIB.

Workers' Compensation Rating and Inspection
Bureau of Massachusetts
101 Arch Street
Boston, MA 02110
phone: 617 439-9030
fax: 617 439-6055
web: www.wcribma.org/mass

Insurance (including workers' compensation) is regulated by:

Division of Insurance
Consumer Affairs
1 South Station, 5th Floor
Boston, MA 02110-2208
phone: 617 521-7794
web: www.mass.gov/doi/

## Michigan

Michigan is not an NCCI state, but maintains its own separate independent rating organization, the Compensation Advisory Organization of Michigan (CAOM)—with an important caveat: in Michigan, there is no regulation of classification codes for voluntary (non-assigned risk) workers' comp. CAOM also administers the Michigan Workers' Compensation Placement Authority, which is that state's assigned risk plan. Michigan also calculates its own separate experience modifier for Michigan exposure; this modifier is not combinable with other states in an interstate modifier. (Modifiers are explained in Chapter 3.)

Compensation Advisory Organization of Michigan
P.O. Box 3337
Livonia, MI 48151-3337
phone: 734 462-9600

fax: 734 462-9721
web: www.caom.com

There is also a very informative web site about Michigan's somewhat unique workers' comp insurance system, maintained by the Michigan Economic Development Corporation: medc. michigan.org/services/workerscomp/.

Department of Labor and Economic Growth
Workers' Compensation Agency
P.O. Box 30016
Lansing, MI 48909
phone: 888 396-5041
web: www.michigan.gov/wca

Insurance is regulated by:

Office of Financial and Insurance Services
P.O. Box 30220
Lansing, MI 48909-7220
phone: 517 373-0220 or 877 999-6442
fax: 517 335-4978
web: www.michigan.gov/cis/0,1607,7-154-10555---, 00.html

## Minnesota

Minnesota operates its own rating bureau, the Minnesota Workers' Compensation Insurance Association. Like Michigan, it does not regulate the classification codes that insurers use on voluntary market WC business. Unlike Michigan, loss and payroll data is reported to NCCI for inclusion in interstate modifiers. (Modifiers are explained in Chapter 3.)

Minnesota Workers' Compensation
Insurance Association
7701 France Avenue South, Suite 450
Minneapolis, MN 55435
phone: 952 897-1737
fax: 952 897-6495

e-mail: info@mwcia.org
web: www.mwcia.org

Insurance is regulated by:

Department of Commerce
Insurance Division
85 7th Place East, Suite 500
St. Paul, MN 55101
phone: 651 296-4026
fax: 651 297-1959
web: www.commerce.state.mn.us/

## Mississippi

Mississippi is an NCCI state. Workers' compensation is provided through private insurance companies. Insurance is regulated by:

Department of Insurance
1001 Woolfolk State Office Building
501 North West Street
Jackson, MS 39201
phone: 601 359-3569 or 800 652-2957
web: www.doi.state.ms.us/

## Missouri

Missouri is an NCCI state. Workers' compensation is provided through private insurance companies. Insurance is regulated by:

Department of Insurance
Division of Consumer Affairs
301 West High Street, Room 530
Jefferson City, MO 65101
phone: 573 751-2640
fax: 573 526-4898
web: www.insurance.state.mo.us/

## Montana

Montana is an NCCI state. Workers' compensation is provided through private insurance companies. Insurance is regulated by:

State Auditor's Office, Division of Insurance
840 Helena Avenue
Helena, MT 59601-4009
phone: 406 444-2040 or 800 332-6148
web: www.state.mt.us/sao/insurance

## Nebraska

Nebraska is an NCCI state, which means workers' compensation insurance premiums are computed in accordance with NCCI manuals and rules. Nebraska does not maintain its own state fund. The assigned risk plan there has become a bit of a political football in recent years, with the operation of this pool changing from one run by NCCI to one run by Employers of Wausau exclusively (in partnership with Aon Corporation) and then more recently to a administered exclusively by Travelers Insurance. Nebraska is currently seeking to restore some additional insurers to its assigned risk plan.

Insurance is regulated by:

Department of Insurance
941 O Street, Suite 400
Lincoln, NE 68508-3639
phone: 402 471-2201
web: www.nol.org/home/NDOI/

## Nevada

Nevada changed in 1999 from a state monopoly WC fund to a system of competitive private insurance and is now an NCCI state. (The former Nevada monopoly state fund has been reconstituted as a competitive mutual insurance company.) Insurance is regulated by:

Department of Business and Industry
Division of Insurance
788 Fairview Drive, Suite 300
Carson City, NV 89710-5491
phone: 775 687-4270
fax: 775 687-3937
web: doi.state.nv.us/

## New Hampshire

New Hampshire is an NCCI state, with workers' compensation provided through private insurance companies. Insurance is regulated by:

Insurance Department
21 South Fruit Street, Suite 14
Concord, NH 03301-7717
phone: 603 271-2261 or 800 852-3416
web: webster.state.nh.us/insurance/

## New Jersey

New Jersey maintains its own non-NCCI rating bureau, the New Jersey Compensation Rating and Inspection Bureau. This bureau has responsibility for creating manuals and rules of classifications and experience rating for New Jersey employers.

New Jersey Compensation Rating and
Inspection Bureau
60 Park Place
Newark, NJ 07102
phone: 973 622-6014
web: www.njcrib.com

Insurance is regulated by:

Department of Banking and Insurance
P.O. Box 325
Trenton, NJ 08625
phone: 800 446-SHOP
web: www.state.nj.us/dobi/

## New Mexico

New Mexico is an NCCI state. Workers' compensation is provided through private insurance. Insurance is regulated by:

Insurance Division
Public Regulation Commission
1120 Paseo de Peralta
P.O. Box 1269
Santa Fe, NM 87504-1269
phone: 505 827-4601
fax: 505 827-4734
web: www.nmprc.state.nm.us/insurance/
inshm.htm

## New York

New York uses its own non-NCCI, independent rating bureau for workers' compensation insurance, the New York Compensation Insurance Rating Board (NYCIRB), which develops its own manuals and rules regarding classification and experience modifiers. (Modifiers are explained in Chapter 3.) Because of this, employers in New York actually lack certain important regulatory protections concerning workers' compensation insurance premiums that employers in many other states enjoy under NCCI manual rules or specific state regulations.

New York Compensation Insurance Rating Board
200 East 42nd Street
New York, NY 10017
phone: 212 697-3535
fax: 212 972-1393 or 212 599-6594
e-mail: info@nycirb.org
web: www.nycirb.org

Insurance is regulated by:

Insurance Department

1 Commerce Plaza
Albany, NY 12257
phone: 518 474-6600
web: www.ins.state.ny.us/nyins.htm

## North Carolina

North Carolina maintains its own independent rating bureau, the North Carolina Rate Bureau, but follows the NCCI model fairly closely. The manual for North Carolina WC is published by NCCI. The North Carolina Rate Bureau promulgates its own in-state experience modifiers, but also reports data to NCCI for use in interstate modifiers. (Modifiers are explained in Chapter 3.)

North Carolina Rate Bureau
5401 Six Forks Road
Raleigh, NC 27609
phone: 919 783-9790
fax: 919 783-7467
web: www.ncrb.org

Insurance is regulated by:

Department of Insurance
1201 Mail Service Center
Raleigh, NC 27699-1201
phone: 919 733-2032 or 800 JIM LONG
(546-5664)
web: www.doi.state.nc.us

## North Dakota

North Dakota maintains a monopoly state fund for WC, meaning that private insurance is not allowed. This fund is administered by:

Workforce Safety and Insurance
1600 East Century Avenue, Suite 1
Bismarck, ND 58503-0644
phone: 701 328-3800 or 800 777-5033

web: www.workforcesafety.com

Insurance (but not workers' compensation) is regulated by:

Insurance Department
State Capitol, Fifth Floor
600 East Boulevard Avenue, Department 401
Bismarck, ND 58505-0320
phone: 701 328-2440 or 800 247-0560
fax: 701 328-4880
web: www.state.nd.us/ndins/

## Ohio

Ohio does not permit private insurance for workers' compensation. Instead, it maintains a monopolistic state fund. However, this state fund has just recently shifted to using the NCCI classification system for workplace exposures. The Ohio workers' comp system is administered by:

Bureau of Workers' Compensation
30 West Spring Street
Columbus, OH 43215-2256
phone: 614 466-4781 or 800 OHIOBWC
(644-6292)
fax: 877 520-OHIO (6446)
web: www.ohiobwc.com

## Oklahoma

Oklahoma is an NCCI state. Workers' compensation is provided through private insurance companies. Insurance is regulated by:

Insurance Department
P.O. Box 53408
Oklahoma City, OK 73152-3408
phone: 405 521-2828 or 800 522-0071
web: www.oid.state.ok.us/

## Oregon

Oregon is an NCII state. Workers' compensation is provided through private insurance companies. Insurance is regulated by:

Department of Consumer and Business Services
Insurance Division
350 Winter Street NE, Room 440
Salem, OR 97301-3883
phone: 503 947-7980
fax: 503 378-4351
web: www.cbs.state.or.us/external/ins

## Pennsylvania

Pennsylvania shares with Delaware a unique non-NCCI classification system. Rules for classification, premium computation, and experience rating are the responsibility of the Pennsylvania Compensation Rating Bureau, a non-government agency licensed and regulated by the PA Insurance Department. The premium portion of overtime pay is not excluded from computation of the workers' compensation premium.

Pennsylvania Compensation Rating Bureau
1 South Penn Square
Widener Building, 6th Floor
Philadelphia, PA 19107
phone: 215 568-2371
fax: 215 564-4328
web: www.pcrb.com

Insurance is regulated by:

Insurance Department
1321 Strawberry Square
Harrisburg, PA 17120
phone: 717 787-2317
web: www.ins.state.pa.us/ins

## Rhode Island

Rhode Island is an NCCI state that also runs a competitive state fund for WC, so workers' compensation coverage can be provided through either private insurance companies or the state fund. However, the state compensation insurance fund created in 1990 was reorganized in 1992 as a mutual insurance company, Beacon Mutual (www.beaconmutual.com).

Insurance is regulated by:

Department of Business Regulation
Insurance Division
233 Richmond Street, Suite 233
Providence, RI 02903
phone: 401 222-2246
fax: 401 222-6098
web: www.dbr.state.ri.us/insurance.html

## South Carolina

South Carolina is an NCCI state. Workers' compensation is provided through private insurance companies. Insurance is regulated by:

Department of Insurance
300 Arbor Lake Drive, Suite 1200
Columbia, SC 29223
phone: 803 737-6160
web: www.doi.state.sc.us/

## South Dakota

South Dakota is an NCCI state. Workers' compensation is provided through private insurance companies. Insurance is regulated by:

Department of Revenue and Regulation
Division of Insurance
445 East Capitol Avenue
Pierre, SD 57501
phone: 605 773-3563

fax: 605 773-5369
web: www.state.sd.us/drr2/reg/insurance/

## Tennessee

Tennessee is an NCCI state. Workers' compensation is provided through private insurance companies. Insurance is regulated by:

Dept. of Commerce and Insurance
Insurance Division
500 James Robertson Parkway
Nashville, TN 37243
phone: 615 741-2218 or 800 342-4029
web: www.state.tn.us/commerce/insurance/
index. html

## Texas

In the wake of a disastrous collapse of its old workers' comp system a decade ago, Texas instituted a number of significant reforms to its system and made it one of the more iconoclastic WC systems in the U.S.

Among other unusual features, Texas allows employers to "go bare"—that is, to not have workers' compensation insurance or self-insurance. Texas also allows employers to negotiate lower experience modification factors with their insurers (if the insurers are willing to accommodate them). Texas is not an NCCI state, but maintains its own manuals of rules and regulations developed by the Texas Department of Insurance (TDI). Workers' compensation is provided through private insurance companies. Regulation is provided by:

Department of Insurance
333 Guadalupe Street
Austin, TX 78701-3938
phone: 512 463-6169 or 800 578-4677

web: www.tdi.state.tx.us

This web site covers all insurance, not just workers' comp. For Texas Workers' Comp information, visit www.tdi.state.tx.us/consumer/wc.html.

## Utah

Utah is an NCCI state. Workers' compensation is provided by private insurance companies. Insurance is regulated by:

Insurance Department
State Office Building, Room 3110
Salt Lake City, UT 88114-6901
phone: 801 538-3800 or 800 439-3805
fax: 801 538-3829
web: www.insurance.state.ut.us

Utah also maintains a competitive state fund, Workers' Compensation Fund (www.wcf-utah.com), which the Utah legislature recently authorized to sell WC in other states as well, through a subsidiary insurance company.

## Vermont

Vermont is an NCCI state. Workers' compensation is provided through private insurance companies. Insurance is regulated by:

Department of Banking, Insurance,
Securities, and Health Care Administration
89 Main Street, Drawer 20
Montpelier, VT 05620-3101
phone: 802 828-3301
fax: 802 828-3306
web: www.bishca.state.vt.us/

## Virginia

Virginia is an NCCI state. Workers' compensation is provided through private insurance com-

panies. Insurance is regulated by:

Bureau of Insurance
Property and Casualty
P.O. Box 1157
Richmond, VA 23218
phone: 804 371-9741 or 800 552-7945
web: www.state.va.us/scc/division/boi/index.htm

## Washington

Washington maintains a monopoly state fund for WC, not allowing private insurance for this exposure.

The fund is administered by:

Department of Labor and Industries
P.O. Box 44000
Olympia, WA 98504-4000
phone: 360 902-5800 or 800 547-8367
fax: 360 902-5798
web: www.lni.wa.gov/

## West Virginia

West Virginia maintains a monopoly state fund for WC. Private insurance is not allowed for workers' compensation. The state fund is administered by:

Workers' Compensation Commission
4700 MacCorkle Avenue S.E.
Charleston, WV 25304
phone: 888 4-WV-COMP (498-2667)
web: www.wvwcc.org/

## Wisconsin

Wisconsin maintains its own non-NCCI rating bureau for determining classifications, premium computation, and experience rating. In state experience modifiers are calculated by this independent bureau, but data is also provided to NCCI for interstate modifiers. (Modifiers are explained in Chapter 3.)

Wisconsin Compensation Rating Bureau
20700 Swenson Drive, Suite 100
Waukesha, WI 53186
phone: 262 796-4540
fax: 262 796-4400
web: www.wcrb.org

Insurance is regulated by:

Office of the Commissioner of Insurance
125 South Webster Street
Madison, WI 53702
phone: 608 266-3585 or 800 236-8517
fax: 608 266-9935
web: oci.wi.gov/oci_home.htm

## Wyoming

Wyoming maintains a monopoly state fund for workers' compensation and does not allow private insurance of this exposure. Workers' compensation is administered by:

Department of Employment
Workers' Safety and Compensation Division
1510 East Pershing Boulevard
Cheyenne, WY 82002
phone: 307 777-7441
fax: 307 777-6552
web: wydoe.state.wy.us/doe.asp?ID=9

It sounds complicated, I know. That's because it is complicated—there's just no getting around that fact. The state-by-state nature of workers' compensation guarantees it. But don't despair, because there's still a large amount of commonality to the most of the state systems as well, enough commonality for it to be possible for most business owners and man-

agers to learn to spot the most common problems that can increase workers' compensation insurance premiums unnecessarily.

## WORKERS' COMP–WHO NEEDS IT?

That may be the first important question that a business needs to address, because not every business is required to purchase workers' compensation insurance. Generally speaking, sole proprietors and partnerships aren't required to purchase workers' compensation insurance unless and until they have employees who aren't owners. Most states will allow sole proprietors and partners to cover themselves for workers' compensation if they choose to, but it isn't required. (An important note, though—these rules vary from state to state and can change over time. So it's always a good idea to check with your particular state's regulatory agency to make sure what the rules are for your state jurisdiction.)

Some states don't require an employee to be covered if he or she is paid solely by commission. Again, check with the workers' compensation regulators in your particular state to see how they handle this.

Interestingly, a few states even give employers the option to not purchase workers' compensation insurance at all. These states are few and far between: Texas and (at least in theory) New Jersey. Remember, though, that just because the state may allow an employer to go without workers' compensation insurance, the employer is still liable under the state's workers' compensation laws for injured workers. Not having workers' compensation insurance, even if allowed by a particular state, does not relieve the employer of financial responsibility for injured workers.

Most states also allow large employers to self-insure for workers' compensation, but the rules about who can and cannot self-insure again vary significantly from state to state.

Typically, your state department of insurance can help you determine if your business is required to purchase workers' compensation insurance. A general rule is that if you have employees who aren't owners of the company, you probably need workers' compensation insurance. Take a look at Appendix D of this book for some more information about state-by-state requirements for workers' compensation insurance.

*Speaking of employees, here's a potential trap to be aware of and avoid: under most state's workers' compensation laws, you might have employees you don't know about.* That's because most states will treat an uninsured contractor or subcontractor as your employee if he or she is injured while doing work for your company.

Let's say you're operating as a sole proprietor and your state doesn't require you to purchase workers' compensation insurance on yourself. Then you hire a painter to paint your office. If that painter doesn't have workers' compensation insurance on himself and gets hurt working on your premises, he may well be able to make a claim against you. The same holds for a roofer, or a glazer, or a cleaning contractor. Anyone you hire to do work for your company could well be held to be eligible for workers' compensation benefits from your company.

That's why many larger companies will contractually require anyone doing work for them to show proof of workers' compensation insurance. A cleaning service operating as a sole proprietor may not be required by the state to purchase workers' compensation insurance, but its clients would be wise to insist on it before hiring that service.

## RIDING THE INSURANCE MARKET

Any business that's had to buy workers' compensation insurance since the dawn of the new millennium has learned more than it ever wanted to know about the fluctuations of the commercial insurance market. The cost of the insurance has increased vastly in just a few years, as the insurance market went from "soft" market conditions in the late 1990s to very "hard" around 2001. As is typical with hard insurance markets, cost skyrocketed and choices for employers contracted sharply.

I find this is always one of the most frustrating and perplexing aspects of workers' compensation insurance, as I work with clients. How can the cost for similar (or identical) coverage this year be twice what it was a year or two before? What other kind of business could operate in such a lurching and chaotic fashion?

Such cycles in the commercial insurance market have been around a long time, although there once was a time when workers' compensation insurance was more insulated from these wild price fluctuations by tighter regulation. But over the course of the past 25 years, state insurance regulators have decided that the benefits of price competition among insurance companies outweigh the negatives. My own opinion is that we may have moved a little too far in the direction of allowing insurance companies to price workers' compensation insurance as they see fit. There is still some degree of regulation, of course. Workers' compensation insurance remains more closely regulated than most other lines of insurance. But insurance companies today have much greater leeway in pricing this necessary coverage than they did when I began my insurance career, back in the mid-1970s. And while it is certainly very helpful for employers when insurance companies compete for business by cutting prices, as they did during the soft market, it can be catastrophic when hard market conditions inevitably return. A little bit more price stability for this vital insurance coverage would be beneficial to employers, I think, even at the cost of losing some of the savings that occur during the soft market.

However, employers will probably have to deal with insurance markets that move from soft to hard and back again to soft for the foreseeable future. Generally speaking, when returns on investment are high, insurance prices tend to be low. Insurance companies can make up a lot of underwriting losses from their investment returns, if those investment returns are healthy. That's part of what happened in this last market turnaround. The very healthy stock market returns that insurance companies had been earning abruptly disappeared and they had to deal with the consequences of years of relatively low prices but claims that had not diminished.

Changes in the commercial insurance marketplace are not that hard to anticipate. A little informed web surfing can provide a fair bit of early warning about upcoming market shifts for commercial insurance. Generally speaking, when insurance markets are soft, employers can expect increased competition for their insurance business. Insurers can and will compete on price for your business, even when your loss history isn't so terrific. This is the time to strike good bargains for cost and coverage and to use the competitive pricing aspects of the modern insurance market to your advantage. It's a time when competitive bidding of your insurance program, particularly your workers' compensation insurance, can produce very striking results.

But when you see signs that the hard market is on the horizon, or once it has struck, understand that price competition among insurers will pretty much be AWOL for the duration. In hard markets, it is essential to do your utmost to provide as much useful information to underwriters as possible, as any and all ambiguities and unresolved questions will be answered using a worst-case scenario.

Also keep in mind that the cost control methods detailed in this book can and will save you money whether the insurance market is hard or soft, but they will yield greater dollar savings on policies written during hard markets. That's because in hard markets any mistake in figuring premiums will be most costly, because rates are so much higher. But it's also because insurance companies often go a little overboard during hard markets and take some actions that sometimes raise premiums improperly and unfairly to a greater degree than they do during soft markets. One might think the opposite would be more likely, with insurers trying to maximize revenue with questionable tactics at times when premiums are lower, but in my experience it's during hard markets that one often finds more violations of the rules.

I've always found it interesting that very few employers would let the IRS figure their tax returns for them, but they typically allow their insurance companies to calculate their workers' compensation insurance premiums without really having their own expert at least review those charges. Yet the rules that govern the calculation of workers' compensation insurance premiums are complex and poorly understood by most employers (and sometimes by insurers as well). The information in this book can help you avoid being overcharged, while making sure you have the workers' compensation coverage you need.

CHAPTER **2**

# Understanding
# Your Policy

THE STANDARD WORKERS' COMPENSA-TION insurance policy is a unique insurance contract in many respects. Unlike other liability insurance policies, it doesn't have a maximum dollar amount limit to its primary coverage. Your auto insurance policy, for example, has certain specified maximum amounts the policy covers per accident; if the cost of a particular accident exceeds that limit, you'll need to look elsewhere for those additional dollars (either your own pocket or an excess or umbrella liability policy). Workers' compensation insurance policies have a dollar limit also, but only for Part Two of the coverage, employers' liability. But Part One, the part that responds to an employer's statutory workers' compensation liability, has no set limit. Once the policy is in force, the insurance company is responsible for all that employer's claims that arise for workers' compensation bene-

fits in the states covered by the policy.

That's the really beneficial aspect of workers' compensation insurance from the employer's point of view. It's impossible to know in advance how great an employer's liabilities may be in a year due to workers' compensation obligations and thus impossible to budget ahead of time with any certainty. A company might run several months with almost no claims and then be hit with a claim that ultimately costs hundreds of thousands of dollars. But an insurance policy has a predictable cost for which a company can plan and budget—at least in theory. Sometimes in practice, this isn't the case. (But more on this later.)

Part One of the standard workers' compensation insurance policy (what used to be called Coverage A, for us old-timers) transfers liability for statutory workers' compensation benefits of an employer to the insurance company, whether that liability turns out to be small, medium, or crushing. If a state increases benefit levels during the term of the policy, the employer doesn't have to make any adjustments to the policy—the policy automatically makes it the responsibility of the insurance company to pay all claims due for workers' compensation insurance for the named employer in the particular states covered by the policy.

Of course, as with all insurance, the devil can be in the details. And there are a few details that are very important for an employer to make sure are handled properly on a workers' compensation insurance policy. The two most important: who is named as an insured under the policy and which states are covered by the policy.

## CHECK YOUR POLICY'S INFORMATION PAGE

I'm always a little amazed at how many businesspeople don't really look over their workers' compensation policy. The fine print of the policy can be a little daunting to the average person, of course, but I'm talking about looking at some of the basic items that almost anyone can find and understand on the policy.

For example, the Information Pages of the policy are normally among the first few pages and those pages show a lot of important information. (Take a look at Figure 2-1 for a sample Information Page.) For one thing, they show what entities are the *named insureds* under the policy. (This is shown in Item I of the Information Page.)

So for starters, is the named insured shown on your policy correct, accurate, and complete? Is your company's name shown correctly? If you operate as a sole proprietorship or partnership,

## GRANDMA'S ROOFER—A CAUTIONARY TALE

Years ago, my late grandmother owned a restaurant. So she had a workers' compensation insurance policy that showed the business as the named insured. One day, she hired a roofer to repair the flat roof on the restaurant. Sadly, the roofer somehow fell off the roof and was killed. It turned out that the roofer didn't carry workers' compensation insurance. He was operating as a sole proprietor and wasn't required to carry workers' comp on himself. But my grandmother hadn't realized that this meant she would be liable for any workers' compensation liability resulting from hiring him to work for her. That was when Grandma discovered that she had a serious uninsured problem—because she owned the building personally and she wasn't named on the policy. She had hired the roofer in her capacity as building owner and the workers' compensation policy showed only the restaurant as named insured.

This illustrates two important lessons regarding workers' compensation. First, in most states, if you use the services of an uninsured independent contractor, you can (and likely will) be held liable for any resulting workers' compensation claims, even if the contractor isn't required to carry insurance by the state, because the contractor is a sole proprietor or partnership. Second, make sure you show as named insured all legal entities related to your business—especially whatever entity owns your real estate, if different from your main business entity.

| Archetypal Insurance Group | Standard Workers' Compensation and Employers' Liability Policy |
|---|---|

INFORMATION PAGE

| Policy Number | From | POLICY PERIOD | To | Coverage Provided By | Agency |
|---|---|---|---|---|---|
| WC 11223344 | 01/01/05 | | 01/01/06 | Archetype Insurance of Virginia | 99887766 |

| ITEM Named Insured and Address | Agent |
|---|---|
| 1. ABC Widget Mfg. Inc. | Mainstreet Insurance Agency |
| 5533 Constitution Lane | 4000 W. Evergreen St. |
| Vienna, VA 22180 | Smallville, VA 22345 |

FEIN: 111222333          NCCI CARRIER CODE NO: 112233

INTERSTATE ID NO: 998877

OTHER WORK PLACES NOT SHOWN ABOVE: SEE ATTACHED SCHEDULE

YOU ARE A CORPORATION

2. POLICY PERIOD- 01/01/05 TO 01/01/06 12:01 AM STANDARD TIME AT THE INSURED'S MAILING ADDRESS

    3.A. PART ONE OF THIS POLICY APPLIES TO THE WORKERS' COMPENSATION LAW AND ANY OCCUPATIONAL DISEASE LAW OF EACH OF THE STATES LISTED HERE:

        MD, VA.

    3.B. PART TWO OF THIS POLICY APPLIES TO EMPLOYERS' LIABILITY INSURANCE FOR WORK IN EACH STATE LISTED IN ITEM 3A: THE LIMITS OF LIABILITY ARE:

             BODILY INJURY BY ACCIDENT     $100,000 EACH ACCIDENT

             BODILY INJURY BY DISEASE      $500,000 POLICY LIMIT

             BODILY INJURY BY DISEASE      $100,000 EACH EMPLOYEE

    3.C. PART THREE OF THIS POLICY APPLIES TO OTHER STATES, IF ANY LISTED HERE:

        ALL STATES EXCEPT AK, ND, OH, WA, WV, AND STATES DESIGNATED IN ITEM 3.A OF THE INFORMATION PAGE.

    3.D. THIS POLICY INCLUDES THESE ENDORSEMENTS AND SCHEDULES: SEE ATTACHED SCHEDULES

4. THE PREMIUM FOR THIS POLICY WILL BE DETERMINED BY OUR MANUAL OF RULES, CLASSIFICATIONS, RATES, AND RATING PLANS. ALL INFORMATION REQUIRED BELOW IS SUBJECT TO VERIFICATION AND CHANGE BY AUDIT. ADJUSTMENT OF PREMIUM SHALL BE MADE: AT POLICY EXPIRATION

| CLASSIFICATION OF OPERATIONS | | EST ANNUAL PREMIUM |
|---|---|---|
| SEE ATTACHED | | $93,502 |
| | PREMIUM DISCOUNT | 8,800- |
| | EXPENSE CONSTANT | 160 |
| MINIMUM PREMIUM    $750 | TOTAL ESTIMATED ANNUAL PREMIUM | $84,862 |
| | TERRORISM RISK INS ACT | $924 |
| | TOTAL ESTIMATED COST | $85,786 |

DATE OF ISSUE    02/15/05

POLICY ISSUING OFFICE: RICHMOND

COUNTERSIGNED _____     BY _____

            DATE                                 AUTHORIZED AGENT

FIGURE 2-1. A typical information page of a workers' compensation insurance policy (continued on the next page)

**Schedule of Operations**

State: MD

| LOC NO. | CLASS CODE | CLASSIFICATION OF OPERATIONS | EST TOTAL ANN REMUN | RATE PER $100 REMUN | EST ANNUAL PREMIUM |
|---|---|---|---|---|---|
| 01 | 3632 | MACHINE SHOP NOC | 1,098,381 | 6.78 | 74,470 |
| | 8742 | SALESPERSONS, COLLECTORS OR MESSENGERS–OUTSIDE | 122,879 | .38 | 467 |
| | 8810 | CLERICAL OFFICE EMPLOYEES NOC | IF ANY | .27 | 0 |
| | | | SUBTOTAL FOR LOCATION 01 | | 74,937 |

State: VA

| LOC NO. | CLASS CODE | CLASSIFICATION OF OPERATIONS | EST TOTAL ANN REMUN | RATE PER $100 REMUN | EST ANNUAL PREMIUM |
|---|---|---|---|---|---|
| 02 | 3632 | MACHINE SHOP NOC | 750,000 | 5.43 | 40,725 |
| | 8810 | CLERICAL OFFICE EMPLOYEES NOC | 825,000 | .29 | 2,396 |

| | | | |
|---|---|---|---|
| TOTAL ESTIMATED MANUAL PREMIUM | | | 118,058 |
| EXPERIENCE MODIFICATION FACTOR | | | .88 |
| SCHEDULE CREDIT   (10%) | | | .90 |
| | | | |
| TOTAL ESTIMATED STANDARD PREMIUM | | | 93,502 |
| PREMIUM DISCOUNT | | | (8.800) |
| EXPENSE CONSTANT | | | 160 |
| TERRORISM RISK INS ACT 2002 | 1,848,381 | .050 | 924 |
| | | | |
| TOTAL ESTIMATED PREMIUM | | | 85,786 |

DATE OF ISSUE: 02/15/05
POLICY ISSUING OFICE: RICHMOND

**FIGURE 2-1.** A typical information page of a workers' compensation insurance policy (continued)

is that shown correctly? Are there additional entities that should be listed, but are not? For example, sometimes a company leases real estate from another company. Sometimes real property is held in a trust. Are those separate legal entities named on the policy, either on the Information Page or on a separate endorsement to the policy? If not, they should be. A building owner could hire someone to do work on the building. If that independent contractor does not have workers' compensation coverage of his or her own and then is injured while working on the building, the contractor could well have a claim against the legal entity that hired him or her. If that legal entity is the building owner but the building owner isn't named on the workers' compensation policy, that policy may well not cover the claim.

While you're looking at your policy, review the list of states that the policy covers to ensure that it includes all the states you need. The policy may not necessarily list every state you do business in, as a few states do not allow private insurance. North Dakota, Ohio, Washington, West Virginia, and Wyoming currently require workers' compensation coverage for their jurisdictions to be provided through their "monopoly" state funds. Other than these five states, make sure that your policy lists all states in which you have employees (or uninsured independent contractors or subcontractors). This is shown in Item 3.A of the Information Page.

In addition, you want to make sure that the policy provides coverage for other states where you might have an *incidental exposure*. Even though you don't have employees working in these other states, it's conceivable someone might seek to make a claim for benefits under a particular state's benefits because the worker was traveling through the state on business or was there on a temporary basis. Other states coverage used to be provided by a separate endorsement, but now it's part of the basic policy language (Part Three of the standard policy). However, you have to make sure that the policy clearly states which other states are covered for such incidental exposures. This is shown in Item 3.C of the Information Page. If this is left blank, then you have no coverage for states other than those listed in Item 3.A.

The best and most comprehensive approach is to have Item 3.C show a broad coverage statement such as "All states and U.S. territories except North Dakota, Ohio, Washington, West Virginia, Wyoming, Puerto Rico, the U.S. Virgin Islands, and those states designated in Item 3.A of the Information Page."

What about employees who are working outside the U.S.? Most states provide that workers who are hired within those states but are injured outside those states are entitled to benefits. But if you have U.S. employees who are working in

foreign countries, you may well want to make endorse your policy with a *voluntary compensation endorsement* for those employees working temporarily outside the U.S. and a *foreign voluntary compensation endorsement* for those who are located in foreign countries for longer-term projects. A foreign voluntary compensation endorsement is not a standardized form, but it typically would provide not only statutory benefits on a voluntary basis but also coverage for endemic disease and the expense of repatriating injured or ill workers. The costs of transporting injured or ill workers back to the U.S. can be substantial, so it can be important to obtain the repatriation expense coverage if you have employees traveling internationally on business.

## FEDERAL WORKERS' COMP EXPOSURES

Although the individual states' workers' compensation statutes are the primary focus of most employers' insurance, there are some federal acts that can also impose liability on an employer. The 1992 revision of the standard workers' compensation insurance policy specifically excludes coverage for federal legislation such as the Longshore and Harbor Workers' Compensation Act, the Nonappropriated Fund Instrumentalities Act, the Outer Continental Shelf Lands Act, the Defense Base Act, the Federal Coal Mine Health and Safety Act, and the Federal Employers' Liability Act. Coverage for these laws can be added to your workers' compensation policy by endorsement, as needed. Here's a brief rundown on who might need these endorsements.

- **Longshore and Harbor Workers' Compensation Act (LHWCA).** This act provides benefits to employees (other than masters or crew members of a vessel) who are injured in maritime employment. So if you have employees loading, unloading, repairing, or building a vessel, you need this coverage endorsed onto your policy. Maritime coverage for masters or members of a crew of a vessel is available with a maritime coverage endorsement.

- **Outer Continental Shelf Lands Act.** This act provides LHWCA benefits to employees (again, other than masters or crew members of a vessel) working on a continental shelf, such as on an offshore oil rig.
- **Defense Base Act.** This act covers civilian workers on military bases, such as if you contract to provide janitorial services to a military facility.
- **Nonappropriated Fund Instrumentalities Act.** This act extends LHWCA benefits to civilian employees of the U.S. military, like PX workers.
- **Federal Coal Mine Health and Safety Act.** This act provides workers' compensation benefits to coal miners who contract black lung disease.
- **Federal Employers' Liability Act.** This act covers employees of interstate railroads, who can be covered by a Federal Employers' Liability Act coverage endorsement.
- **Migrant and Seasonal Agricultural Worker Protection Act.** This act protects migrant and seasonal agricultural workers and establishes a private right of action against employers and contractors who violate housing and safety requirements. Coverage can be obtained through a Migrant and Seasonal Agricultural Worker Protection Act endorsement.

## EMPLOYERS' LIABILITY COVERAGE

We've already made reference to Part One and Part Three of the coverage provided by the workers' compensation insurance policy. But we haven't yet talked about Part Two—employers' liability coverage. Most workers' compensation claims come under Part One of the coverage— the statutory state benefits for injured or ill workers. But don't ignore Part Two, as it can be very important to make sure this sometimes overlooked area of the policy is set up correctly.

This is the section of the policy that *does* have a set dollar limit. But employers' liability coverage is not always well understood by employers (or even by some insurance people). Employers' liability insures the employer for liability to employees for work-related bodily injury or illness that isn't subject to the statutory benefits imposed by state or federal regulations. For example, a lot of states exclude certain employees from the statutory benefits covered by Part One or Part Three of the policy. Employers' liability coverage would insure the employer for liability to such employees (as long the particular state where the injury or illness occurs is shown in Item 3.A or Item 3.C).

Employers' liability also insures an employer in cases such as third-party over suits, where an injured worker files suit against a third party and that third party then seeks to hold the employer responsible. For example, an employee injured by a piece of machinery at the workplace might file suit against the manufacturer of the machinery. The manufacturer might claim that the employer modified the machinery or used it improperly and is thus responsible for the liability.

But since employers' liability has a set limit, it is vital that this limit be correctly coordinated with the excess or umbrella liability coverage that is purchased separately. If the amount of employers' liability coverage on the workers' compensation policy is lower than the amount that the umbrella or excess policy requires for underlying coverage, there can be an uninsured gap. So it is vital to make sure that the employers' liability limit on the workers' compensation policy matches what is shown on the umbrella or excess liability coverage that sits on top of the primary workers' compensation policy.

## DIFFERENT KINDS OF WORKERS' COMP POLICIES

All legitimate workers' compensation insurance policies provide the same coverage. There is no difference between the coverage provided by one insurer's policy and the coverage provided by the policy of a different insurance company. The policy language has been standardized, reviewed, and approved by regulators, so the only real difference among workers' compensation policies is in how premium charges may be computed. Even in this regard, there is a high degree of standardization, but developments over the course of the last decade or so have eroded some of that standardization in how premiums are computed. More than ever, employers need to understand the details of how insurance companies calculate premiums, as regulation of workers' compensation pricing is not as vigilant as it once was.

### Guaranteed-Cost Policy

The most basic and most common type of workers' compensation insurance policy is known as a *guaranteed-cost* policy. Bear in mind,

though, that insurance terminology can sometimes be misleading to those outside the insurance industry. "Guaranteed cost" does not mean that the premium for the policy is a fixed dollar amount. It means instead that the premium will be computed as a rate times hundred dollars of payroll, computed according to some fairly complicated rules that aren't all spelled out in the policy itself. But the rate that will be multiplied by payroll is shown on the policy, so in theory as long as payroll costs are known, an employer should know the cost of insurance.

All workers' compensation insurance policies start out with an estimated premium, because the payroll numbers for the policy period cannot be known exactly. The actual premium will vary depending upon what the actual payrolls turn out to be for the policy period. So even a "guaranteed-cost" policy has a premium that is only an estimate at the outset, subject to adjustment once actual payroll is determined. But the premium for a guaranteed-cost policy is adjusted only based on payroll fluctuations, not on the cost of claims incurred or paid out under the policy. Remember that the premium for even a "guaranteed-cost" policy will be subject to a payroll audit and thus there may be additional premium charges due after the policy expires, if the actual payroll for the policy period was higher than estimated. If the estimated payrolls are significantly lower than actual, you could be in for a large bill due after the policy expires.

We'll go into more detail about how these premiums are calculated in the next chapter. Now, let's take an overview of the other types of workers' compensation policies employers may encounter.

## LOSS-SENSITIVE PLANS

There are other types of workers' compensation policies, however, that do adjust the premium based on losses incurred or paid out under the policy. Such policies are generally known as *loss-sensitive plans*, and there are a number of types. Loss-sensitive plans still use the rate times hundred dollars of payroll to calculate premiums, but then make further adjustments based on the losses under the policy. These adjustments may lower premiums if losses are low or may raise premiums even higher than the guaranteed cost premium would have been if losses are high. Here are the common types of loss-sensitive policies.

## Retrospective Rating Plans

These policies compute premiums following the same rules as guaranteed-cost policies, but then make further adjustments by using a formula that incorporates the cost of claims that occur during the policy. These adjustments can make premiums lower than they would have been under a guaranteed-cost policy (if the losses are low) or higher than they would have been under a guaranteed-cost policy (if losses are high).

Under these policies, the major component of the cost becomes the losses covered by the policy. Because the total cost of the claims can't really be known until after the policy has ended, the *retrospective* premium adjustments are made after the policy ends. Such adjustments usually continue for a number of subsequent years, as the cost of claims can change over time. Thus, retrospective rating policies can sometimes create substantial additional costs for an employer long after the policy has ended.

## Deductible Plans

Another category of loss-sensitive plans is known as deductible plans. They come in two basic types: *small-deductible* plans and *large-deductible* plans.

Small-deductible plans have deductibles of relatively low dollar amounts, such as $1,000 per claim. In return for accepting responsibility for paying these deductible amounts, the employer gets a discount on the premiums. This premium is computed according to the same rules as for a guaranteed-cost policy, but the rates have been discounted and the employer is responsible for reimbursing the insurer for the claims costs that fall under the deductible amount.

A large-deductible plan operates in similar fashion, but the size of the deductible is much larger, typically starting at $25,000 per claim and going upward from there. Like small-deductible plans, there is a discount given on the premium charges to reflect the deductible assumed by the employer. Most states that allow large-deductible plans allow insurers to offer them only to employers whose premium size is above a certain threshold amount, so that these plans are typically available only for employers paying substantial premiums.

## Dividend Plans

These types of plans used to be used much more commonly, but have been largely supplanted by other types of loss-sensitive plans in more recent years. Still, in particular states employers may encounter these kinds of plans. A dividend plan returns some portion of the guaranteed-cost premium to the employer based on loss experience. Decades ago, mutual insurance companies paid dividends to policyholders based on the company-wide loss experience, but such plans are rare now.

*Sliding-scale* dividend plans were a refinement of earlier dividend plans and returned dividends to the employer based on the loss experience of that particular employer during the term of the policy. Thus, sliding-scale dividend plans can reduce premium costs if losses are low, but typically do not hold the possibility of premiums that are higher than guaranteed cost if losses are excessive.

## COMMON COVERAGE ENDORSEMENTS

Although the standard workers' compensation policy tends to provide very broad coverage, there are some endorsements that are commonly used to provide additional coverage. Here are some important endorsements that are used to extend or restrict coverage in certain situations.

**Alternative employer endorsement** extends coverage for employees working at another employer, for example, workers from a temporary agency. This would typically be used to extend coverage to the client company of the temp agency for workers provided by the temp agency.

**Employers' liability coverage endorsement (stopgap)** is used to provide employers' liability coverage for employees in a monopoly state. Monopoly state funds do not provide the employers' liability coverage provided by Part two of the standard workers' compensation policy, so this endorsement extends Part Two coverage to employees covered under such monopoly fund programs.

**Joint venture as insured endorsement** is used when the named insured on the policy is a joint venture. It clarifies that coverage extends to the members of the joint venture, but only regarding their

capacity as members of the joint venture. If you also have other business enterprises separate from the joint venture, you will need separate workers' compensation coverage.

**Medical benefits exclusion endorsement** is used in states that allow employers to pay medical benefits directly, instead of through a workers' compensation policy. This endorsement excludes medical benefits for specified states and makes the employer responsible for payment of these benefits.

**Partners, officers, and others exclusion endorsement** is used when partners and executive officers wish to exclude themselves from coverage, and thus their remuneration will be excluded from premium computation.

**Sole proprietors, partners, officers, and others coverage endorsement** extends coverage to sole proprietors, partners, and officers who are not required to be covered but who choose to extend coverage on themselves.

**Voluntary compensation and employers' liability coverage endorsement** is used to extend coverage to certain employees who are not required to be covered for workers' compensation benefits in a state, such as domestic or farm workers and commission-only salespeople.

**Foreign voluntary compensation endorsement** extends coverage to employees who are working outside the country for an extended period. Importantly, this also can include repatriation expense, which can be a significant expense for injured workers who are out of the country.

**Waiver of our right to recover from others endorsement** means the insurance company waives its right of subrogation against third parties who may be responsible for some losses under the policy. The particular parties who are covered by this waiver should be named in the endorsement.

## THE EMPLOYER'S DUTIES UNDER THE POLICY

The workers' compensation policy imposes certain duties upon the policyholder in the event of a claim:

- Duty to notify the insurer if an injury that may be covered occurs;
- Duty to provide for immediate medical and other services required by the applicable workers' compensation statutes;
- Duty to provide the insurer the names and addresses of the injured persons and of witnesses, as well as other information needed by the insurer, and to promptly give the insurer all notices, demands, and legal papers related to the injury;
- Duty to cooperate with the insurer and to assist in the investigation, settlement, or defense of any claim.
- Duty to do nothing after an injury occurs that would interfere with the insurer's right to recover from others.

Remember that if you do anything to violate these duties, the insurance company may be able to claim breach of contract and void the policy.

The workers' compensation policy also lists five conditions that apply. These conditions deal with inspections, long-term policies, the transfer of the named insured's rights, cancellation of the policy, and the sole representative on behalf of all insureds.

The *inspections* section gives the insurance company the right to make an inspection of the workplace at any time. Historically, these inspections were done for the purposes of loss-control and safety engineering, but then some insureds took legal action against insurers, claiming that the insurance companies had failed to notify the employers of safety matters that eventually caused serious problems. So nowadays the insurance policy makes it clear that these inspections are not intended to be a comprehensive safety program and are really intended so that the insurance company can make sure it's underwriting exposures properly. Safety and loss control are still services offered by insurers, but they don't want to be held responsible for any alleged deficiencies or shortcomings in those services.

The *long-term policies* section states that, if a policy is written for longer than one year and 16 days, then all provisions in the policy apply as if under a new policy. Thus, the annual renewal of the policy would be an automatic rewrite of the existing policy terms and conditions.

The *transfer of rights* section prohibits the policyholder from transferring their rights or duties to another party without written consent from the insurance company.

## FEDERAL WORKERS' COMPENSATION COVERAGE

Although workers' compensation is primarily a matter of obligations and rules established by the individual states, there are some federal laws that come into play in certain situations.

The United States Longshore and Harbor Workers Compensation Act (LHWCA) was enacted in 1927 to provide benefits to employees other than seamen who worked in maritime employment. Employees working upon the navigable waters of the United States are generally not covered by state workers' compensation laws. The coverage of the LHWCA is pretty broad, applying to compensation for disability or death of an employee injured while working on the navigable waters of the United States, including any adjoining pier, wharf, dry dock, terminal, marine railway, or other area customarily used in loading, unloading, dismantling, or building a vessel.

However, the LHWCA does not apply to an officer or employee of the federal government or any state or local governments, or any employee injured solely due to the employee's intoxication or to a fellow employee's willful intention. And the definition of "employee" under the LHWCA excludes clerical, secretarial, security, or data processing. It also excludes employees of camps, restaurants, recreational facilities, or retail outlets; employees of marinas; aquaculture workers; workers who build, repair, or dismantle recreational vessels under 65 feet long; masters or members of a crew of a vessel; and workers loading or unloading or repairing a vessel under 18 tons.

There is also the Jones Act, also known as the Merchant Marine Act of 1920. This mandates benefits for seamen injured in the course of their employment due to the negligence of the owner, master, or fellow crew member. The act itself does not define the term "seaman," so this has been left to the courts to resolve. Over the years, courts have determined through their decisions that certain factors determine if a worker is considered to be a "seaman." Some of these factors are that the vessel in question must be in navigable waters, the worker must have a permanent connection to the vessel, and the worker must be aboard to aid in the navigation of the vessel, that is, be part of the actual operation of the ship.

## CHECKLIST TO AVOID COMMON POLICY PROBLEMS

Here are six suggestions for avoiding common problems with workers' compensation policies.

- Name all related business entities (including land trusts, if any) on the policy.
- List all the states where you operate in Item 3.A of the Information Page.
- Make sure that the Other States Coverage shown in Item 3.C of the Information Page shows all states except those in Item 3.A and the monopoly states.
- Review operations to see if any federal coverage must be endorsed onto policy.
- Verify that the employers' liability limit matches what is shown on the umbrella or excess liability policy.
- Make sure that estimated payrolls are reasonable when the policy begins, to avoid a large additional premium due after the policy expires.

## STEPS TO TAKE TO EVALUATE YOUR STATE-BY-STATE WORKERS' COMP EXPOSURES

1. Examine your company's possible exposures to workers' compensation claims from different states. If you have employees who live in or who travel through or in other states, you need to make sure you are properly covered in each state. Remember, many states treat uninsured independent contractors or subcontractors the same as an employee of yours.
2. If you have workers in monopoly-fund states, you will need to arrange coverage through those state funds. Private insurance

cannot satisfy coverage requirements for monopolistic states.

3. If you are based in a monopoly-fund state but have some workers elsewhere, you will need to arrange coverage for those states separate from your state fund.

4. If you are self-insured in your primary state of operations but have some employees or uninsured contractors in other states, you will need to arrange coverage for those other states.

5. If you are operating in multiple states, check into possible different classification definitions that apply in different jurisdictions for your operation. Make sure you are properly classified in each state, to avoid either hidden overcharges or an unpleasant audit surprise of additional premium.

6. A few states do not use the interstate experience modification factor system, but instead calculate a modifier only for use within that state, based on prior losses and payrolls within that state. These "standa-lone" states are California, Michigan, Pennsylvania, Delaware, and New Jersey. If you have operations in these states but also operate elsewhere, make sure proper experience modifiers are used for the stand-alone states.

## QUICK REVIEW

- Make sure the named insured on the workers' compensation policy includes all related corporate entities.
- Make sure the policy lists all states where you have operations.
- Make sure policy is endorsed with any federal workers' comp endorsements your company may need, such as Longshore and Harbor Workers or Defense Base coverage.
- Make sure the employer' liability limit on the workers' comp policy matches what is required under any umbrella or excess liability policy.
- Make sure estimated payroll on policy are reasonable to avoid large premium adjustments at audit.

# CHAPTER 3

# Understanding How Premiums Are Calculated

## GUARANTEED-COST POLICIES

IN CHAPTER 2 WE TOUCHED UPON WHY THE phrase "guaranteed cost" can be misleading. When insurance people talk about a "guaranteed-cost" workers' compensation insurance policy, they mean that the policy's premium is not adjusted to reflect the cost of claims covered by the policy. The actual premium for the policy can and will still be adjusted to reflect the actual payroll of the insured business, so the premium shown on the policy is not the final premium due for the coverage. It is always an estimate, subject to later revision. In my experience as an agent and consultant, I've learned that, while many of those adjustments that insurance companies seek to make are proper and done according to the rules, *many are not.*

I don't think I can stress this enough. Insurance companies make lots of mistakes in computing workers' compensation insurance premiums. Human nature being what it is, they tend to catch the mistakes that cost them money—mistakes that make premiums lower than they should be. They are nowhere near as vigilant about catching mistakes that increase premiums.

And to avoid paying premium charges that are not correct and not according to the rules, businesses need to learn the basics about how workers' compensation insurance premiums are calculated—*and sometimes miscalculated.*

## Calculating Premiums

Not all workers' compensation policies are guaranteed cost. But all policies use the guaranteed-cost premium computation formula as the starting point. *Loss-sensitive* plans make additional adjustments to premium, but they are based on the same formulas and rules as are used for guaranteed-cost premiums, so understanding guaranteed-cost premiums is fundamental to understanding how all workers' comp premiums are calculated.

## Rate Times Hundred Dollars of Remuneration

This is the fundamental calculation at the heart of workers' compensation insurance premiums. Virtually all workers' compensation premiums are calculated by multiplying a rate times hundred dollars of payroll. (For domestic employees, premium is calculated on a per-capita basis.) There have been efforts in recent years to allow construction-related employers to calculate premiums by work hours instead of payroll but this has been approved only in the State of Washington to date. The idea is that payroll fluctuations roughly match up with fluctuations in workplace exposure to injury. It's also a verifiable number that insurance companies can audit without undue difficulty.

Actually, we talk about payroll being the basis for premium, but that's not technically true. It's really *remuneration*. Payroll typically is the main component of remuneration, but it isn't the only component. The insurance industry, in its wisdom, figured out that if it based premium solely on payroll, some employers would inevitably try to hold down payroll costs (to minimize workers' comp premiums) and compensate employees in other ways as much as possible. Insurers feared this would inevitably distort matters and shortchange them on premiums, so "remuneration" is defined pretty broadly to discourage such maneuvers. Of course, for most employers, remuneration is almost exclusively payroll, but sometimes an employer can

get tripped up by not understanding just what constitutes remuneration under the rules of workers' compensation premiums.

Under National Council on Compensation Insurance rules, remuneration *includes:*

- Regular pay, including salary or hourly
- Commissions
- Bonuses
- Overtime pay, less the premium portion
- Holiday, vacation, and sick pay
- Payments by the employer of contributions required by law to statutory insurance or pension plans such as Social Security that would otherwise be paid by the employee
- Piecework, incentive plans, profit-sharing plans
- Payments to employees for hand or power tools supplied by employees
- Rental value of housing provided to employees
- Value of lodging provided by the employer
- Value of meals provided by the employer
- Value of store certificates, merchandise, or credits given to employees by the employer

Remuneration *excludes:*

- Tips and gratuities received by employees
- Payments by the employer to group insurance plans
- Value of special awards paid for invention or discovery
- Dismissal or severance pay, except for time worked or accrued vacation
- Value of employer-provided aircraft
- Value of employer-provided automobiles

- Value of employer-provided free or discounted aircraft flights
- Value of employer-provided incentive vacation (contest winner)
- Employer-provided discounts on property or services
- Employer-provided tickets to entertainment events
- Employer payments to military reservists called to active duty, payments that make up the difference between military pay and employees' pay prior to conscription

## ▼ NATIONAL COUNCIL ON COMPENSATION INSURANCE

The National Council on Compensation Insurance, as mentioned in Chapter 1, writes the rules that are used in most (but not all) states concerning the computation of workers' compensation premiums. It is a private, for-profit corporation that services the insurance industry. It essentially acts as a centralized organization for workers' compensation ratemaking, giving a large degree of standardization to the industry. It has historically been known as a *rating bureau*, although regulators nowadays seem to prefer the term "advisory organization." We'll get into more detail about NCCI and the other rating bureaus (sorry! "advisory organizations") later.

So now that we know what constitutes *remuneration* for the purposes of computing workers' compensation insurance premiums, what about the *rate* that gets multiplied times the hundred dollars of payroll? Where do those rates come from?

## Manual Rate

First there is a *manual* rate. Workers' compensation rating systems assign kinds of work to different classifications; each classification within a state has its own rate per hundred dollars of payroll. Thus, the manual rate for clerical work is typically around 30 to 50 cents per hundred dollars of payroll. This will be shown on the policy, along with a code number and a brief description of the classification. The manual rate is the rate that's applied by the insurance company to all insureds in a state for a particular classification. In other words, the manual rate isn't varied to reflect your company's loss record or any other underwriting evaluation done by the insurance company. The manual rate is really a starting point for calculating your premiums; that rate is then adjusted to reflect your company's particular loss history and other credits or charges made by the insurer.

Years ago, there was just one set of manual rates that were used by all insurers in a state. So every insurance company would use the same manual rate for clerical work, for instance. But that has changed dramatically over the course of the past two decades, as most states have introduced some form of competitive rating to workers' comp insurance. This means that in most states insurance companies are encouraged to develop their own schedules of manual rates, with the idea being to foster price competition among insurance companies. So the manual rate for Code 8810 (clerical work) could be 35 cents from Mega Colossal Insurance, Inc. but 43 cents from Jolly Roger Mutual.

## The Classification Problem

Of course, most companies aren't exclusively clerical in their work exposures. And the key to making sure your manual rate is correct is making sure your insurance company is using the right classification code for your particular workplace exposures. Classification systems for workers' compensation insurance aren't always as clear-cut and easy to administer as might be hoped for, so mistakes in assigning the correct classification (and thus the correct manual rate) are far from uncommon. Sometimes the differences between qualifying for one classification (at a low rate) and another classification (at a higher rate) are subtle.

One important principle of workers' compensation classification is that, generally speaking, it is the overall business enterprise that is classified, not necessarily particular job functions. So, for example, a janitor in a manufacturing plant is not assigned to a janitorial classification but instead to the overall classification used for that kind of manufacturing.

We'll get into much greater detail about the classification system in Chapter 4, but at this point just keep in mind that your company's manual rates will depend upon which particular classifications are used by your insurance company. Each classification has its own manual rate, which is multiplied by the payroll for the employees who fall into those classifications. Multiplying payroll by manual rates produces *manual premium.*

## Experience Rating

The manual premium gets further adjusted for most employers. The most widely used adjustment is *experience rating*, which uses the *experience modification factor*. This is a multiplier that is calculated based on your company's reported workers' compensation losses. If your company's reported past losses are lower than average, you might earn a credit modifier. If your past losses are higher than average, you will probably get a debit modifier.

Whatever your modifier is calculated to be for a policy period, the manual premium gets multiplied by that factor. So if your manual premium is $100,000 but you have a .75 experience modifier, your *modified premium* is then $75,000. If your experience mod were 1.25, for that same $100,000 in manual premium, your modified premium would instead be $125,000.

Most employers whose annual workers' compensation insurance premiums exceed $5,000 qualify to be experience rated. The particular thresholds to qualify for experience rating can vary from state to state and are also adjusted over time, but generally speaking all but relatively small employers should qualify for experience rating. Again, we'll get into much greater detail later about how to check your experience modifier and avoid being overcharged due to mistakes in its calculation or application.

## Merit Rating

Some states—Alabama, Arkansas, Georgia, Oregon, South Dakota, and Vermont—have programs in place that offer credits or debits on the premiums of employers that are too small to qualify for experience rating. These programs are known as *merit rating*. For example, in Alabama, an employer that is not experience rated and whose annual premium is less than $5,000 qualifies for merit rating as follows:

| | |
|---|---|
| No claims in most recent year | 10% credit |
| No claims in most recent two years | 15% credit |
| One claim in most recent year | no credit or debit |
| Two or more claims in most recent year | 10% debit |

## Other Premium Credits or Debits

Many states also allow discretionary credits or debits by insurers. These are generally known as *schedule credits or debits* and they work much like the experience modification factor. They are percentage adjustments to the modified premium. A 25 percent schedule credit will further reduce the modified premium by 25 percent. Conversely, a 25 percent schedule debit will increase the modified premium by 25 percent.

These schedule credits and debits are filed by insurers with state insurance regulators and are supposed to be used on a rational and specified basis. That is, an insurer will file with state regulators that it wants to be approved for a maximum percentage of schedule credit or debit, say 40 percent; if regulators in that state approve it, the insurer can choose to apply up to a 40 percent credit or a 40 percent debit for a particular policyholder. Within those overall limits, insurers file sub-limits for particular criteria they propose for these adjustments. For example, if an insurer filed for a 50 percent maximum credit or debit, it would use criteria something like the following:

### Schedule Rating Plan Credits and Debits

| Criteria | Maximum credit or debit % |
| --- | --- |
| Premises | 10% |
| Classification Peculiarities | 10% |
| Medical Facilities | 5% |
| Safety Devices | 5% |
| Employee Selection, Training, and Supervision | 10% |
| Management Cooperation with Insurance Carrier | 5% |
| Management-Safety Organization | 5% |

However, in actual practice, many state insurance regulators pay little or no attention to how closely insurers actually follow these criteria. Therefore, insurers normally use schedule credits and debits with a complete and utter disregard for the actual criteria they have filed with regulators. They abide by the overall maximum amounts they have filed, but use these credits/debits as discretionary adjustments to manipulate premiums for their own purposes. Thus, when insurance markets are soft, insurers will typically use schedule credits to lower premiums in order to compete for an account that they view as attractive. When insurance markets are hard, insurers will use schedule debits to increase premiums, essentially operating on a "what the market will bear" philosophy. An insurance company will offer significant schedule credit to a policyholder one year and then, only a year or so later, when the insurance market has hardened, insist on significant schedule debit charges for the same employer. Nothing has changed in any of the specified criteria that the insurer filed with regulators—it just wants more money and feels it can get away with it in the hard insurance market.

Unfortunately, insurance regulators tend to not hold insurance companies accountable for such abuses of schedule credits and debits, so from a practical standpoint there is not a lot employers can do to hold insurers to the specific criteria filed. However, state insurance regulators might probably require a carrier to be able to document any change among filed criteria if the carrier were seeking to change the schedule credit or debit during the policy term.

## Other Premium Credits

Many states have enacted other premium credits

that can apply to certain employers within their jurisdictions. A number of states have enacted contractor premium adjustment programs, which can give contractors who pay high hourly wages some percentage credit. Other states have enacted discounts for operating drug-free workplaces or for employers who elect to utilize managed care arrangements. Figure 3-1 shows the kinds of premium credit programs offered by different states.

One thing to bear in mind with these programs is that the insurance industry has generally been successful in setting up these programs in such a way so that the employer is responsible for making sure an applicable credit is calculated and applied to its policy. Experience modification factors are calculated automatically for qualified employers, but these other premium credits are not. So it can be important for employers to review what particular credits may be available in their states and to make sure to complete and send in whatever paperwork is needed to obtain those credits.

## Standard Premium

Once the manual premium has been adjusted by the experience modification factor and any other credits and debits that apply, the resulting adjusted premium is known as the *standard premium*. This standard premium is used as a reference point by many loss-sensitive policies, but on a guaranteed-cost policy there is one last adjustment that is made: the *premium discount*.

## Premium Discount

A premium discount is a size discount that is applied to workers' compensation insurance premiums that exceed $5,000. It's also a *sliding*

*scale discount*, so that as the standard premium grows, the percentage of premium discount increases. As an example, a policy with a standard premium of $100,000 might receive a premium discount factor of 10.3 percent. This further reduces both the estimated premium paid on a policy and the audited premium that is figured after the policy expires.

## Summary of Calculating Premiums for Guaranteed-Cost Policies

So that's how the premiums for guaranteed-cost policies are computed. The manual premium is figured by determining what classifications apply for a particular employer and then multiplying the rates for those classifications by payroll. The manual premium is then adjusted by an experience modification factor, schedule credits or debits, and any other credit that may apply (such as contractors' premium adjustment plan credits or drug-free workplace credits). Finally, the premium discount factor is applied.

Remember: the premium on a policy, even a so-called "guaranteed-cost" policy, is only an estimate, because the payrolls are, by necessity, an estimate. Only after the policy has ended can actual payrolls for the policy period be determined and then a final, audited premium for the policy can be calculated by plugging in the actual payroll numbers.

Figure 3-2 shows a sample premium calculation of a guaranteed-cost policy, with estimated premiums as would be used when a policy begins. Figure 3-3 shows how that same guaranteed-cost policy premium could change once actual, audited payrolls are known.

| State | NCCI or Independent Rating Bureau | Drug or Program Credit | Merit Rating Plan | Contractor's Credit | Experience Modification* | Safety Certified Risk | Monopoly State Fund |
|---|---|---|---|---|---|---|---|
| Alabama | NCCI | Yes | Yes | | 1 | | |
| Alaska | NCCI | | | Yes | 1 | | |
| Arizona | NCCI | | | | 1 | | |
| Arkansas | NCCI | Yes | | | 1 | | |
| California | Independent | | | | 2 | | |
| Colorado | NCCI | | | | 1 | | |
| Connecticut | NCCI | | | Yes | 1 | | |
| D.C. | NCCI | | | | 1 | Yes | |
| Delaware | Independent | | | | 2 | | |
| Florida | NCCI | Yes | | Yes | 1 | Yes | |
| Georgia | NCCI | Yes | | | 1 | | |
| Hawaii | NCCI | | Yes | Yes | 1 | | |
| Idaho | NCCI | Yes | | | 1 | | |
| Illinois | NCCI | | | Yes | 1 | | |
| Indiana | Independent | | | | 1 | | |
| Iowa | NCCI | | | | 1 | | |
| Kansas | NCCI | | | | 1 | | |
| Kentucky | NCCI | | | | 1 | | |
| Louisiana | NCCI | | | | 1 | Yes | |
| Maine | NCCI | | | | 1 | Yes | |
| Maryland | NCCI | | | Yes | 1 | | |
| Massachusetts | Independent | | | | 1 | | |
| Michigan | Independent | | | | 2 | | |
| Minnesota | Independent | | | | 1 | Yes | |
| Mississippi | NCCI | Yes | | | 1 | | |
| Missouri | NCCI | | | Yes | 1 | | |
| Montana | NCCI | | | Yes | 1 | | |
| Nebraska | NCCI | | | Yes | 1 | | |
| Nevada | NCCI | | | | 1 | | |
| New Hampshire | NCCI | | | | 1 | | |
| New Jersey | Independent | | | | 2 | | |
| New Mexico | NCCI | | | Yes | 1 | | |

**FIGURE 3-1.** Premium credits offered by states (continued on next page)

| State | NCCI or Independent Rating Bureau | Drug or Program Credit | Merit Rating Plan | Contractor's Credit | Experience Modification* | Safety Certified Risk | Monopoly State Fund |
|-------|-----------------------------------|------------------------|-------------------|---------------------|--------------------------|-----------------------|---------------------|
| New York | Independent | | | Yes | 1 | | |
| North Carolina | NCCI | | | Yes | 1 | | |
| North Dakota | Monopoly Fund | | | | 2 | | Yes |
| Ohio | Monopoly Fund | | | | 2 | | Yes |
| Oklahoma | NCCI | | Yes | Yes | 1 | | |
| Oregon | NCCI | | Yes | | 1 | | |
| Pennsylvania | Independent | | | | 2 | | |
| Rhode Island | NCCI | | | | 1 | | |
| South Carolina | NCCI | Yes | | | 1 | | |
| South Dakota | NCCI | | Yes | | 1 | | |
| Tennessee | NCCI | Yes | | | 1 | | |
| Texas | Independent | | | | 1 | | |
| Utah | NCCI | | | | 1 | | |
| Vermont | NCCI | | | | 1 | | |
| Virginia | NCCI | | | Yes | 1 | | |
| Washington | | | | | 2 | | Yes |
| West Virginia** | Monopoly Fund | | | | 2 | | Yes |
| Wisconsin | Independent | | | Wisconsin | 1 | Wisconsin | |
| Wyoming | Monopoly Fund | | | | 2 | | Yes |

*For Experience Modifiers: **1** means that loss and payroll data will also be used to calculate an interstate experience modifier, if employer has operations in other states. An interstate experience modifier is used to adjust premiums in all participating states for an employer. **2** means that loss and payroll data for operations in that state are not reported for use on an interstate experience modifier if employer has operations in other states.

**West Virginia is in the process of moving away from its monopoly state fund system and transitioning to a private insurance system.

**FIGURE 3-1.** Premium credits offered by states (continued)

## ASSIGNED RISK PLANS

Since workers' compensation obligations are essentially imposed upon employers by government, yet most states utilize private insurance companies to enable employers to meet those obligations, what happens when those private insurance companies do not wish to offer the insurance to a particular employer? After all, as private businesses, insurance companies have the right to decline to underwrite certain risks. In recognition of the imposed necessity of workers' compensation insurance, the various states all provide some kind of "insurer of last resort" mechanism, usually known as the *assigned risk plan*.

In states that operate a state fund, that state fund operates as the insurer of last resort. But

| Classification | Code | Rate | Payroll | Premium |
|---|---|---|---|---|
| Clerical | 8810 | 0.32 | $100,000 | $320.00 |
| Outside Sales | 8742 | 0.78 | $75,000 | $585.00 |
| Machine Shop | 3632 | 6.75 | $750,000 | $50,625.00 |
| Manual Premium | | | | $51,530.00 |
| Experience Modification Factor | | | | 0.78 |
| Modified Premium | | | | $40,193.40 |
| Schedule Credit | | −25% | | $30,145.05 |
| Drug-Free Workplace Credit | | −5% | | $28,637.80 |
| Standard Premium | | | | $26,637.80 |
| Premium Discount | | −10.3% | | $25,688.00 |
| Discounted Premium | | | | $25,688.00 |

FIGURE 3-2. Sample premium calculation

| Classification | Code | Rate | Payroll | Premium |
|---|---|---|---|---|
| Clerical | 8810 | 0.32 | $88,567 | $283.00 |
| Outside Sales | 8742 | 0.78 | $76,875 | $600.00 |
| Machine Shop | 3632 | 6.75 | $877,543 | $59,234.00 |
| Manual Premium | | | | $60,117.00 |
| Experience Modification Factor | | | | 0.78 |
| Modified Premium | | | | $46,891.41 |
| Schedule Credit | | −25% | | $35,168.56 |
| Drug-Free Workplace Credit | | −5% | | $33,410.13 |
| Standard Premium | | | | $33,410.13 |
| Premium Discount | | −10.3% | | $29,969.00 |
| Discounted Premium | | | | $29,969.00 |

FIGURE 3-3. Sample premium calculation after audit

states that do not have state-administered workers' compensation fund have established assigned risk plans. Sometimes, employers are not even aware that their policies have been written

through the assigned risk plan, because agents do not always make this clear. An assigned risk policy looks just like a regular workers' compensation insurance policy. It shows the name of a regular insurance company—"American Obtuse Insurance" or some other well-known name—and doesn't make any obvious mention of being an assigned risk policy. But in many states, assigned risk policies carry much higher premiums than the same coverage would have if written on a *voluntary market* basis. ("Voluntary market" is the insurance industry term for insurance written not on an assigned-risk basis.) Another key phrase to watch for is *residual market*; this is another name for assigned risk.

The assigned risk plans in many states are pooling mechanisms, where claims are not actually paid by the insurance company whose name is on the policy. Instead, the claims and the premiums all go into a pool. Every insurance company that writes workers' comp on a voluntary basis in the state is responsible for a pro-rata share of the claims from that pool if the claims exceed the premiums paid into the pool, as often happens. So even though good old American Obtuse Insurance has its name on your assigned risk policy, American Obtuse isn't responsible for the claims that come due under the policy—the assigned risk pool is. American Obtuse is just paid a servicing fee to produce the policy and service it. That's probably why so many people covered by assigned risk plans complain that the service they receive from the insurance company is so poor.

An assigned risk premium is calculated just like that of any other policy—with a few changes that make premiums a lot higher (at least in most states). For starters, the manual rates are usually higher in the assigned risk plans. Thus, if the manual rate for Code 3632 in the voluntary market is $6.23, in the assigned risk plan in the same state the manual rate for 3632 might well be $7.58.

To make matters worse, in most NCCI states you lose the premium discount factor when you're in the assigned risk plan.

Finally, many states impose an additional surcharge factor known as *ARAP*, or *assigned risk adjustment program*, which essentially is a percentage debit charge for insureds with a debit experience modification factor that are in the assigned risk plan. This means that if you are insured through the assigned risk plan and have an experience modifier higher than 1.00, you get hit with an additional debit factor.

To be fair, assigned risk plans in many states have hemorrhaged money year after year, becoming a serious hidden tax on the insurance industry. (Remember: if the premiums collected by the assigned risk plans are insufficient to pay all claims, the insurance companies doing business in that state get assessed to make up the shortfall.) So these additional charges on assigned risk business are just attempts to make the plans self-funding to whatever extent possible. But it also means that if your company is in the assigned risk plan, you have a powerful motivation to try and get your workers' compensation insurance written through the voluntary market.

If you are in a state that uses its state fund as the assigned risk mechanism, then you aren't being assessed these higher rates and surcharges. For the most part, such surcharges are a feature of assigned risk plans administered in NCCI states. Because of these higher rates and surcharges, it can be very advantageous for an employer who is insured through one of these assigned risk pro-grams to move to voluntary market coverage whenever it is feasible. We'll go into greater detail about this later in the book.

## RETROSPECTIVE RATING PLANS

A relatively recent development of NCCI assigned risk plans is that policies above a certain premium size (typically $200,000) must now be written on a loss-sensitive plan. The particular loss-sensitive program utilized is a form of *retrospective rating*. Retrospective rating can lower premiums if losses are favorable, but can significantly increase premiums if losses under the policy are not so favorable.

All forms of retrospective rating policies (or "retro" policies, as they are often called) make adjustments to the premium based on losses reported during the term of the policy. Since you can't know how expensive the claims have been for the policy term until the policy ends, these adjustments are always made after the policy has expired. They perform a further rating calculation that looks back at losses that occurred during that policy period, hence the "retrospective" aspect of these policies. And because the dollar value of those claims will usually vary as time goes by, the retrospective premium adjustments are normally revised on an ongoing annual basis. Thus, the ultimate cost of a retrospective rating policy may not truly be known until years after that policy expires.

Retrospective rating policies calculate these subsequent premium adjustments by taking the standard premium (premium before application of the premium discount factor) and the losses for the policy year and running them through a formula that has been agreed upon in advance.

A classic retrospective rating formula works like this. You determine the basic premium, which is a percentage of the standard premium. Then you take the losses for the year and multiply them by a *loss conversion factor*. This gives you *converted losses*. You then add the basic premium to the converted losses and multiply that total by a *tax factor*. (States charge premium taxes that are built into the rates charged for guaranteed-cost policies but are calculated separately for retro policies.) This gives you your retro premium.

For example, if the standard premium on a policy effective January 1, 2004 through January 1, 2005 were $100,000, the basic premium percentage were 30 percent, losses for the period were $45,000, the loss conversion factor (LCF) were 1.15, and the tax factor were 1.03, the retro premium would be calculated as follows on the first retro adjustment, based on losses for 2004-05 as they were valued as of July 1, 2005:

| | |
|---|---|
| (a) basic premium | $30,000 ($100,000 standard premium x .30) |
| (b) converted losses | $51,750 (losses of $45,000 x 1.15 loss conversion factor) |
| sum of a + b | $81,750 |
| tax factor | 1.03 |
| retro premium | $84,202.50 ($81,750 x 1.03) |

So under this hypothetical retro plan, the premium would be lower than the standard premium—and lower even than it would have been if premium discount had been applied, as it would have been under a non-assigned-risk guaranteed-cost policy.

But consider what might happen for the same policy on the next retrospective adjustment, done a year later. Now losses for the 2004-05 policy have increased to $66,000, valued as of July 1, 2006.

| | |
|---|---|
| (a) basic premium | $30,000 |
| (b) converted losses | $75,900 ($66,000 x 1.15 loss conversion factor) |
| sum of a + b | $105,900 |
| tax factor | 1.03 |
| retro premium | $109,077 |

Now the retro premium is higher than the standard premium. And if losses go higher in later adjustments, the premium will continue to increase.

If you haven't dealt much with workers' compensation insurance, you might be asking why the claims costs would increase so much over time. (If you have dealt with workers' comp for a while, you probably know all too well why.) There are two parts to this question. First, many workers' comp claims don't get fully settled or paid out during the term of the policy. So a year later, when our second retro adjustment above was done, the cost of those claims was higher. Second, many retro plans use *incurred losses* as their basis—which means not just claims costs actually paid out by the insurance company, but also their estimates, or *reserves*, for what they think the ultimate cost of those claims will be.

So in our second retro adjustment above, not only could the paid-out claims for 2004-05 be now higher than a year earlier, it might well also be that the reserves set for some claims could be higher, as some claims that had earlier appeared to be not so expensive have been re-evaluated in light of changing circumstances.

So one drawback to retro plans is that until all the claims for the year are settled and paid and closed out, there can be additional charges for the policy that aren't even known until years later. Thus our hypothetical employer in the example above could be paying additional premium charges for the 2004-05 policy year until 2010 or even later.

There is one retro factor that helps limit this exposure—the *maximum premium factor* (max). This sets a ceiling on how high the retro premium can go, no matter how high the claims cost ultimately go. The max is usually set as a percentage of the standard premium. So, for instance, if the above plan had a maximum premium factor of 1.30, the most that could be due under the policy would be 130 percent of the standard premium, or $130,000. This means that, for this particular policy, incurred losses over $83,664 would not increase premiums further.

| | |
|---|---|
| (a) basic premium | $30,000 |
| (b) converted losses | $96,214 ($83,664 x 1.15 loss conversion factor) |
| sum of a + b | $126,214 |
| tax factor | 1.03 |
| retro premium | $130,000 |

So if on the adjustment done in 2007 incurred losses for the 2004-05 policy should be reported as $90,000, the premium would still only be $130,000, even though the retro formula would otherwise have called for more.

Retro policies also have a *minimum* premium factor, again usually a percentage of the standard premium. A minimum premium of .35 would mean that the minimum premium chargeable under the plan, even with zero losses would be 35 percent of the standard premium, or in this case $35,000.

## DEDUCTIBLE PLANS

Another common type of loss-sensitive plan involves the use of a deductible. These plans come in two varieties, small deductibles and large deductibles. A small deductible might be $1,000 per claim. Large deductibles can range from $25,000 per claim up to several hundred thousand dollars per claim.

In these plans, the employer agrees to reimburse the insurer for the amount of the claims that falls under the deductible limits. This is a little different from deductibles in other kinds of insurance, where the insured is responsible for paying the deductible amount outright. With workers' compensation, regulators want to make sure injured workers have their claims paid without worrying about whether the employer can afford to pay promptly. So in workers' comp deductibles, the insurer is still responsible for paying the claims, but it then has a right to demand reimbursement from the employer for those claims costs that fall within the deductible limits.

Large-deductible plans normally have both a *per-occurrence* deductible limit and an *aggregate* deductible limit. The aggregate limit sets a maximum amount for all claims covered by the policy for which the employer owes reimbursement.

In return for accepting these deductibles, the premium rates charged for the insurance are discounted. In small-deductible policies, a percentage premium credit is applied. In large-deductible plans, a percentage discount is applied to the manual premium. A very large-deductible plan may discount manual rates by a considerable percentage.

This means that under large-deductible plans, there are essentially two separate kinds of charges that an employer will have to pay the insurance company: a premium charge for the insurance over the deductible and the reimbursement for claims under the deductible limits.

Actually, in practice, large-deductible plans tend to be a bit more complicated than outlined above. To begin with, the insurance company is going to insist upon some kind of written agreement guaranteeing that it will be reimbursed for claims falling within the deductible limits. These agreements often can get fairly complex, as they will usually require reimbursement not just for claims paid out but also for charges for claims-handling expenses, all spelled out in insurance company jargon.

Additionally, insurance companies want some financial guarantees that they will actually be reimbursed for claims within the deductible limits. After all, the insurance company is on the hook for those claims whether or not the employer makes good on the reimbursement. Insurance companies being the cautious creatures they are, they tend to want to make sure they will actually receive that reimbursement. So the agreements for large-deductible plans also normally set forth terms for prefunding claims accounts that will be used to pay those claims under the deductible limits and terms under which the employer will have to replenish those accounts to maintain a certain level of funding even as claims occur and start to deplete that account.

Finally, the insurance company will want some kind of guarantee to make sure it is ultimately reimbursed for those claims. This is almost always in the form of a letter of credit from the insured.

Nowadays it is not uncommon to see plans offered by insurance companies that essentially act as a sort of combination of both large-deductible plans and retro plans. These typically are offered to larger employers (defined as those employers paying larger workers' comp premiums). But insurance companies have been lowering the thresholds at which they offer such complicated plans, so where once a million dollars of standard premium might have been required to be eligible for such programs, in some states the thresholds have been lowered to only several hundred thousand dollars of standard premium. We'll get into more detail about some of these more complicated plans later in the book and describe some of the potential benefits and potential pitfalls of these programs.

## QUICK REVIEW

- A workers' comp premium is almost always calculated using rate per hundred dollars of *remuneration*.
- *Remuneration* is largely payroll, but can also include other items of value.
- Changes in payroll can result in changes in the premium, even for so-called "guaranteed-cost" policies.
- For many employers, premium is adjusted based on prior losses and payrolls, by means of the *experience modification factor*. This is calculated yearly by a rating bureau like the National Council on Compensation Insurance and then applied by the insurance company to compute the premium.
- *Retrospective rating* policies make a further adjustment to the premium based on the losses

that occur during the term of the policy.

- *Deductible policies* discount the rates charged per hundred dollars of payroll in return for the employer accepting responsibility for claims falling under the deductible amount. Deductible plans come in two general types: small deductibles and large deductibles. Large-deductible plans can use deductible amounts of $100,000 or more, and offer greatly discounted rates.

# CHAPTER 4

# The Classification System

## WHO WRITES THESE RULES?

As should be obvious by now, how your business is classified can make a very large difference in your workers' compensation insurance premiums. After all, classification determines manual rate, which makes up the most significant component of your premium (unless you're on a loss-sensitive plan).

The classification systems used for workers' compensation insurance are unique. They don't match up directly with other business classification systems, like the Standard Industrial Classification (SIC). Even a lot of insurance professionals don't always understand these classification systems as well as they might. Most employers understand them poorly; this creates a situation where mistakes can happen. The insurance companies do a pretty good job of catching classification mistakes that run counter to their interests—mistakes that would lower premiums. But they are nowhere near as good at catching mistakes that increase premiums. So, to avoid being penalized by such mistakes, it helps to understand how these rules work.

Notice that we're talking about classification systems—in the plural. That's because there isn't one single nationwide classification system. The one used in the most states is the NCCI classification system. We'll talk a lot about that system, then, because it's so widely used. But a number of states do not use the NCCI system. In a few states, the classification system is very different from the NCCI system, so it's important to keep those situations in mind also. Still, there is a significant amount of commonality among all these systems.

Of course, all of these classification systems have been devised over the years by the insurance industry—insurance companies and the organizations created to work with them. We've mentioned the NCCI, the National Council on Compensation Insurance. NCCI is the workers' compensation advisory organization—aka rating bureau—used in a majority of U.S. jurisdictions. And NCCI produces the manual of rules that governs how businesses in those states are classified for workers' comp insurance. At this writing, the NCCI classification system utilizes around 600 classification codes. (In contrast, the classification system used by Pennsylvania and Delaware uses only around 300 classification codes.)

NCCI was created back in the 1920s, in response to pressure from state insurance commissioners to standardize and consolidate a lot of the rules for ratemaking for workers' compensation insurance. Over the years, NCCI has somehow acquired an aura of being some kind of quasi-governmental entity. I've sometimes heard even insurance professionals talk as if NCCI were a government agency. But that's not accurate. NCCI is an independent organization that works as a sort of interface tween insurance companies and insurance regulators. NCCI works to develop the manuals of rules that govern the computation of workers' compensation premiums and performs a lot of statistical work used to develop rates for particular kinds of work in particular states, and they calculate the experience modification factors that are used in most (but not all) states.

The idea that NCCI is a government agency might arise in part because some other rating bureaus are indeed government-established bodies. In those states that use non-NCCI rating

bureaus, some of those other rating bureaus are run by the state government.

This confusion might arise, in part, because some other rating bureaus are indeed government-established bodies. In those states that use non-NCCI rating bureaus, some of those other rating bureaus are une by the state government.

No matter which rating bureau is used in a particular state, that rating bureau sets the rules regarding how certain business enterprises are classified for purposes of computing workers' compensation insurance premiums. The NCCI produces a manual that details what is intended to be included in each classification code, *The Scopes® of Basic Manual Classifications*—the "Scopes® Manual" for short.

Even though this manual largely determines how your business will be classified (for operations in NCCI states, at least), it's copyrighted material that is published and sold by NCCI. So if you want to read the details of what's in this manual, you could order a copy from NCCI. But most employers don't need to go to that expense. For one thing, you can all NCCI and get information about particular classifications at no cost. NCCI maintains customer service people who will be glad to discuss the details about how particular work exposures should be classified. Just keep in mind that the customer-service people have to rely on the information you provide over the phone to give accurate classification advice. So try to be as thorough and accurate as you can be in describing your situation.

A lot of times we get calls from people asking where online they can find the details of what's covered by certain classifications. In this day and age, it's understandable that people think that any and all such information should be available on the internet somewhere. But as this copyrighted material that NCCI sells to insurance companies and insurance agents (and to consultants like me) they really can't just make it available free on the internet, but they will discuss it freely if you call the number above. A policyholder should also be able to get information about their specific classifications from their insurance agent or broker. My company provides a lot of information about classification matters at our web site, www.cutcomp.com, but we can't provide copyrighted contents of the Scopes® Manual. We'll gladly answer questions about particular classifications at our toll-free number of 800-288-9256.

## WHICH STATES USE NCCI?

It's actually easier to list the ones that don't. Here are the states that maintain their own independent rating bureaus, with their own sets of manual rules:

California
Delaware
Indiana
Massachusetts
Michigan
Minnesota
New Jersey
New York
North Carolina
Pennsylvania
Texas
Wisconsin

Keep in mind that there are also the so-called "monopoly" jurisdictions where workers' compensation can be written only through a state-administered fund:

North Dakota
Ohio*
Puerto Rico
U.S. Virgin Islands
Washington (state)
West Virginia**
Wyoming

*Ohio maintains its monopoly state fund for worker's compensation with that state, but it has recently transitioned to using the NCCI classification system for the state fund in place of their own distinct classifcation system.
**West Virginia is in the process of transitioning to a private insurance system as of this writing.

Every other state jurisdiction uses the NCCI system of manual rules for determining classifications, computing premiums, and calculating experience modifiers and other adjustments to the premium. There can still be important differences between one NCCI state and another, because each state can and often does enact particular rules and statutes that can affect workers' comp premiums. NCCI states operate under a unified set of manual rules, but those rules have a lot of exceptions for particular states.

## HOW CLASSIFICATIONS AFFECT PREMIUMS

Each particular classification will carry a particular rate per hundred dollars of payroll. So making sure your business is classified properly is vital to making sure your premiums are calculated properly. All classification systems used, whether NCCI or other, have some common characteristics that you should familiarize yourself with.

## The Governing Classification

Even the most basic kind of company will typically have more than one classification code used on its policy. The workers' compensation classification systems generally will try to classify the overall business enterprise, rather than breaking down each different kind of work done by employees. So janitors in a manufacturing plant won't go into a janitorial class, but instead into the overall classification assigned to that manufacturing operation. The classification on a policy that has the most payroll assigned to it is known as the *governing classification*; this is the classification that is used to cover the overall business enterprise.

But for almost all kinds of businesses, the classification systems recognize certain *standard exceptions*, which are kinds of work that are almost always broken out into their own classification. Clerical work is considered a standard exception for almost all employers. So, unlike our janitor in the manufacturing plant, the office workers in that same manufacturing company will have their payroll assigned to Code 8810, the class for clerical work. (Janitorial work is considered a *standard inclusion* in most classification codes.) Another important standard inclusion for most classifications is for shipping and warehousing. Although there is a separate classification for warehouse operations, the warehousing operations of a manufacturer are not assigned to this class. Instead, they are treated as a standard inclusion, so the shipping and warehousing employees of a manufacturing plant would be included in whatever the governing classification for that manufacturer is.

Another standard exception is for "Outside Sales." Almost all governing classifications allow outside salespeople to have their payroll broken out into its own classification. Drivers are another common standard exception, although there are a number of governing classifications that include drivers within their descriptions, so one has to look more carefully at the governing classification to determine if drivers can be broken out or not.

Although most businesses are allowed to break out clerical work into its own (inexpensive) classification, some kinds of businesses are not allowed to do so. Recently, I was retained to assist a public broadcasting satellite uplink facility. It had been assigned the classification code used for broadcast television and radio stations and, under the NCCI classification rules, that kind of business is not allowed to break out clerical payroll into its own classification. The details of this prohibition were not spelled out in the policy—but only in the Scopes® Manual.

I should point out that of this writing, NCCI indicates it is planning a major review of such classification codes beginning in 2005 and continuing over the next five years. So it is possible that some of these details may change in the near future. Take a look at Figure 4-1 for a representative sample of the kind of detail the Scopes® Manual goes into. Some of the Scopes® Manual entries for a particular classification can cover an entire page or more of the manual, although many entries are shorter than this.

One problem with the classification system is that it's difficult to keep it current with developments in the business world. There are many kinds of businesses that didn't exist ten years ago—and many that have changed how they do their work in fundamental ways. The classification system, whether it uses 600 classes or 300, is

The NCCI publishes a manual, known as the Scopes® Manual, that contains detailed descriptions of what is intended to be included under each classification. Here is an excerpt from that manual, to give some idea of the kind of detail they go into.

Each NCCI classification has a unique four-digit code number. This particular Scopes® entry is for Class code 5213, Concrete Construction NOC. The NOC designation stands for Not Otherwise Classified. This means that this classification is used when some other more specific classification does not fit a policyholder's operations.

5213

**PHRASEOLOGY** CONCRETE CONSTRUCTION NOC. Includes foundations or the making, setting up or taking down of forms, scaffolds, false work or concrete distributing apparatus. Excavation, pile driving, all work in sewers, tunnels, subways, caissons or cofferdams to be separately rated. Codes 5222–Concrete Construction in Connection with Bridges and Culverts–and 5506 and 5507–Street or Road Construction–shall not be assigned at the same job or location to which Code 5213 applies.

**CROSS-REF.** Cleaning or Renovating Building Exteriors (N/A MN; WI); Concrete: Construction-Private Residences-Monolithic: Guniting-Not Chimneys-All Operations-guniting on chimneys to be separately rated as Code 5222–Chimney Construction (N/A MN; WI); Hod Hoist or Construction Elevator Installation, Repair or Removal & Drivers (N/A MA)–the following operations will be classified as:

    5213 Concrete or Concrete Encased Buildings or Structures

    5057 Iron or Steel Buildings or Structures

    5022 Masonry Buildings or Structures

    6003 Piers or Wharfs

    5403 Wooden Buildings or Structures Including Those Designed for Dwelling Occupancy

*Satellite Dish Installation: Applies to Ground or Roof-Mounted Installations; Installation of Concrete Mounting Pad (N/A MA) Silo Erection: Concrete; Silo Erection: Pre-Cast Concrete Staves; Wrecking: Building or Structures–Not Marine–All Operations*–includes salespersons and clerical at wrecking site. Wrecking or demolition operations shall be classified as follows:

    5403 Wooden Buildings or Structures Including Those Designed for Dwelling Occupancy

    5213 Concrete or Concrete Encased Buildings or Structures

    5057 Iron or Steel Buildings or Structures

    5022 Masonry Buildings or Structures

    6003 Piers or Wharfs

Where wrecking or demolition involves buildings or structures of more than one type of construction, the highest rated classification applies (N/A MA, WI). State Special: California–Concrete Construction-NOC–including foundations or the making, setting up or taking down of forms, scaffolds, false work or concrete distributing apparatus–NPD with Code 5222–Concrete Construction-Wood or Code 5506 or Code 5507–Bridge Building-Metal, Code 6003(3)–Bridge or Trestle Construction–Wood, or Code 5506 or Code 5507–Street or Road Construction-excavation, reinforcing steel installation, pile driving and all work in connection with sewers, tunnels, subways, caissons or cofferdams shall be separately classified.

**FIGURE 4-1.** Representative detail of the Scopes® Manual (continued on next page)

SCOPE Code 5213 applies to all commercial types of concrete building construction, self-bearing floors, foundations, piers, culverts, silos, grain elevators, etc., and includes making and erecting forms, placing reinforcing steel and stripping forms. Code 5213 would apply to each of the aforementioned steps in the concrete construction process whether all work is performed by the principal contractor or portions of the job, such as making and erecting forms, are completed by a special subcontractor.

The term "self-bearing floors" mentioned above is used as a basis for distinguishing between self-supported concrete floors, assignable to Code 5213, and ground-supported concrete floors, assignable to Code 5221. A self-bearing floor is elevated above the ground, and, being an integral part of the concrete construction itself, is assigned to Code 5213—Concrete Construction NOC. A ground-supported floor of a building which is poured either at the beginning or end of the construction job involves the type of concrete or cement work contemplated by Code 5221.

Concrete walls that are poured in flat forms on ground level are assigned to Code 5221, provided that the pouring insured does not tilt up the walls and secure them in place. This operation is assigned to Code 5221 since the exposure is the same as that of pouring a ground-supported concrete floor. Code 5213 is assigned to an operation in which an insured both pours the concrete and ground level to create a wall and subsequently tilts the wall into place......

*This particular Scopes® entry goes on for another page, but you probably get the idea. Many of the Scopes® entries are similarly detailed, with exceptions noted for particular states and lots of technical details. Fortunately, many other Scopes® classification definitions are shorter and easier to follow. But this illustrates the point that when it comes to classification, the devil can really be in the details. And remember that some states don't use the NCCI system, so in those states the details can be different for a particular kind of work than they would be in an NCCI state.*

*Scopes® Manual excerpt © 1990-2005 The National Council on Compensation Insurance, Inc.*

**FIGURE 4-1.** Representative detail of the Scopes® Manual (continued)

hard-pressed to anticipate all the varieties of work that exist in the modern world.

So looking at the Scopes® Manual can sometimes give you a glimpse of the history of the American workplace. You will find a few very old-fashioned-sounding classification codes still in existence, such as macaroni manufacturing, but software programmers and computer chip manufacturers did not get specific separate classifications approved until 1992. The upcoming NCCI review of its classification system will undoubtedly update things significantly, but the workplace exposures of the real world will always be a moving target.

## Classification by Analogy

There is another aspect to workers' comp classification that can create problems for employers: the limited number of classifications used. With a limited number of classifications available, it's inevitable that many kinds of work will not fit neatly and exactly into a particular code. When that happens, NCCI and other rating organizations will try to find the classification that comes closest to fitting an employer. Since that usually involves a judgment call to some extent, classification by analogy can sometimes be open to dispute.

This situation is being exacerbated by a long-term trend toward fewer classifications overall.

Just recently I helped a client successfully appeal a classification, and the solution actually involved classification by analogy. NCCI had assigned Class Code 8010, Store: Warehouse NOC to this employer, who recycles computer and other electronic equipment by disassembling it and salvaging usable parts. NCCI had recommended 8010 by analogy, saying that the employer was in the business of buying and reselling computers. Thus, a wholesale store classification. But we helped this employer successfully argue before the appeals board that they were essentially a manufacturer in reverse. That is, they performed the same kinds of work that a computer manufacturer did, only they did it in reverse sequence. We argued that since the work was the same, only in reverse, they should be classified the same as a manufacturer of such computer equipment, Code 3574. The appeals board agreed with this logic, and assigned Coded 3574, with a large reduction in rate and premium.

Thus, each remaining classification tends to be used for a wider variety of businesses, increasing the classification-by-analogy approach.

Here's an example of how classification by analogy can be problematic for employers. A few years back I reviewed the classification of a manufacturer of fuel and oil filters for heavy machinery. This particular operation was done in a modern, new computer-assisted factory that minimized the exposure of employees in the manufacturing process. But NCCI practice is to classify all filter manufacturers, by analogy, in the classification used for the manufacture of folding paper boxes. This means that our modern, high-tech manufacturer of filters get the same classification (and manual rate) as companies that make cardboard boxes in workplaces with much greater exposure to workplace injury. While experience rating will (theoretically) adjust those manual rates eventually (assuming the loss experience of the high-tech filter manufacturer really is lower than the loss experience of the box makers), the experience rating formula doesn't remove the entire penalty from this inappropriate classification. And as the number of overall classifications is decreased in the future, such problems can only increase. With fewer classifications, each classification will be broader and less precise, increasing the number of times that an employer gets lumped in with other kinds of companies whose injury exposure is higher.

## IMPORTANT RULES REGARDING CLASSIFICATIONS

For manufacturers and other non-construction-type businesses, the *single enterprise rule* is important to keep in mind when it comes to determining proper classification. The single enterprise rule states that it is the overall business of the employer that is classified, not necessarily each and every job function done there. (So the janitor and the shipping and warehousing people go into the company's governing classification.) But there can also be important exceptions to the single enterprise rule.

For instance, if a company does a kind of work that is not contemplated by the governing classification, a second classification may be assigned (other than a standard exception class) in certain circumstances. But the rules that govern how and when this may be done are specific.

Under NCCI manual rules, an employer may have additional classifications that are not standard exceptions under certain circumstances:

- When each separate legal entity insured under a policy should be assigned to the classification that describes its overall business within a state;
- When the basic classification requires (per the manual) that certain operations be broken out into a separate classification;
- When the employer does construction or erection work, farm work, or repair operations or operates a mercantile business;
- When the employer operates more than one business in a state.

Keep in mind: the assignment of certain classifications is limited to separate and distinct businesses because, according to NCCI, "they describe an operation that frequently is an integral part of a business described by another classification." These rules are not contained in the Scopes® Manual, but instead are in another manual published by NCCI, *The Basic Manual for Workers' Compensation and Employers' Liability Insurance*. Each non-NCCI state typically has its own manual of rules published by its respective rating bureau.

For a concrete example of how this rule works, consider a case I worked on years ago. A trucking company also maintained a separate repair facility. Normally, such a repair facility would be considered an integral part of the trucking company and would not be eligible for a separate classification. But this particular client operated its repair facility as a separate business and worked on vehicles of third par-

ties as well as those of the trucking company. In that instance, I was able to get a separate (and less expensive) class approved for the company's repair work.

It isn't always the rules about classifying the business that can trip up employers; the rules about assigning payroll of individuals within the company can also get complicated. According to the NCCI *Basic Manual*, the payroll of an employee can be divided between approved classifications that apply to an employer, as long as payroll records are kept that record how much time the employee actually spends in the different kinds of work. An estimate of how much time is spent in each occupation is not acceptable, nor are percentages of overall time (as in "He works 20% of the time painting and 80% as a carpenter").

In practical terms, this division of payroll for individual workers typically applies primarily to those in construction or erection work. For one thing, NCCI rules don't allow a worker's

> I had one client whose insurance company tried to take this physical separation rule to an absurd extreme. Their insurance company had insisted on lumping the company secretary/treasurer into the machine shop class because she had to walk through the shop every morning on her way to the physically separated office area. Fortunately, we were able to get that decision overturned by working with NCCI and the department of insurance. In fact, while I was at it, I got the classification used for their shop operations changed to one that had a rate half that of its original classification.

payroll to be divided between the clerical class and another class, even if proper payroll records are kept. The same is true for the outside sales classification: you can't divide the payroll of an individual between this class (#8742) and another class, even if proper payroll records are kept.

Also, for employers that operate in tight quarters, keep in mind that NCCI rules require that clerical work be done in a "physically separate" area in order to qualify for the inexpensive clerical classification. "Physically separated" means separated by walls and a door.

## Mercantile Risks

Under NCCI rules, each separate location of a mercantile type risk is classified separately according to the kind of work done at that location.

## Important Rules for Construction Employers

The NCCI rules are different for construction-type risks in one important aspect. It is common for more than one type of work to be done by the same employer. Thus, it is more likely that payroll for certain employees may have to be divided between or among more than one classification. NCCI rules now allow the payroll of any employee to be divided between classifications, if those classifications are approved for a particular employer. But the exception to that rule is that you can't divide payroll of an individual between either the clerical class or the outside sales class and another class. Since most non-construction employers don't have more than one class on their policy (other than clerical and outside sales), it's relatively rare for payroll of non-construction employees to be divided that way. It's much more

common for construction risks, because their policies often have several construction classifications approved and employees often divide their time among different kinds of construction work. Consider the following example.

A client of mine made, repaired, and installed industrial furnaces. Under NCCI rules, when a company works on furnaces on its own premises, the payroll goes into a manufacturing class. But when that same company's employees work on furnaces on the clients' premises, payroll goes into a millwright classification. When I got involved in reviewing things, the insurance company auditor had been deciding for several years that the payroll records did not allow him to tell when employees were working on the company's premises and when they were working offsite at a client's location. So all payroll for these employees was thrown into the expensive millwright classification.

Fortunately, by reviewing their records carefully, I was able to reconstruct when employees were actually out at clients. This left the remainder of the payroll eligible for the lower furnace manufacturing classification, for a premium reduction of about $8,000 per year. If either the insurance agent or the insurance auditor had explained all this ahead of time to the employer, payroll records could have been set up to clearly differentiate between these two kinds of work. But, as is common in workers' compensation insurance, no one had bothered to explain to the employer why it would be important to keep such records. This happened even though it was clear to the insurance company from prior policies that a significant portion of payroll properly belonged in the manufacturing classification.

## What a Difference a State Makes

A few years back I worked with a company that manufactured steel reinforcing bars used in concrete construction. The employees also installed these steel bars at construction sites. The owners came to me after a serious problem developed.

A few years earlier, they had expanded from Arizona into California. They build a manufacturing plant there, in addition to their original plant. When they set up their California policy, they used the same classification codes as they had been using for years in Arizona.

Everything was fine the first year. Then a dispute arose regarding the proper classification for the California policy. The employer had purchased coverage through the California State Fund, a competitive state fund. In California, as in some other states, the state-run fund competes with private insurers.

The employer began to receive monthly statements from the California fund showing a different classification—one with a significantly higher rate than the old class. He discussed it with his Arizona agent and with the state fund staff and was told it must be just an error. So the employer corrected the invoices by hand, replacing the higher class with the lower-rated old one, and paid the premium due under the less expensive class.

But eventually the California Rating Bureau and the state fund told the client that there had not been an error after all. The higher classification was correct under California rules and this employer now owed several hundred thousand dollars in back premiums.

Arizona is an NCCI state, while California has its own independent rating bureau. The lower class was right under NCCI manual rules but wrong under the California definitions. To make matters worse, the California State Fund insisted that these back premiums be paid promptly or else the California current policy would be cancelled.

If someone had only explained to this employer at the outset that California classification rules were different from Arizona rules, he would have been able to plan differently to avoid the problem. But this employer did not learn the true cost of his California workers' compensation insurance until the year was over and so the jobs they had bid on for that policy period had not been priced with the actual cost of insurance. They had inadvertently underpriced their product for that entire year. When the company finally understood the true costs of the California workers' compensation coverage, my client eventually moved its operations out of California.

## COMMON CLASSIFICATION MISTAKES

In our consulting work with employers, we see a number of mistakes in assigning classification codes. Here are some of the more common ones:

- The employer's operations have changed over time, but the classification(s) used on the workers' comp policy has or have not kept up.
- A classification mistake was made years ago and has been repeated year after year, as the insurance agent and insurance company underwriter don't bother to think for themselves, but instead just copy what's on the prior policy.
- A recent inspection by NCCI or other rating bureau has misunderstood the nature of the employer's operations in some regard and assigned an erroneous new classification.
- The classification used is correct for many

other states but not for a particular state the employer has workers in.

■ Classifications have been changed mid-policy in a state that does not allow such midterm changes.

Time and again, as we correct classification mistakes for clients, we hear employers express surprise that these mistakes haven't been caught in the normal course of the work done by their insurance agent or the insurance company. Indeed, sometimes these mistakes are caught that way. But far too often they are not. The lesson employers need to learn is that no one else has as much incentive to catch mistakes that raise premiums as the one paying the premiums. If you sit back and trust that everything is working the way it should in a perfect world, you may be setting up your company for serious premium overcharges.

The common classification mistakes listed above aren't theoretical—as evidenced by the following cases from our files.

We recently worked with a client that had been manufacturing several products for decades—but its product mix had changed. Many years ago, most of their sales were of a cloth-based wrap that was applied with a hot sealant to industrial pipelines. But over time, a different product came to dominate their sales: a sort of industrial-strength duct tape that was also used on pipelines, but this product wasn't cloth-based and wasn't applied with a hot sealant. As you might expect, the manufacturing processes for these two products were very different. But the classification on the company's policy was based on the old product, which now generated only a minority of its sales. Correcting the classification to reflect the cold-applied product reduced pre-

miums substantially (in the range of 35 percent). The classification had once been right, but somehow the evolution of the product line (and manufacturing process) had never been reflected on the workers' comp policies.

Or consider this problem we fixed a couple of years ago. The client was in the business of selling home furnishings to interior decorators. Its showroom wasn't open to the public, but only to those in the decorating business. In the showroom they displayed samples from various suppliers they represented. It turned out to be that, although the classification code used on their policies was right in most NCCI states, the particular state where this client was located had what is known as a *state special* classification for their particular kind of employment—and that state special had considerably lower rate.

That's one more tricky part to the NCCI classification system—individual states that use the NCCI system can create special rules for certain industries that apply just in their jurisdiction. So a classification code that is right in one NCCI state can be wrong in the NCCI state right next door.

This situation gets exacerbated by a trend in the insurance industry in recent years of consolidating underwriting in regional offices. Combined with other trends like downsizing and turnover, it means that many underwriters tend to be younger, less experienced, and handling more states than their predecessors of a decade or two past.

*Sometimes, even when a class is right, it can be wrong.* That's because different state jurisdictions place different restrictions on when a classification can be changed to a more expensive class. The NCCI *Basic Manual* itself places some restrictions on how late in a policy such changes can be made, but some NCCI states place even tighter restrictions on this. But insurance underwriters and auditors are often unaware of such state restrictions and operate as if they were free to make such changes at will. Thus, an insurance company will sometimes change the classification code (and thus the rate) used on a policy well after the policy has begun. But if this change is against manual rules or a state statute, it may not be allowable even if the classification change is correct per other manual rules. Insurance companies often will unknowingly violate such limitations, but if you bring it to their attention you can get them to reverse their actions.

Here's an example of how this can work and how different states impose different limitations in this regard. We recently worked with an employer that specialized in painting commercial aircraft. They had operations in both Florida and New Mexico. Their insurer had changed their classification code three months into the policy to a more expensive classification that was, it turned out, correct for their kind of work under NCCI rules. But New Mexico has statutory limitations on the ability of an insurer to change to a more expensive class more than 60 days after the policy begins. (It allows such changes after 60 days only if there has been a change in the insured's operations.) So we were able to get the insurance company to reverse its change in New Mexico (at least for that year), but we couldn't fight the change for Florida, because Florida allows such changes to be made within the first 120 days of the policy.

## The Ways Your Classifications Can Go Wrong

1. If the rating bureau has not inspected your business, your insurance company may have assigned the wrong classification because it misunderstood your operations or the fine details of the classification definition.

2. If the rating bureau has inspected your business, there might be an inaccurate description of your business (or at least some part of your business) in the inspection report that hasn't been caught.

3. If the rating bureau has inspected your business, and even if the description of your operations is accurate, the inspector's interpretation of the classification rules might be wrong. (This happens more often than one would think.)

4. If there is more than one business entity insured on your policy, one of the businesses may be eligible for a separate and lower classification.

5. If your company does business in a non-NCCI state as well as an NCCI jurisdiction, the classification definitions for the non-NCCI state might differ significantly. The classification that's right in the NCCI state may not be right in the non-NCCI state.

6. There may be an unusual exception in your state (even if it is an NCCI state) about your kind of work that allows your company to take a less expensive classification than if you were in some other NCCI state.

7. If your operations have changed over time,

the classification used currently may no longer be right. You may now be eligible for a less expensive classification, but the insurance underwriters do not realize this.

8. Whether or not the rating bureau has inspected your business recently, the definition of pertinent classifications may have changed. At the time of this writing, NCCI was in the early stages of a major review of all its classifications and the definitions for them. What was right a year ago might be wrong by next year.

## NCCI Basic Manual Rules

The NCCI *Basic Manual* sets forth some limitations on changes to a more expensive classification code after policy inception. A few states have tougher restrictions on this practice than are contained in the NCCI manual. Also, the limitations in the *Basic Manual* also have some important exceptions. The manual states that changes in classification that result in lower premiums shall be made retroactive to the inception date of the policy. But changes in classification that result in higher premiums shall be made as follows:

- During the first 120 days of coverage, a change can be made retroactive to policy inception.
- After first 120 days but before final 90 days of coverage, a change can only be made pro rata as of the date the company discovers the cause for such a change.
- In the final 90 days of coverage, a change in classification that results in a higher premium cannot be made to the policy, but only to the next renewal policy.

## State Restrictions

But a few states place different restrictions upon the ability of an insurance company to change to a more expensive classification after a workers' compensation insurance policy begins. They are as follows.

*Connecticut* allows a change to a more expensive class during the first 60 days of the policy to be made retroactively back to the inception of the policy. After first 60 days but before the final 90 days, the change can be made effective only as of the date the insurance company endorses the policy. And during the final 90 days of the policy (or later, in the case of an audit), the insurance company cannot change to a more expensive class (although it can change the next renewal policy).

*Florida* allows a change to a more expensive class during first 120 days of policy to be made retroactive to inception. After first 120 days but before final 90 days, a change can only be effective as of the date the company endorses the policy with the change. During the final 90 days of the policy (or later), the change to a more expensive class cannot be made. Florida does not exempt those in the construction or erection business from these limitations (the way the NCCI *Basic Manual* rules do), but the Florida rules state explicitly that any error or omission in describing the employer's operations will allow the more expensive classes to be added as of the effective date of the policy.

*Georgia* follows the NCCI manual rule, but clarifies that a reallocation of payroll is considered to be a change in classification; this can be an important difference from standard NCCI manual rules.

*Illinois* does not allow a change to a more expensive class after the policy begins unless there has been a change in the insured's operations during the term of the policy or if the policy was the first year for which that particular insurance company had written coverage for that employer. Illinois does not exempt those in construction or erection work from these limitations.

*Kansas* has a strict policy that does not allow changes at all to a more expensive class after the policy begins. No exceptions are made for these strict limitations, so those in the construction and erection business are also protected.

*New Mexico* allows changes to a more expensive class within the first 60 days of the inception date of the policy. After 60 days, such changes are allowed only if there has been a change in the insured's operations or if there was some misrepresentation or omission to the insurance company about the operations by the employer or its insurance agent. But these limitations do not apply to those in the construction or erection classifications; these classes can be changed anytime back to policy inception.

*Oklahoma* allows changes to a more expensive class only within the first 90 days of the policy.

*Oregon* allows changes in classification to be made anytime. It does not even allow the limited protections offered by the NCCI *Basic Manual*.

*Wisconsin* allows changes to a more expensive class within the first 120 days to be made retroactive to policy inception. After 120 days, more expensive class cannot be added to the policy. These limitations apply equally to those in the construction or erection classes.

## Reallocation of Payroll

This is an area that often gets involved in disputes about changes in classification.

Reallocation of payroll means that the insurance company decides that work that was assigned to one classification on your policy really belongs in another classification that is also on your policy. The effect on premium is essentially the same as changing a classification, although no new classification is added to the policy.

Oftentimes insurers will list several classes on a policy with payroll shown as "If Any"—so no payroll is used to compute the premium on the initial policy, but if someone at the insurer later decides that payroll should be moved into this class, the insurer is able to do so. Under NCCI *Basic Manual* rules, reallocation of payroll is not prohibited and is not considered to be a change in classification.

Now that we've learned about how the workers' comp classification system works (and what can go wrong), let's move on to Chapter 5, where we can cover how to get mistakes in classification fixed.

## QUICK REVIEW

- The rules governing classification of an employer's operations for determining workers' compensation insurance premiums are written by rating bureaus such as the National Council on Compensation Insurance (NCCI).
- Most but not all states use the NCCI system. Some states operate independent rating bureaus.
- For most non-construction employers, the rating bureau will try to determine an overall classification that best fits the overall work of the employer.
- A few workplace operations are normally broken out into their own classifications: clerical, outside salespeople, and (often, but not always) drivers.
- Different states may classify employers doing the same work differently.

- Classifications need to be regularly reviewed to make sure the employer isn't being overcharged through use of an out-of-date classification.

- Some states limit the ability of an insurance company to change an employer to a more expensive classification after the policy has been in effect for a while, even if the classification change is correct under manual rules.

# CHAPTER 5

# Correcting Classification Mistakes

## HOW AN EMPLOYER GETS CLASSIFIED

SO HOW EXACTLY DOES AN INSURANCE COMPANY decide which classifications to use for a particular employer? Understanding the various ways this is done (and what can go wrong) can be an important step in the process of correcting classification mistakes.

## A New Business

For a brand new business that has never been insured for workers' compensation insurance, the initial step in determining classification will be with the insurance agent, who will probably help you complete an application. At this stage, it is important to make sure your agent really understands your operations and the exact nature of the work you do. This is true whether your business is a new venture or not, but it is particularly important when applying for your first workers' comp policy.

It's natural to want to rely upon the experience and expertise of your insurance agent at this stage. It's also common for many businesspeople to find insurance application forms a bit frustrating and user-unfriendly. The terminology can be unfamiliar and sometimes the questions asked don't seem to be particularly applicable to your line of work. But one mistake that can be made at this point is to leave too much of the application process to the agent.

First of all, the level of experience and expertise among insurance agents can vary greatly—your agent may inadvertently give you the impression that he or she knows more about the process than is really true. Many insurance application forms ask only relatively cursory information or don't leave a lot of room for detailed answers. But from your point of view, it is important that you provide really thorough and complete information about the nature of your work. The better job you can do in that regard, the more you decrease the chances of a mistake in classification that will cause problems for you down the road.

Not only do you want to give the agent and underwriters thorough and accurate information to help them do their job, you also want to document that there was no omission or misrepresentation made at this stage of the process. In Chapter 4 we saw that some states limit the ability of insurance companies to change to a more expensive class after the policy begins, as long as there has been no misrepresentation by the employer. If you do a thorough job of explaining what you do at the outset and document exactly what information you provide, you can defend yourself against any later charges that you misrepresented what you do.

For a new business, the insurance company will rely upon whatever is on the application form, along with any brochures and other information provided. So you want to double-check any information that the insurance agent has written on the application and make sure it is complete and accurate. Give the agent lots of supporting documentation like brochures and web sites and *keep your own file that documents exactly what you have provided.* Keep a copy of the completed application, along with copies of all brochures and other documents you provide, and keep the file with your insurance documents in case you need it later.

The completed and signed application, along with supporting documents, will be sent to one

or more insurance companies, where an underwriter will review them and (in theory) exercise independent judgment about the classification codes used on the application form. However, in practice, sometimes underwriters don't always invest sufficient time and effort at this stage of the game. That's how mistakes in classification can arise and why insurance companies will sometimes want to try and change classifications after the policy has begun.

This can be especially true if your policy is being written through an assigned risk plan. In many jurisdictions, insurers handle assigned risk plans as a necessary cost of doing business—something that has to be done, but that they aren't real enthusiastic about doing. So an assigned risk underwriter may not be able to take a lot of time and effort to check the classification codes the agent has put on the application. If the agent has made a mistake, it may take a while before someone at the insurance company figures it out.

In general, the employer is much better off if the classifications are right from the outset. Changes to a more expensive class can be a very costly and unpleasant surprise when they are done in midterm. You have already made your business plans, figuring on a certain cost for workers' comp, and finding out halfway through the year that your cost projections were way off can throw a real monkey wrench into your business plan.

If your insurance company tries to change you to a more expensive class sometime after the policy has begun, you may be able to resist it based on the state restrictions we detailed last chapter. But you may need to show that the mistake wasn't due to misrepresentation or omission by you or the agent.

## An Established Business

With a business that isn't applying for workers' comp insurance for the first time, agents and underwriters pay a lot of attention to what classifications have been used on prior policies—sometimes too much attention. A normal part of the insurance underwriting process is to look at prior audits and at experience modification factor worksheets. Both of these kinds of documents show what classification codes have been used in recent past policies for your company; insurance agents and insurance company underwriters rely heavily on these to guide them about how to classify your operations. The problem, of course, is that any past classification mistakes will just get perpetuated that way.

Many times when my consulting practice discovers a classification mistake for a client, we see that the mistake has been going on for many years. As we'll discuss later, most states allow an employer to recover such overcharges only for a few past years. So if the insurance company has been overcharging you due to a classification mistake, it will be able to keep its unwarranted premiums for all but the most recent few years. It can be vital, therefore, to be alert for such mistakes. But the tendency of so many agents and underwriters to rely on past classifications can work against uncovering long-standing classification mistakes.

## THE ROLE OF THE RATING BUREAU

Rating bureaus like NCCI not only write the classification manual rules, but they are also supposed to assist and guide member insurance companies in applying those rules correctly. And in a perfect world, mistakes would usually get caught by a system of checks and balances among insurers, rating bureaus, and insurance regulators. Guess what! We don't live in a perfect world.

A long time ago, in an insurance industry far, far removed from the current one, rating bureaus and regulators kept insurance companies on a tighter leash. But here and now, the old checks and balances just aren't working as well. Still, rating bureaus like NCCI can and do play a role in correcting classification mistakes made by insurers.

Perhaps the most common mechanism for doing this is the inspection process. As part of its duties, NCCI performs inspections of workplaces in order to determine proper classifications. These used to be done at nominal cost to employers, but nowadays the cost of an inspection can be seven or eight hundred dollars. This is all part of a change at NCCI that began a decade or so ago, shifting away from assessments on member insurance companies to a fee-for-services model for its revenues. This has made inspections more expensive and thus less likely to be requested by insurance companies or employers.

An inspection can officially resolve classification disputes between insured and insurer. But since inspections have become expensive, employers want to do their homework first and make sure the results of an inspection will be positive. Additionally, they should try to negotiate for responsibility for the inspection to lie with the insurer or at least for the inspection to be done on a "loser pays" basis.

Sometimes, if an insurance company suspects that the classification used historically for an employer is too low, it will request an NCCI inspection on its own. We often find that employers have been the subject of an NCCI inspection without being aware of it. We've never figured out how these inspections are so often done in a kind of "stealth" mode, but perhaps when the inspector shows up the shop personnel believe it's just an "insurance inspection" and never understand that the NCCI inspection is unique. At any rate, it can be a good idea to check with NCCI or other appropriate rating bureau to see what inspections it may have on file for your company, as employers are often unaware of inspection reports.

If there is an inspection report on file, you definitely want to get a copy and check it over carefully. Sometimes small errors in describing your operations can make a difference between a costly classification and a much less expensive class—potentially worth thousands or tens of thousands of dollars a year in premium charges.

## WHAT CAN GO WRONG WITH INSPECTIONS

Like so much else in the insurance system, the inspection system has been going through significant changes in recent years. NCCI has been trying different methods of getting inspections done, with varying results. For many years, NCCI used only its own in-house inspectors to do this work. While not foolproof, using its own specially trained inspectors ensured that inspectors were knowledgeable and experienced in the NCCI classification system.

However, in an attempt to increase efficiency and reduce costs, NCCI moved to a system of outsourcing to third-party inspectors. This approach seemed to reduce the quality of the field inspections and NCCI has now moved to return to using its own inspectors. But this means that

---

### The Value of Working for Third Parties

Here's an interesting example of how a part of an employer's operations can be misclassified, due to a misunderstanding of a small detail. This particular employer operated a trucking company. Also covered under the workers' compensation insurance policy were mechanics who worked on those trucks. Now, normally, mechanics are classified into a much less expensive class code than the one used for trucking companies. But the NCCI had inspected and informed the employer that under NCCI rules the mechanics went into the trucking classification, because mechanics working for a trucking company are classed into the governing classification of trucking. And this is correct.

Except that this particular trucking company operated the repair work as a separate business. The trucking company was a corporation while the repair work was done by a separate company that was a sole proprietorship and the mechanics not only worked on the trucks of my client, they also did repair work for third parties. Under these circumstances, the mechanics were eligible, under NCCI rules, to be separately rated in a much less expensive classification.

We eventually got NCCI to understand these details and to revise its decision. This lowered the client's premiums to $6,000 a year.

---

some inspections done in recent years may have problems due to the less expert third-party inspectors who were used for several years.

Even with well-trained inspectors, things can still go wrong with inspections. Typically, the field inspector writes a report that is then reviewed by an office-bound classification expert. So the final classification decision is made by someone who has not seen your operations firsthand, but is relying on the field inspector's description. If the field inspector misunderstands some crucial aspect of your operation or leaves out some detail from the written report, the classifier may assign an incorrect classification. So it is vital to review written inspections with the proverbial fine-tooth comb, to make sure all details are correct and nothing has been left out.

Figures 5-1 and 5-2 show two checklists that can be used to review inspection reports by those in manufacturing work and those in construction work.

Notice that each checklist has an entry for checking work done by either subcontractors with their own insurance or leased/temp employees who are insured on someone else's policy. This can be important, as sometimes this can make a difference in the classifications that are assigned to your company. If some particular work function is done exclusively by subcontractors or employees insured elsewhere, it can make a big difference. Consider this example.

The client was a concrete contractor. The classification assigned—concrete contractor—seemed appropriate. But when we looked into the case, we saw there were some factors that made that classification far too expensive.

Part of the problem was caused by the insured company's name—Suncrete, Inc. (This is a fictionalized version of its actual name.) The company constructed buildings using a proprietary concrete-based formula, hence the "crete" part of its name. For years, it had been classified in the

| | Actual | Inspection Report |
|---|---|---|
| Raw Materials Used | | |
| | | |
| | | |
| | | |
| Description of Operations | | |
| | | |
| | | |
| | | |
| Operations Conducted as a Separate Business Enterprise | | |
| | | |
| | | |
| | | |
| | | |
| | | |
| | | |
| Machinery and Equipment Used | | |
| | | |
| | | |
| | | |
| Finished Products | | |
| | | |
| | | |
| | | |
| Work Done by Leased or Temp Employees Insured Elsewhere | | |
| | | |
| | | |
| | | |

**FIGURE 5-1.** Checklist for manufacturers to check inspection and classification reports

expensive concrete contractor class.

But we learned during our review that the

| | Actual | Inspection Report |
|---|---|---|
| Actual Work Operations Performed by Own Employees | | |
| | | |
| | | |
| | | |
| | | |
| Work Operations Performed by Subcontractors with Own Insurance | | |
| | | |
| | | |
| Permanent Yard Employees | | |
| | | |
| | | |
| Usual Kinds of Worksites (Residential, Commercial, Multistory, etc) | | |
| | | |
| | | |
| Trades Employed | | |
| | | |
| | | |
| | | |
| | | |
| | | |
| | | |
| | | |
| | | |

**FIGURE 5-2.** Checklist for construction employers to check inspection and classification reports

actual work with the special concrete material was performed by subcontractors that had their own insurance. The client's own employees performed a variety of construction and carpentry operations, but did not actually work with the concrete. All of the correct classifications for the work actually performed by the client's employees were much less expensive.

Fortunately, we were able to produce certificates of insurance for the subcontractors and convince the NCCI that the client's employees did not do the concrete work. The NCCI approved a number of carpentry classifications that carried about half the rate of the concrete classification. The result was a substantial reduction in premium and a refund of $60,000 for prior years when the wrong classification had been used.

## The *Scopes® Manual*—a Vital Tool

As we've mentioned earlier, the Scopes® Manual published by NCCI contains detailed descriptions of what each of the classification codes in the NCCI system is intended to cover. To check if the classification codes used for your business are correct, you really need to look at what the codes on your policy are intended to cover.

If you're in an NCCI state, the Scopes® Manual is the bible of classifications. You can order a copy from NCCI or subscribe to an online edition, but be aware that it can be a little expensive. So you might instead want to ask your insurance agent to send you a copy of the pertinent Scopes® entries for the classes on your policy. Most insurance agents who write workers' comp insurance will probably have access to this manual.

The only problem with relying on just some excerpts from the manual that your agent can send you is that this might limit your checking too much. Having access to the entire manual can enable to you to look at other possible classifications and decide if another is really more appropriate for your operations. Remember, also, to check for state special classifications that might apply in your state. State special classifications are detailed in a separate section in the back of the Scopes® Manual.

Of course, the Scopes® Manual is an NCCI publication. Thus, it will not apply to every state, because some states do not use the NCCI classification system. Here's a rundown of some states where the Scopes® Manual is not going to be authoritative. To get details about the non-NCCI rating bureaus used in these states, consult the state-by-state directory at the end of Chapter 1. These states don't use the NCCI classification system, but still allow private insurance for workers' comp. There are also states that don't allow private insurance for this, but instead require employers to obtain coverage through a state-administered fund. Their rules about classification of employers also will vary from the NCCI system. The following states allow private insurance, but don't follow NCCI classification rules.

**California.** This is the largest single state market for workers' comp and it operates completely independently of NCCI. The pertinent manuals are published by the Workers' Compensation Insurance Rating Bureau of California (WCIRB). While many classes are very similar to those in the NCCI system, there can be very important differences as well. In order to find out what each classification in California is intended to cover, you need to review the manuals published by WCIRB.

**Delaware and Pennsylvania.** These two states share their own unique rating system. Their rating bureaus are completely independent of NCCI and their classification system is radically differ-

ent. The NCCI system has about 600 classes; the system used by Delaware and Pennsylvania has just over 300 classifications. Even the numbering system is different for these two states: three digits, not four as in the NCCI system and elsewhere.

**Indiana.** Even a lot of insurance people seem to think that Indiana is an NCCI state, but this is not accurate. Indiana has an independent non-NCCI rating bureau, but it follows NCCI rules to a large extent (but there can be differences, too).

**Massachusetts.** This is a non-NCCI state with its own rating bureau, and thus its classifications can vary from NCCI standards in the Scopes® Manual.

**Michigan.** Michigan takes a rather unusual approach. It maintains its own rating bureau, but this bureau has real jurisdiction only over classifications used on assigned risk policies. For policies written in the voluntary market, the state doesn't enforce manual rules about classifications, so insurance companies can use their own judgment about classifications.

**Minnesota.** Minnesota takes the same approach as Michigan: when it comes to classifications, only assigned risk policies are subject to strict jurisdiction of a rating bureau. For voluntary market policies, insurance companies are free to exercise their own judgment about classes.

**New Jersey.** This state maintains its own independent rating bureau that writes the manuals and then determines proper classifications.

**New York.** This state has an independent non-NCCI rating bureau that publishes its own manuals regarding classifications and other rules governing workers' compensation insurance in that state.

**North Carolina.** This state maintains an independent rating bureau, the North Carolina Rate Bureau, which calculates experience modifiers for use in North Carolina. Although it operates independently, it uses the NCCI Scopes® Manual as the basis for classifications.

**Texas.** This is another non-NCCI state. Texas doesn't exactly operate its own rating bureau; the Texas Department of Insurance (TDI) has a separate workers' compensation unit that writes the manual rules that apply in Texas, including classification rules.

**Wisconsin.** This state maintains a non-NCCI rating bureau that writes its own manual rules for classification. The classification system is generally similar to the NCCI one, but can differ in some classification particulars, so to be sure you need to consult that rating bureau's manuals.

## Inspection or No Inspection, Classes Can Be Wrong

It may sound like a bad joke, but the truth is that there are two ways your business can be misclassified—if you haven't been inspected … or if you have. If you haven't been inspected, it means that your classifications have been determined by some insurance underwriter using his or her best judgment, based on information provided. And while insurance underwriters try to do their best, the system is complex: mistakes happen. And even if you have been inspected, the same still applies: the system is complex and even rating bureaus make mistakes.

You really can't rely upon the traditional insurance system to reliably catch mistakes in classification. Typically, the system is a lot better at catching mistakes that lower premiums than at catching mistakes that increase premiums. Insurance agents may assure you, either directly or indirectly, that they review such things for you, but in my experience the ability of insurance agents to actually determine if classifications are right or not varies widely. Maybe your agent really is knowledgeable about classifications—but maybe not. Frankly, the odds are better than even that he or she doesn't know as much in this area as you've been led to believe.

But with a little time and effort, you can do some checking on the classifications used for your business. After all, you don't need to become expert about all the classifications—just the ones that are being used for your business or that might be used.

So dig out your policy and recent audits, make a list of the classification codes being used, and then do some research into what those classes are intended to cover. Your agent can probably be helpful in obtaining copies of the manual descriptions of what's covered by each class. If you agent can't or won't help with this, it's probably an indicator that you need to consider finding a new agent.

If what you see in the manuals isn't a spot-on match for what your company does, dig further. Talk with people at NCCI or the other appropriate rating bureaus to see what they think. Although the quality of the advice available over the phone from rating bureaus isn't always as consistently good as one might wish, it can still be valuable. And talk with your competitors, if possible, to learn what classification codes are used on their policies. If you don't have competitors who are friendly enough to share this information, check with any industry-specific associations you belong to. Often, they've already done some research and have experience in this area that they would be happy to share with you.

## FIXING CLASSIFICATION MISTAKES

OK, so let's assume you've done all the above and you've found something you feel really isn't right. How do you get your insurance company to correct it?

Two keys to getting such situations fixed are patience and attention to details. Insurance company underwriters and auditors often receive communications from policyholders

### When Inspections Go Awry

This client was a private school in Vermont. NCCI had recently inspected it at the behest of its insurance company, and the inspector changed the way a number of their employees were classified, resulting in a large premium increase that would raise premiums from that point forward.

This school ran group homes and dormitories for students, and the NCCI inspector had decided that their residential counselors were nonprofessional staff, who were classified as Code 9101 with a rate of $8.01 per hundred dollars of payroll, rather than as Professional Employees, Code 8868, with a rate of $0.78 per hundred dollars of payroll.

This obviously had a huge impact on their premiums. The inspector was adamant in his interpretation of the classifications. The school had already asked him to reconsider, but he stuck to his guns.

However, we forwarded this matter to a more senior (and more experienced) classification expert at NCCI. We pointed out that these Residential Counselors were responsible for working with and supervising students, had to be certified in first aid and CPR, planned and ran recreational activities for the students, and were part of the treatment team for the students.

The more experienced classification supervisor at NCCI overruled the inspector and returned these counselors to the professional classification, and the crisis over vastly increased workers' compensation premiums was averted.

In this case, the problem wasn't so much an inaccurate description of the employees' work as it was an incorrect interpretation of rules by an inspector. But it we hadn't gotten the matter reviewed by a more experienced NCCI person, the change in classification would have stuck, resulting in severe financial problems for the school.

Remember that even if an inspector insists that he or she is right, appealing the inspection (either formally to the appeals board or informally to higher-ups at the rating bureau) can often get an unfavorable inspection overturned. The key is to look carefully at the classification definitions and then to present convincing information and documentation to support the classification change you are requesting. An inspection by a rating bureau may seem like the final word, but it doesn't have to be. If you're convinced that an inspection has assigned an incorrect classification to your operations, don't take no for an answer.

that are long on indignation but short on detail. Most of these insurance folks are genuinely honest and ethical and will want to do the right thing, if only you can overcome their natural human tendency to resist admitting (even to themselves) that they've made a mistake.

Your agent can be of real assistance here, as many insurance companies can be pretty stubborn about wanting such communications to be funneled through the agent. Sometimes this isn't possible, if the agent just isn't giving you much service or if you're complaining about a prior policy that was written with a different agent. But as a general principle, you probably want to start the process of fixing a classification mistake by working through your agent.

Put in writing exactly why you feel the classification(s) used is or are wrong for your business. Be as specific and details as possible. Make reference to the specific descriptions in the manuals (like the NCCI Scopes® Manual) that you feel support your case. And then follow up like your life depended on it.

Insurance agents and insurance companies are swamped with paperwork, e-mail, faxes, and pressing deadlines. So it can be very easy for something like a communication about a mistake in classification to get lost in the shuffle, even with the best of intentions. Nobody else has as much incentive as you do to make sure this gets addressed, so don't assume that agents and companies will properly review or act upon your initial communications.

Whatever their response to your initial complaint is, make sure you get it in writing. You want to set up a file and document it carefully with every letter, fax, and e-mail you receive on this subject. Keep a detailed record of all phone conversations you have about this as well, noting date, person you spoke with, and what was said or agreed to. If they commit to a deadline or timetable for action, be prepared that you may have to initiate follow-up when those key deadlines arrive.

Sometimes, even with all this effort, I have seen insurance companies just try to "make the problem go away" by responding with double-talk or just plain insisting that they're right and they're not going to reconsider their position. If you feel that they're just being stubborn and refusing to respond to your legitimate concerns, you still have options open to you.

## If There Is a Rating Bureau Inspection

When your company already has been inspected by NCCI or other rating bureau, you can communicate with the rating bureau and point out the specific areas in the report that you feel are inaccurate or incomplete. I have often been successful in getting NCCI to change something in a classification report, even after the client had been told that the classification decision was final, just by sending detailed information to someone higher up at NCCI who has more experience with the classification system.

So in these situations you want to work your way up through the rating bureau bureaucracy and find someone higher up the food chain who is more experienced and knowledgeable in classification matters. Then send a detailed written communication to this person.

If this is unsuccessful, and you still feel your argument has merit, every state has some kind of appeals mechanism that employers can use to try and get classification decisions reversed. Your state's department of insurance can explain what the process is for your particular state. Normally you can appear before such bodies without having to hire an attorney.

Keep in mind that these appeals boards operate with certain restrictions. The time allotted for your presentation will probably be limited. That means you have to focus on the particular reasons you feel the classification needs to be changed. You may want to consult with an insurance agent or consultant before doing this, as I sometimes see employers who do this on their own spend their limited time going off on a tangent away from the heart of the classification problem. Sometimes employers and managers are just too close to the situation to see that the point they most passionately want to make isn't really germane to the classification in question.

The second important thing to keep in mind is that the appeals process in most states isn't a legal hearing. This means that your testimony about your operations isn't under oath—and the people who are listening to your presentation know it. So your own verbal testimony about what your company does and how you do it may not necessarily be compelling to an appeals board. To whatever extent possible, document every important point that makes a difference to the classification. Have written documentation that backs up your testimony and have it in such a form that you can give copies to the appeals board.

It may be irritating to think that the people listening to your appeal might take your testimony about your company's operations with a grain of salt, but I have sometimes seen appeals boards discount uncorroborated testimony. So document everything you can. If video of your operations will be enlightening about some unique aspect of your work, arrange to have a television and playback equipment at the hearing.

Keep in mind that in most states you can even make a further appeal, if you feel it is warranted. I have helped several clients successfully appeal decisions made by the Workers' Compensation Appeals Board of California. Again, talk to your state's insurance regulators to find out what the particular process is for that state.

## If There Is No Inspection

If you can't make headway working with your insurance company and if the rating bureau hasn't inspected your company, you may want to consider requesting an inspection. Keep in mind that many rating bureaus like NCCI now charge significant fees for an inspection, so if at all possible you want to negotiate for the insurance company to pay for the inspection. If you fight hard enough for this, you can often get it to accept responsibility for paying for the inspection. If this can't be worked out, you should at least insist that the inspection be done on a "loser pays" basis, so that if the inspection upholds your request for a change in class, the insurance company pays the bill. Only if the inspection upholds the decision of the insurance company would you be responsible for the charges.

Once the inspection is arranged, don't be a passive participant in the process. I have seen many such inspections go awry because the employer wasn't properly prepared. Before the inspector arrives, you should review the key points you want to make sure he or she understands. Don't assume the inspector will know to ask the right questions. Do your homework ahead of time, know what the important differences are between the classifications involved in your dispute, and make sure you have available documents and key people who can verify the key elements in your assertions.

If the results of the inspection aren't favorable, be sure to carefully review a written copy and see if there are any inaccuracies or omissions. If there are, immediately send in a written correction and then follow up to make sure it is taken into account. If necessary, consider using the appeals process as detailed above.

## After You Win

If you are successful in getting a rating bureau to approve a new classification, through either a new inspection or an appeal, be prepared to have to do some work with your insurance company. In an ideal world, winning at the appeals board should make everything else automatic, but it often doesn't work that way. The rating bureau will typically only insist that your current insurance company correct the classification on the current policy. But if you've been misclassified for past years, you should insist that your insurance company return any premium overcharges that have occurred in the past. Many states allow you to go back only three or four years. One state, Illinois (my home state), allows refunds going all the way back to 1987, if you can document the facts of the matter. Again, the insurance regulators in your state can inform you about how far back you can go in that state.

Expect that your insurance company may attempt to avoid making such refunds even after you press your case with them. They may say, for instance, that rating bureau inspections only require classification corrections to be made from that date forward. That's technically true, but if you can document that there has been no change in your operations, you should be able to persuade state insurance regulators to support your claim to go back at least three years into the past.

The standard workers' compensation insurance policy has language in it that makes it the responsibility of the insurance company to get your classification right. Under Part Five— Premium, paragraph B entitled "Classifications" it reads:

> Item 4 of the Information Page shows the rate and premium basis for certain business or work classifications. These classifications were assigned based on an estimate of the exposures you would have during the policy period. *If your actual exposures are not properly described by those classifications, we will assign proper classifications, rates, and premium basis by endorsement to this policy*. (Emphasis mine.)

Notice that the policy doesn't say, "We will try to use the correct classification" or "We will use the correct classification to the best of our ability." It says, "If your actual exposures are not properly described by those classifications, we will assign proper classifications, rates, and premium basis...." The policy contains a promise by the insurance company that it *will* use the correct classifications and rates, even if different from what's on the policy. You might need to remind a recalcitrant insurer about this policy language, as sometimes underwriters and auditors haven't really read the fine print of their own policy. But if push comes to shove, this is your written guarantee that your insurance company has promised to use the correct classifications and rates for your policy. You should definitely hold it to that promise.

## Temporary or Leased Employees

Earlier, we discussed how it can sometimes affect your overall classification if you use temporary or leased employees for some portions of your work. This is because such employees are usually insured under the policy of the temporary agency or the employee-leasing firm (often called a PEO, *professional employer organization*). The use of temporary workers and leased workers has grown considerably in recent years and has caused some real ripples in the workers' compensation insurance field.

Once upon a time, temporary agencies provided someone to sit in for your secretary while he or she was on vacation and not much else (or so it seemed, anyway). Do you remember the movie *Dave*, about the temp agency owner who impersonated the president of the United States? Kevin Kline played the titular character as a small-town everyman who was honest but naive and loved finding temp work for maiden-aunt types. If you don't have occasion to use modern temporary agencies, that may be your image of the industry. But if you spend more time running your business than watching cable-TV reruns, you probably already know just how different reality is. Nowadays, so-called *alternative employers* like temp agencies and PEOs provide workers for factories, distribution centers, and construction sites on a large scale. The growth of these kinds of employers has caused significant stresses and strains in the workers' compensation arena, and one of the most significant stresses has been in the area of classifications.

If you use such alternative employment techniques, it may seem that you have outsourced your worries about the workers' compensation insurance for those employees. And that's certainly true to a large extent, but not entirely. The first and foremost thing to watch carefully when using such alternative employment sources is to make sure that your temp agency or PEO maintains valid workers' compensation insurance. I know this sounds elementary, but not all temporary agencies or PEOs are created equal in this regard.

Earlier in this book, we talked about how insurance markets cycle between soft markets and hard markets. Alternative employers like temporary agencies and PEOs are often hit hardest by shifts to hard markets. Part of the whole business model that makes temporary agencies and PEOs feasible is that they can arrange for employee benefits and insurance with economies of scale that allow them to take care of these business expenses at a cost lower than their client companies could do on their own. When it comes to workers' compensation insurance, however, it often becomes very difficult for such alternative employers to find economies of scale when the insurance market turns hard.

A few years ago, one of the largest PEOs in the U.S. was abruptly and unexpectedly driven out of business in significant part by the sudden shifting of the workers' compensation market to hard conditions. It didn't happen all at once, of course, but rather in a horrific sort of slow-motion collapse over the course of a year: during that time, the PEO struggled and failed to obtain valid workers' compensation coverage for all those employees it had leased to client companies all over the country. And many of those client companies that were allowing those leased employees to work in their shops and offices learned to their regret that the PEO was unable to keep the promises it had made about those workers being covered by its policy. So guess where those injured workers got coverage. They were covered by the policies of those client companies, even though those companies had already paid the PEO to cover those workers. And of course the insurance companies insisted on getting premiums for all those workers who were supposed to be covered elsewhere, but weren't. So the client companies ended up paying for workers' comp twice for those workers—once to the PEO and again to their own insurance carriers.

The other thing about temp agencies and PEOs is that they can be terribly difficult for insurance companies to classify properly for workers' comp purposes. That's because the standard insurance policy was just not designed with such employers in mind. And the insurance industry hasn't tried very hard to come up with innovative solutions to the classification problems of such employers, preferring to try and shoehorn them into a policy format that was really designed for more traditional kinds of employers.

The standard workers' compensation policy was designed for employers that would have only a few classifications. A typical manufacturer has one governing classification and two or perhaps three standard exception classifications (for clerical, outside sales, and perhaps drivers). A typical contractor may have a few more, because the contractor may be performing several kinds of construction-related work at job sites that require separate classes. But a temporary agency or employee leasing company might have dozens, even hundreds of classifications on

## How to Check Your Company's Workers' Comp Classifications

1. List the classification codes used on your workers' compensation policy.

2. Compare these with the classifications used on the audits of recent past policies. Any changes? If so, look more carefully into the reasons for this change.

3. Examine the definitions for your classifications with the appropriate rating bureau for the states involved (NCCI for most states or the independent rating bureau for non-NCCI states). Your agent or broker should be able to give you copies of the definitions of the classifications involved. Make sure your company's operations seem to fit these definitions.

4. Make sure to check if there are any "state special" classifications that may apply to your operations in some states.

5. Call the rating bureau and see if there has been an inspection of your operations in recent years. If yes, request a copy of the inspection report so you can review it and make sure the description of your operations is accurate.

6. If there is any question about the accuracy of the classification assigned to your operations, discuss this with an experienced and knowledgeable classification expert at the appropriate rating bureau. See if this person agrees with the results of your inspection.

7. Contact competitors in your same line of work, if feasible, to see how they are classi-

fied. If they are classified in a less expensive class than your company, they may be willing to share this information. Business groups and associations for your field of work may also have information on this subject.

8. Discuss the classification with the experienced agent, broker, or consultant, to determine if your classification may be wrong. Do not request an NCCI inspection without first determining the cost of such a request. NCCI inspections are often fairly expensive, with costs possibly running close to $1,000. You may not wish to incur this expense. You may be able to correct a classification error in other ways without paying for an NCCI inspection. Non-NCCI rating bureau inspections tend to be less costly.

9. If you can't get the rating bureau to change your classification and you feel you belong in another class, you can request an appearance before the appeals board in your state. Contact your state's insurance regulators to find out the details about how to request an appearance. There is no cost involved with appearing before the appeals board.

its policy or audit.

Properly classifying such alternative employers can create real problems for both the insurance company and the employer. The insurance company wants to get fair and proper premium for the real exposures of those workers who are out in all those workplaces, yet the mix of workplaces can change from year to year, even from month to month. The standard policy just doesn't have the flexibility to work very well with large numbers of classifications that can change often.

It's just as bad from the point of view of the policyholder-employer. The cost of workers' compensation insurance is a vital factor in pricing the fees charged by temp agencies and PEOs. But how do you project the actual cost of the insurance if the insurance company can radically change the classifications (and rates) for the work after the policy has expired? I have worked with temp agencies that have received audit bills for twice or three times the premium they had expected, because the insurance company has retroactively changed a lot of the classification codes used to compute the premium.

The NCCI manual rules that protect other employers from those kind of late-in-the-game class changes don't apply to temporary agencies and employee-leasing companies in many states, so these alternative employers are far more vulnerable to this tactic by insurers. And make no mistake: it can be devastating.

## The Alternative Employer Trap

People who run temp agencies or PEOs may not fully realize how this trap can ensnare them. A lot of such employers have no recourse but to be insured through assigned risk plans. This means that not only are they probably paying much higher premiums than they might in the voluntary market, but they are probably also receiving a lower level of service in terms of underwriting and loss control. That's a pretty broad generalization and a harsh one that some in the insurance industry might disagree with. I know that insurers don't like to think they are really shortchanging assigned risk policyholders, but I can only tell what I've seen over the years in the field. Because insurers aren't really playing with their own money on assigned risk plans, they have a reasonable tendency to hold down expenses on policies that aren't making them much money and where they aren't really on the hook for the claims.

That oversimplifies things a bit, I know, because ultimately insurers will be assessed to make up shortfalls in the assigned risk pools, and so in recent years some NCCI and some member insurers have focused significant resources on doing a better job with assigned risk policies. But part of the problem is that they focus those resources in ways that don't necessarily make life easier for policyholders.

The unique aspect of alternative employers like temporary agencies and PEOs is that their policies can have lots of classifications on them. Where a typical manufacturer might have only three or four classes, a temp agency or PEO can have dozens or even hundreds. And the workplace exposures of employees can change in an instant, if the policyholder signs up a new client that is in a different kind of work.

The standard workers' compensation insurance policy just wasn't designed with such alternative employers in mind. The policy was really designed to work for more traditional kinds of employers. But instead of developing policy forms that would address these problems, the insurance industry has just tried to shoehorn alternative employers into the existing policy format, with predictable difficulties ensuing.

The real trap for such alternative employers is that underwriting of assigned risk policies can often be a bit cursory, as nowadays NCCI and

insurers concentrate much more effort on the audit. So they are less concerned that a policy isn't written with all the appropriate classes and rates, because they figure they can just catch any problems at the audit. But doing a stringent audit for such employers, when the underwriting process tends to be the opposite and the classification rules are complex and arcane, is a recipe for disaster for policyholders.

So it is vital for alternative employers to expend some considerable effort in learning the complexities of the classification system. This is not an easy task. The workers' comp classification system, as we have mentioned earlier, does not correspond with any other classification system, such as SIC codes. Even insurance professionals make mistakes in assigning classifications, because of the complexity. Yet if an alternative employer does not make this effort, its insurance company may be demanding huge additional premiums after doing an audit, because it has changed classifications codes. During the course of the policy, the alternative employer has priced its charges to clients based on the classes and rates on the policy, not realizing that the insurance company might come in after policy expiration and double the rate being charged for some kinds of work. Needless to say, this is not a situation any sane business owner wants to be in.

If you are an alternative employer and you find yourself in such a situation, review the audit billing done by the insurer very, very carefully. Because of the complexity of the classification system and the insurer's limited understanding of the work done at your clients, many of the classification changes sought may not really be valid. Depending on what your state insurance regulations say, you may also have some protection there from changes made on the audit.

To avoid these problems, review carefully exactly what kind of work will be done at each of your clients and then work with your insurer and NCCI to try to determine the proper classification. You may not always like the answer you get, but it's far better to get that information before you bid on a job than only when the policy is audited.

The insurance industry does not make the classification system user-friendly, so be prepared to have to do some heavy lifting to get good information. As mentioned earlier, many agents and brokers are not as knowledgeable as you might hope in this regard. And since it is your company that will ultimately have to deal

▼
### A Complicated Case of Classification Correction

Correcting classifications isn't always easy, but if you're convinced that the change is correct then persevere—it can pay off handsomely, as this case illustrates.

The agent had appealed the classification used for this employer before we got involved. This attempt was unsuccessful, but the employer wasn't ready to throw in the towel. They contacted my office for further assistance and we got to work.

Our review of the inspection report showed that it accurately described the employer's operations. However, we couldn't justify the higher-rated classification that had been assigned, based on our reading of the pertinent

manuals. This particular employer was based in Indiana, and Indiana has a unique relationship with NCCI. Technically, Indiana operates an independent rating bureau, but that rating bureau follows NCCI manual rules pretty closely and relies on NCCI for a lot of services. At that time, the NCCI office that had handled the inspection and classification assignment was based in Illinois. (Since then, NCCI has consolidated its operations down in Florida.) Based on our different interpretation of the classification description, we sent a copy of the inspector's report, along with appropriate sections from the NCCI Scopes® Manual, to a senior classifier at NCCI. He reviewed this and agreed that the classification decision had been in error. He then assigned the lower classification we felt was more appropriate. But things got complicated.

Remember, this employer was headquartered in Indiana, a state that is technically independent of NCCI. And even though NCCI had agreed with us that a less expensive classification code was warranted, the independent Indiana rating bureau didn't want to go along with this decision. In their files, they had found a copy of an old decision made by Indiana's governing committee, their precursor to modern appeals boards. In the late 1960s, this particular employer had appealed before this governing committee, and it had assigned the expensive classification. Indiana said that NCCI did not have the authority to overrule that earlier decision by the committee—even though that decision was nearly 25 years old at that time.

But we went back to the governing committee and presented the same evidence that had persuaded NCCI to agree with us. The committee agreed that the new, lower classification was warranted and approved its use for this employer. The lower classification was ultimately approved for use in all states in which this employer operated, with a reduction in annual premium of about 25 percent.

The moral of this story? When you're sure you're right, keep on working the system, even when things get complicated. The odds are that you can prevail, if you just keep at it.

with the audit premium, no one else has as much incentive to get things right as you do.

## QUICK REVIEW

- Mistakes in classification are one of the most common causes of overcharges in workers' compensation premiums for employers.
- Rating bureaus like NCCI have authority to determine proper classification for employers and can overrule the classification decisions of the insurance company.
- Even rating bureaus can make mistakes in assigning classifications, so employers need to be involved in reviewing and researching if classifications used are really correct.
- If a classification mistake is suspected, employers often need to work with the rating bureau, not the insurance company, to get the problem corrected.
- The classification system is complex, particularly for employers such as temporary agencies or employee leasing companies. Particular effort may be needed to avoid overcharges due to misclassification by insurance companies.

# CHAPTER 6

# Experience Modification Factors

W HEN I DO PRESENTATIONS ON THE subject of experience modification factors, I often use a graphic of Egyptian hieroglyphics up on the screen. It usually gets a chuckle of recognition from some in the audience who get my little joke: to a lot of folks who buy insurance (as well as a lot of folks who sell insurance), the calculation of experience modification factors is about as understandable as that ancient Egyptian graffiti. Perhaps that's why problems with experience modifiers constitute the second most common source of premium overcharges that I see in my consulting practice.

Most employers who pay more than a few thousand dollars per year for workers' compensation insurance are familiar with the experience modification factor, sometimes called an *EMR* for *experience modification rating*, or just *mod*. It can be found

down toward the bottom of the premium calculation, right after manual premium and before premium discount. The experience modifier is designed to adjust the current premium based on prior losses. This is done by comparing loss information for a particular employer from three prior years (typically) with expected losses (calculated based on average losses of similar companies) for those same prior years.

*Expected losses* are calculated by taking the audited payrolls for those same past years and multiplying them by an *expected loss ratio* (ELR). The ELR for each classification is figured by averaging the losses of all businesses in that classification in a state per hundred dollars of payroll. So the ELR for classification 8810 (clerical) in Illinois is calculated each year as the average loss per hundred dollars of payroll for all employers in Illinois reporting payroll in code 8810.

## DECIPHERING YOUR EXPERIENCE MOD

If your company is large enough to be experience rated (most companies paying more than $5,000 per year in workers' comp get experience rated), then you should be receiving a worksheet each year from the rating bureau that calculates your modifier. Yes, the same rating bureaus that write the rules about classification also are in charge of calculating experience modifiers. And those same rating bureaus write the manual of rules that governs how modifiers are to be calculated. For most states, the rating bureau is NCCI. But again, some states don't use NCCI:

California
Delaware
Indiana
Massachusetts
Michigan
Minnesota
New Jersey
New York
North Carolina
Pennsylvania
Texas
Wisconsin

These states still calculate experience modifiers for employers; it's just that the formulas that these non-NCCI states use to calculate modifiers differ a little from the formula used by NCCI. Employers don't really need to understand all of the fine details of these formulas in order to check their mods, but in this chapter we'll give you the tools you need to be able to check your company's modifier and spot common mistakes that increase mods improperly.

## Common Misconceptions About Modifiers

Over the years, I've heard a lot of things said about experience modifiers that just aren't true. Perhaps most common is that "the state" calculates them. As you may have gathered, this just isn't so. Rating bureaus are not part of state government. The biggest rating bureau, NCCI, is a not-for-profit corporation that serves member insurance companies. It's a private corporation. Even the non-NCCI rating bureaus are not really part of state government, although some of them are established by state statute and are more quasi-governmental than NCCI.

Another inaccuracy I've heard about experience modifiers is that they compare your past losses with your past premiums. Again, not true. As mentioned above, the mod formula compares your past reported losses (subject to some important limitations) with *expected losses*. Those expected losses are calculated by multiplying your audited payroll for those same past years times statewide expected loss factors for each classification code.

## Past Years' Payroll Audits Should Match Modifier

Since past audited payrolls are used to calculate experience mods, this is the easiest part of experience modification factors for employers to check on their own. The information used here should match up exactly with the audited payroll information on your past years' audit billing statements for your past workers' compensation insurance coverage.

Remember: workers' compensation insurance begins by the insurer estimating which payroll amounts fall into which particular classifications.

After the policy ends, the insurer does an audit—either by sending out its own auditor to review your payroll records or by asking you to report actual payrolls to it (usually the case for smaller employers). You then receive an audit billing statement that shows the final audited premium for the policy, based on actual payrolls. The numbers on that audit billing statement should match up exactly with the payroll numbers used to calculate your experience mod. If they don't match, it may well indicate that incorrect information was used to calculate your modifier.

## Intrastate or Interstate Modifier

If your business has always operated in just a single state, you'll get an *intrastate* modifier—calculated using expected loss data for just that one state. But if you've operated in more than one state, you may well get an *interstate* mod.

Most states coordinate with NCCI so that companies that operate in multiple states get a single integrated experience modifier. An interstate modifier combines payroll and loss data for multiple states and the resulting experience mod applies to your current policy for all states that participate. Even some states that maintain separate non-NCCI rating bureaus take part in the interstate rating mechanism.

For example, in Wisconsin the Wisconsin Rating Bureau calculates modifiers. But if Wisconsin employers have operations in other states, they may qualify for interstate rating. Then NCCI will calculate the mod for them, utilizing payroll and loss data for both Wisconsin and the other states. This is a fairly recent change, though. Ten years ago, Wisconsin didn't coordinate with NCCI for interstate rating. And some other states still operate that way.

## Stand-Alone Modifiers

California, for instance, does not (as of this writing, late 2004) coordinate with interstate experience rating. So a company's California payroll and loss data will not be integrated into its interstate mod and its separate California mod will be calculated based solely on past payroll and losses from California operations. The resulting modifier will apply only to California premium calculations, even if it's as part of a policy that covers other states as well. Delaware, Michigan, New Jersey, and Pennsylvania also operate the same, not coordinating with interstate rating. For these states, separate "stand-alone" modifiers will apply to premiums for those states, assuming that the employer meets the premium size requirements in each state to be eligible for experience rating.

## REVIEWING YOUR EMR WORKSHEET

Take a look at the sample experience modification rating worksheet that follows (Figure 6-1). This is a mod worksheet for a fictitious company using the formula and worksheet layout used by NCCI. Modifiers calculated by non-NCCI rating bureaus will use formulas and layouts that differ in some details, but the general principles will be similar.

In this sample worksheet, the expected loss ratio (ELR) for Class 7380 is 3.52. This means that the average claims of everyone in Class 7380 were computed to be $3.52 for every hundred dollars of payroll. So, by multiplying the audited payroll reported in Class 7380, we get

**NCCI**

**Sample NCCI Mod Worksheet**

NAME OF RISK

RISK IDENT. NO

EFFECTIVE DATE  10/01/00

STATE  ILLINOIS

| 1 CODE | 2 ELR | 3 D-RATI | 4 PAYROLL | 5 EXPECTED LOSSES | 6 EXP PRIM LOSSES | 7 CLAIM DATA | 8 IJ | O F | 9 ACT INC LOSSES | 10 ACT PRIM LOSSES |
|---|---|---|---|---|---|---|---|---|---|---|
| CARRIER 10 | | 502 | POLICY NO. | WC96046695 | | EFF-DATE | 10/01/96 | | EXP-DATE | 10/01/97 |
| 7380 | 352 | 23 | 113838 | 4007 | 922 | 13482850 | 4 | F | 8988 | 5000 |
| 8018 | 236 | 27 | 315682 | 7450 | 2012 | 13476882 | 5 | F | 9834 | 5000 |
| 8742 | 022 | 24 | 27143 | 60 | 14 | NO.   2 | 6 | * | 830 | 830 |
| 8810 | 014 | 25 | 332137 | 465 | 116 | | | | | |
| 9807 | ADDITIONAL | | PREMIUM | ( 0) | ( 0) | | | | | |
| | | | | | | | | | | |
| POLICY-TOTAL | | | 788800 | (SUBJECT | PREMIUM = | 28017 | ) | | 19652 | |
| | | | | | | | | | | |
| CARRIER 10 | | 502 | POLICY NO. | WC97046695 | | EFF-DATE | 10/01/97 | | EXP-DATE | 10/01/98 |
| 7380 | 352 | 23 | 125088 | 4403 | 1013 | NO.   2 | 6 | * | 1513 | 1513 |
| 8018 | 236 | 27 | 300597 | 7094 | 1915 | | | | | |
| 8742 | 022 | 24 | 5293 | 12 | 3 | | | | | |
| 8810 | 014 | 25 | 336787 | 472 | 118 | | | | | |
| 9807 | ADDITIONAL | | PREMIUM | ( 0) | ( 0) | | | | | |
| | | | | | | | | | | |
| POLICY-TOTAL | | | 767765 | (SUBJECT | PREMIUM = | 25748 | ) | | 1513 | |
| | | | | | | | | | | |
| CARRIER 10 | | 502 | POLICY NO. | W04669506 | | EFF-DATE | 10/01/98 | | EXP-DATE | 10/01/99 |
| 7380 | 352 | 23 | 119187 | 4195 | 965 | NO.   1 | 5 | * | 634 | 634 |
| 8018 | 236 | 27 | 369360 | 8717 | 2354 | NO.   4 | 6 | * | 2540 | 2540 |
| 8810 | 014 | 25 | 320577 | 449 | 112 | | | | | |
| 9807 | ADDITIONAL | | PREMIUM | ( 0) | ( 0) | | | | | |
| | | | | | | | | | | |
| POLICY-TOTAL | | | 809124 | (SUBJECT | PREMIUM = | 27845 | ) | | 3174 | |

RATING REFLECTS A DECREASE OF 70% MEDICAL ONLY PRIMARY AND EXCESS LOSS DOLLARS WHERE ERA IS APPLIED.

(ARAP) IF APPL.: 1.00

| (A) | (B) | (C) EXPECTED EXCESS (D-E) | (D) | (E) | (F) ACTUAL EXCESS (H-I) | (G) | (H) | (I) |
|---|---|---|---|---|---|---|---|---|
| 010 | | 27780 | 37324 | 9544 | 8822 | 15900 | 20921 | 12099 |

\# Total by Policy Year of all cases $2,000 or less.
\# Limited loss.

| | (11) PRIMARY LOSSES | (12) STABILIZING VALUE | (13) RATABLE EXCESS | (14) TOTALS | |
|---|---|---|---|---|---|
| PAGE NUMBER  1 | | (C) X (1-W) + (G) | (A) X (F) | (J) | (15) EXP.MOD. |
| ACTUAL | (I) 12099 | 40902 | 882 | 53883 | (J) / (K) |
| DATE  05/24/00 | (E) | (A) X (C) | (K) | | 1.01 |
| EXPECTED | 9544 | 40902 | 2778 | 53224 | |

2839

the expected losses for a company of its size in its state. In the first year of the sample worksheet, payroll of $113,838 in Class 7380 generated $4,007 of expected losses. This amount was arrived at by dividing the payroll of $113,838 by 100, then multiplying it by the ELR of 3.52.

## The D-Ratio

But as you can see from the sample worksheet, there is another column immediately to the right of the expected loss ratio, the *discount ratio* (*D-ratio*). This is a further calculation done to expected losses, to determine how much of those expected losses are *primary* and how much are *excess*. (These terms are explained below.) This is done to reflect similar differentiation of actual losses into primary and excess. The D-ratio determines what percentage of expected losses is considered primary. I know this gets a little technical, but it's an important part of the NCCI experience rating formula, so let's review it so that worksheet becomes a little more understandable.

In its experience rating formula, the NCCI recognizes that not all claims dollars should be counted equally. One employer might have a single, unlikely event that costs $100,000, while another employer has a pattern—five separate claims, each for $20,000. The two employers have each had the same dollar total of claims, but the experience rating formula is designed to discount that single $100,000 claim. So the employer with the five $20,000 claims will have a higher modifier than the employer with the single $100,000 claim, all other things being equal. The single large claim could well be atypical, a fluke that's unlikely to recur, while the five $20,000 claims indicate a pattern that is more

likely to be repeated in the future.

The NCCI experience rating formula discounts reported claims over a certain amount, so to be consistent the expected losses need to have that same discount applied. The D-ratio reflects how much of expected claims (on average) exceed that primary cutoff. Currently, the NCCI experience rating formula discounts each individual claim over $5,000. That's why at the far right of the worksheet there are two columns that contain actual reported losses for this company. The first column shows "Actual Incurred Losses." Take the second claim listed, for $20,000. In the column labeled "Actual Primary Losses," that claim is shown for only $5,000, because only the first $5,000 of the claim is counted as primary.

## Actual Incurred Losses

This is one of those great insurance terms that is often poorly understood by the people buying insurance, yet it is an important concept that makes a lot of difference in the cost of workers' compensation insurance. Incurred losses include not just what the insurance company has actually paid out for the claim, but also the *reserves* that the insurance company has established for the claim. Reserves represent what the insurance company thinks the ultimate cost of the claim will be—and it is an educated guess at best. But in the experience rating formula, those best guesses get counted exactly the same as hard dollars actually paid out.

## Medical-Only Claims Discounted

The current NCCI experience mod formula also heavily discounts *medical-only* claims—that is, claims for which the only cost is medical care, without any lost-time benefits being paid. In calculating an NCCI experience modifier, the dollar amount paid for these claims is discounted by 70 percent. This means that only 30 percent of the cost of medical-only claims is actually counted in computing a modifier under the NCCI formula. (Remember: non-NCCI states don't include this feature, as they follow different rating formulas.) This discount was instituted by NCCI to encourage employers to turn all claims to their insurer, even minor ones. In the past, some employers would pay such small claims themselves without reporting them to the insurer, with the idea of holding down their future experience modifier. The problem with such a practice is that sometimes minor claims can balloon into major claims; then, if the insurance company wasn't notified in a timely manner, it can deny responsibility for the claim. So unofficially "self-insuring" small claims isn't a good idea, especially if your experience modifier is calculated by NCCI. Additionally, many states have approved so-called *small-deductible* programs, in which an employer can officially self-insure small medical-only claims. If you want to self-insure small medical-only claims, it's best to do so officially. You get a premium credit (if your state has approved a small-deductible plan) and you avoid the possibility of having an insurer deny responsibility for a small claim that later turns out to be not so small.

## Combination of Entities

Under the rules of experience rating, business entities that have more than 50 percent common ownership are supposed to be combined. That is, the past payroll and loss data for all such entities

are supposed to be combined into a single experience modification factor. But problems and errors can also occur in this area, so business owners and managers are well advised to review this area carefully to make sure that mistakes aren't making the modifier higher than it really should be.

▼

### Fathers and Sons and Experience Mods: A Legacy

A few years back I was called in to review the workers' comp premium charges for a small masonry contractor. The company had been started a few years earlier by two young men. As a new business, it had started out with a 1.00 experience modifier, as new businesses should under the experience rating rules. However, in my review I found out that these young men had formed their new company by combining two companies that had been owned by their fathers. So this "new" company wasn't really new after all, but instead a combination of two old companies. Under the rules, the "new" company should have had an experience mod calculated based on the combined experience of the fathers' companies. This experience had been favorable, so the proper mod for the "new" company was significantly lower than 1.00.

The insurance agent and the insurance company had not done a very good job at all of explaining how these rules of experience rating worked, so the two partners were unaware that they should have inherited the favorable experience of their fathers' companies. They had been given the appropriate form to fill out (the NCCI ERM-14), but no one had explained why they should fill it out or how, so it had gotten lost among various other papers relating to their insurance. So I had them fill out the ERM-14 and send it to NCCI. Then I followed up and made sure the resulting lower modifiers were calculated for all appropriate years and then that the insurance company revised those premium charges and refunded all the overcharges that had resulted from the use of the higher, incorrect modifiers.

Remember: it's not just the employer who can request that the rating bureau determine if separately rated entities can be combined. The insurance company can also initiate the process, but sometimes the system doesn't follow the rules carefully.

Of course, sometimes the problem occurs in just the opposite direction: sometimes companies are combined for experience rating when they really shouldn't be and the resulting experience mod is higher than it should be. Consider the following two cases from our files, situations in which NCCI combined entities in a fashion that I felt did not really follow its own rules.

### A Husband and a Wife and Two Companies

A husband and a wife each owned a separate temporary employment agency. ABC Temps (not the real name, of course) was owned 100 percent by the husband. XYZ Temporary Services (also not the real name) was owned 100 percent by the wife. Both companies had been insured through the assigned risk mechanism in their state, on separate policies.

But XYZ had much worse experience than ABC. The insurance carrier requested that NCCI review the matter. The result was that NCCI ruled that the two companies were combinable for experience rating purposes. This greatly increased premiums for ABC, based on the poor past loss experience of XYZ.

However, by appealing this ruling to their state department of insurance, we were able to get the NCCI decision reversed. After all, the NCCI experience rating manual said that, to be combined, two entities had to have more than 50 percent common ownership. These two separate corporations had 0 percent common ownership.

However, NCCI had relied upon another section of the manual that stated that a transfer of assets between two entities was also a basis for combination. XYZ had placed some workers who had formerly been placed by ABC, so NCCI decided that this constituted the transfer of an asset.

But the NCCI manual did not define what constituted an "asset." We argued (successfully, it turned out) that the temporary workers placed by these two separate agencies could not constitute an asset, as these workers were not owned by the temporary agencies and thus did not constitute an asset of either company.

## Changes in Ownership

Folks who have been working with workers' comp insurance may remember a time when, if a company's ownership changed, the experience mod reset back to 1.00. But that changed a long time ago. Under current NCCI experience rating rules, a change in ownership doesn't mean that experience resets, unless the company's operations also change enough to change the classification assigned. Of course, if the change in ownership involves a merger or acquisition of another entity that already has a published experience mod, then the new combined entity should get a modifier that is the result of the combined loss and payroll histories. But if new ownership takes over a company and that new owner doesn't have a published experience mod, then the business continues to have the modifier it's earned from its past experience.

> More recently, I worked with two private schools in the New England area that had been combined for experience rating, even though they had only 50 percent common ownership. Remember: NCCI rules for combining require more than 50 percent common ownership. What was particularly interesting in this case was that separating the two entities produced a lower mod for both schools, even though one had a better loss record than the other. Normally, one would expect that separating two such entities would lower the mod for the one with the better loss record and produce a higher mod for the other. But not in this instance. Due to some quirks in the formula, both schools benefited from having their experience mods calculated separately—a large benefit for one and a lesser benefit for the other.

## COMMON MOD MISTAKES

Here are common mistakes I find in experience modifiers:

- Missing or inaccurate data
- Increase in experience modifier applied late in states that prohibit this
- Mistake in the combination of entities— either combined when they shouldn't have been or not combined when they should have been
- Modifier not revised to reflect change in classification

Let's take a closer look at each of these kinds of mistakes and how to correct them.

## Missing or Inaccurate Data

Just recently, I worked with a small residential masonry contractor. In reviewing their recent experience modification factor worksheets, I saw that a year of data was missing. I checked with the contractor and found that in the missing year losses had been low; in fact, they had no claims that year. However, the payroll had been significant. So I set about getting that missing data incorporated into their mod calculation. That was easier than usual, because a phone call to NCCI revealed that it had the missing data but just had somehow not incorporated it into the mod calculation. The addition of this data reduced the contractor's mod from a 1.00 to a .91.

Now, it isn't usually that easy to correct missing data, because normally it's missing because an insurance company has failed to file what's called a *unit statistical report*—a unit stat report, as it's often called. And typically the rating bureau like NCCI won't take action to get the carrier to file that missing report. So the employer has to contact the insurance company and then persuade or cajole those folks into filing the missing report with the rating bureau. Of course, before doing so, it would be in the employer's interest to determine that the result would produce a lower experience mod. Performing this calculation is pretty technical, so an employer would probably be well advised to ask its agent (or a consultant like me, if the agent can't do this) to perform the calculation to make sure the corrected mod would be lower.

In recent years, data is sometimes missing because a past insurance company is no longer in business. If that's the case, you can probably provide the missing data to NCCI or other rating bureau in a form other than a unit statistical report. If you can document the audited payrolls and classes used in the missing year, along with the claims for that year, the rating bureau should be able to incorporate the missing data. Similarly, if data is missing because your company was covered by some kind of self-insurance program, you can report those past payrolls and losses to the rating bureau and get them incorporated into your mod.

## Increases in Modifier After Policy Inception

In some states, the rules allow an insurance company to increase the experience modification factor for a policy after it starts. But not all states allow this. The easiest way to determine whether your state prohibits such practices is to contact your state's department of insurance. (See the directory in Chapter 1.) If you think that your insurance company must already know which states allow this and which states don't, you would be mistaken.

Last year, I reduced the workers' comp premiums for a client by almost $600,000 by catching such a mistake. The experience modifier had

been calculated correctly, but it had been calculated late and endorsed onto the policy months after it had begun. In Tennessee, where this client operated, this is prohibited by a section of the state insurance regulations. Once we pointed out the mistake to the insurer, it corrected the mistake. But if we had not done so, it would have pocketed almost $600,000 in premium charges that it was not entitled to.

## Mistakes in the Combination of Entities

Earlier in this chapter, I shared two case histories about these kinds of mistakes, one about a company whose mod should have been combined from two prior companies and the other about two companies that had been combined improperly. Generally, two entities are required to be combined if they have more than 50 percent common ownership. (Pennsylvania does not make this a requirement, but rather an option that the employer can choose.)

So if your company was formed in recent years by combining entities, you may well want to take a close look at the modifier used on your policies since that combination.

Conversely, if your experience modifier has been calculated on the basis of combining two or more separate entities, you may well want to verify that this was really done properly and check if separating the entities would be beneficial to one or both.

I mentioned that Pennsylvania does not require commonly owned businesses to be combined. This was an issue in a recent case. There, an insurer combined two commonly owned entities for the experience rating, because the insurer wasn't aware that the rules were different in Pennsylvania. Being accustomed to the way things are done in NCCI states, the insurer initiated the process of combining the companies without getting the consent of the policyholder. As it turned out, the policyholder found it preferable to have the two companies experience-rated separately, so we had to work with the carrier and the Pennsylvania rating bureau to untangle the improper combination.

Again, keep in mind that calculating the effect of making changes in combination of entities is a technical process; you will probably need the assistance of someone with experience in this to make sure the end result will benefit your company.

## Modifier Not Revised to Reflect a Change in Classification

This is also a relatively common mistake. When an insurer makes a change in classification code on a policy, the experience modifier used on that policy is supposed to be recalculated in a reciprocal fashion. So if an insurance company changes your classification to something more expensive, a good part of that increased rate (not all of it, but a good part) is supposed to be offset by a lower experience modification factor. In essence, the experience modifier should be recalculated as if your company had always been in this more expensive class. But again, I often find that the insurers do not initiate this. They tend to worry about getting the classification change done and don't make sure the rating bureau makes the reciprocal change in the modifier.

So if your company is subject to a classification change to a more expensive class and you

can't successfully fight that change, then you at least want to make sure the experience modifier has been revised to reflect the updated classification.

The earlier sample modifier worksheet used the NCCI experience modification factor formula. But remember that some states don't use the NCCI experience rating formula and their mod worksheets can look a little different. Figure 6-2 shows a sample California experience modification factor worksheet.

This second experience mod worksheet shows the same kind of information as the first, only laid out in a little different format. Instead of showing payroll and loss information for each year in one block, this worksheet breaks payroll information and loss information out into different areas.

One other important difference you may note on this California experience modifier worksheet: the medical-only claims are not discounted as they were in the NCCI calculation. Also, the California formula discounts actual losses above $2001.00. So some of the details of the formula are different from the NCCI calculation, but the calculation is still done in a very similar fashion, comparing actual historic losses for a particular employer with expected losses that are calculated using historic payroll information.

As I said at the beginning of this chapter, experience modification factor worksheets can seem like hieroglyphics to many employers. But reviewing these calculations can be well worth the effort, as there can be significant mistakes buried in those rows of numbers.

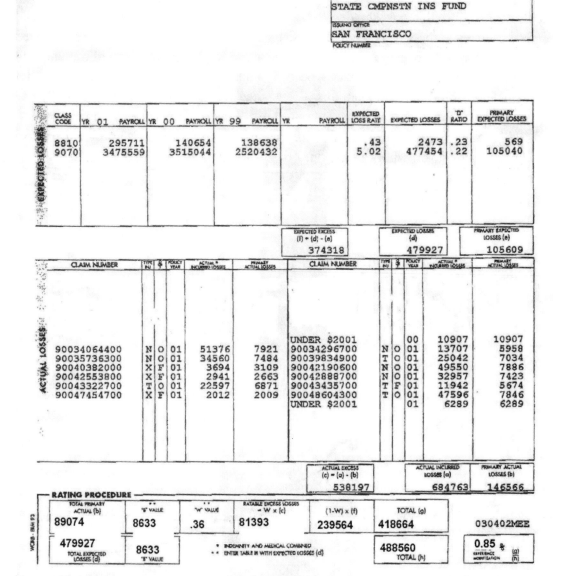

**FIGURE 6-2.** Sample California experience modification factor worksheet

## QUICK REVIEW

- Experience modification factor is the way insurance companies adjust current premiums based on prior years' losses and payrolls.

- Experience modification factors are calculated by rating bureaus based on loss and payroll information reported by an employer's past insurers.

- Errors by insurance companies regarding past losses and payrolls can cause experience modification factors to be wrong. Employers need to review the worksheets carefully to spot such errors.

- Changes in ownership can also affect experience modification factors. Employers should review the modifiers being used on their policies to make sure they takes into account current ownership.

- Some states limit the ability of insurance companies to increase experience modification factors after a policy begins. Employers should check what protection is provided by their particular state.

- A change to a more expensive classification means the experience modification factor should be recalculated downwards. There is a reciprocal relationship between classification and modifier, but often when class change is made the change to the modifier is overlooked.

# CHAPTER 7

# The Premium Audit

ARLIER IN THIS *ULTIMATE GUIDE TO Workers' Compensation Insurance,* we covered how the premium for a workers' compensation insurance policy is only an estimated premium when the policy starts. The actual premium for the coverage is determined through an audit. The audit is usually done after the policy has expired, although sometimes an insurance company will want audits done earlier, during the term of the policy, to make sure the estimated premium isn't too far off the mark. The premium audit that's performed after policy expiration is mainly about payroll—because for almost all kinds of employments, payroll is the basic unit that is applied to the rate to determine the premium.

For smaller employers, an insurance company may just ask that the employer fill out a form about the final payroll and send it in to the insurer. But for larger employers, they will want to send out a *premium auditor* to determine the actual premium for the policy period. In such cases, the premium auditor will contact the employer to schedule an appointment for the auditor to come out and review payroll records and operations for the audit.

There has been some evolution in recent decades in the profession of premium auditor. When I first began working with workers' compensation insurance, back in the mid-1970s, most premium auditors worked directly for an insurance company. But since then the trend has been for much of this work to be outsourced to third-party firms. A lot of the people working for these third-party firms are the same people who used to work directly for the insurance companies, but now they're under a lot more pressure to do the audits in less time. So more than ever, an employer that prepares wisely for a premium audit can benefit by avoiding over-charges.

## PREPARE FOR YOUR AUDIT

It can be vital to spend a little time and effort preparing for your premium audit, because if the auditor can't readily determine from your records certain important details, he or she will just assume the worst-case scenario and bill you on that basis. Because the auditor is under pressure to do the audit as quickly and efficiently as possible, he or she will resolve any unclear areas by assuming the worst. So, for example, if your payroll records don't let the auditor quickly and easily determine how much of your payroll is for overtime, you won't get the adjustment that eliminates the premium portion of overtime pay. (Most states, but not all, allow for overtime pay to be reduced down to straight time when computing workers' comp premiums.)

So before the auditor arrives, review your payroll records and make sure they allow the auditor to easily determine how much payroll for the year was for overtime, so that the adjustment can be made that eliminates the premium portion of the overtime pay. If your company has situations where you pay more than time-and-a-half, make sure the payroll records allow the auditor to readily determine that. Double-time would be adjusted by half, as long as the payroll records allow the auditor to readily determine the actual amount of the premium pay.

I've sometimes consulted with employers whose records didn't spell out this vital information for the auditor, at least not in a usable form. Even though these employers used a well-known payroll service, the records didn't allow the auditor to easily determine overtime pay for the year. The

overtime was broken out, yes, but only pay period by pay period—and only for each individual employee. The auditor would have had to spend a lot of time going through the records and compiling the overall overtime amount. And the auditor just didn't have the time to do that. So the insurance company did not exclude the premium portion of the overtime pay and, as a result, the employer paid significantly higher premiums.

So take the time to review your payroll records a couple of weeks before the auditor is due to stop out. See if you can tell, by looking at your actual records, the following kinds of information:

- Overtime pay summarized by department and calculated on annual basis.
- For construction-type work, records kept of how many hours worked at different kinds of employment that are eligible for different classifications.
- Separation of payroll for different departments that are eligible for different classifications.
- Certificates of insurance readily available for all subcontracted work.
- Executive officers clearly identified.

Take the time to review the audit billing statements and audit work papers from recent past audits. This can give you an idea of what areas might be issues for your company in the upcoming audit. Make sure you've got a designated person available to answer any questions the auditor might have about company operations. Take some time to review the manual descriptions of the classifications on your policy, to anticipate any questions the auditor might come up that could potentially lead to changes in classification.

## Other Pay Differential Programs

Occasionally I have worked with employers that had other kinds of pay differential systems in place for employees. So instead of paying time-and-a-half for overtime, they would do things like pay employees for an additional day (even though the employee hadn't worked that day). The problem with all such alternative schemes for pay differential is that the workers' compensation rules only allow for traditional adjustments to overtime pay (either time-and-a-half or double-time) and no other. So if you've agreed to pay an employee for time that the employee isn't actually working, that pay will be picked up when it comes time to compute your workers' comp premiums, even though the employee wasn't physically exposed to the workplace. It's the same for sick time and vacation pay: under the rules, all these things are picked up, even though the employee isn't physically present. In fact, all kinds of compensation to employees can be counted when computing the workers' compensation premium. Here again is the official list of what's counted as *remuneration* and what's not, per NCCI rules, as presented in Chapter 3:

Remuneration *includes:*

- Regular pay, including salary or hourly
- Commissions
- Bonuses
- Overtime pay, less the premium portion
- Holiday, vacation, and sick pay
- Payments by the employer of contributions required by law to statutory insurance or pension plans such as Social Security that would otherwise be paid by the employee
- Piecework, incentive plans, profit-sharing plans

- Payments to employees for hand or power tools supplied by employees
- Rental value of housing provided to employees
- Value of lodging provided by the employer
- Value of meals provided by the employer
- Value of store certificates, merchandise, or credits given to employees by the employer

Remuneration *excludes:*

- Tips and gratuities received by employees
- Payments by the employer to group insurance plans
- Value of special awards paid for invention or discovery
- Dismissal or severance pay, except for time worked or accrued vacation
- Value of employer-provided aircraft
- Value of employer-provided automobiles
- Value of employer-provided free or discounted aircraft flight
- Value of employer-provided incentive vacation (contest winner)
- Employer-provided discounts on property or services
- Employer-provided tickets to entertainment events
- Employer payments to military reservists called to active duty, payments that make up the difference between military pay and employee's pay prior to conscription

## CONTROL THE AUDIT PROCESS

One red flag I watch for, when reviewing audits, is if the audit was performed away from the company premises, at the accountant's offices. That's because the accountant, while he or she knows the payroll numbers well and has lots of records, may not always know the details of the work being done by the employer. And since part of the auditor's job is not just to determine payroll but also to review the classifications used, if questions arise about the kind of work being done by the company or by certain departments, the accountant may not be able to give accurate information.

If your company uses subcontractors or independent contractors, make sure you have on file certificates of insurance documenting that these 1099 people have their own workers' compensation insurance. If you don't have certificates of insurance from them, but they did carry their own workers' compensation insurance, make sure to get certificates before the audit. Otherwise, your company may well be charged for this exposure. Similarly, if you've used temporary employees or workers from a professional employer organization, make sure you have evidence that they were covered elsewhere.

Remember that most *construction-type* companies can use more than one classification code for their operations; they can even divide the payroll of an individual employee between or among classifications. But the payroll records must document the actual hours spent by such employees in each of the workplace exposures. An estimate will not suffice. If the payroll records do not document the hours spent in each kind of work, all of an employee's payroll will go into the most expensive classification applicable.

## CHECK YOUR WORK PAPERS

I mentioned earlier that it can be a good idea to review the audit work papers from prior years in preparation for a current audit. But not all employers get copies of the audit work papers—and that can be an expensive mistake.

Audit work papers are computerized records of how the auditor conducted the audit, listing the documents consulted, the auditor's description of his or her understanding of your operations, notes on any changes in classifications made, a detailed description of the payroll numbers and all adjustments (like overtime and executive officer limitations), and what's done by various departments and what classifications have been assigned to those workers. In other words, the audit work papers are a roadmap that details how the auditor arrived at the payroll numbers that will be used to determine the final audited premium for the policy.

Audit work papers are not automatically provided to policyholders. They have to be requested. If the policyholder requests a copy, the insurer will provide it. But if the policyholder doesn't ask, it typically isn't provided. So by all means, request a copy of the audit work papers from the auditor. Then review them carefully to make sure there are no mistakes or misunderstandings that have improperly inflated your premiums. The next case study illustrates how comparing one year's audit with the next can reveal questionable changes.

This client was a medium-sized paint manufacturer, with plants in several Midwestern states. The company was large enough to have its own corporate airplane, with a pilot and co-pilot on staff. The audited payroll for the pilot and co-pilot alerted me to a problem with the audit.

While reviewing the audits for several past

years, I noticed that the payroll for the pilot and co-pilot's classification had jumped from $50,000 one year to $200,000 the next. When I questioned this, I was told there had been no big increase in the aircraft personnel payroll. So I began investigating the audit. This client, headquartered in a small Iowa city, had used the one large accounting firm in the area for its payroll work. The premium auditor had gone to the accountant's offices to perform the workers' comp audit, so I went to those same offices to find out where those payroll numbers for the flight personnel had come from.

As I worked through the payroll records, less of what I saw made sense. The correct payroll for the pilot and co-pilot was still $50,000. However, a copy of an early trial balance I found in the accountant's files had mistakenly assigned $200,000 in payroll to the flight personnel. All of the other payroll numbers on the audit matched this trial balance, also. Yet the actual payroll records for the policy period did not match.

The trial balance had mistakenly been used as the basis for the audit. I am still not sure how much fault lay with the insurance company premium auditor and how much with the accountant. Obviously, no one had checked the final product very carefully. There were several significant errors in the audit besides the aviation payroll: the overtime payroll was off and several departments had been placed into the manufacturing class instead of the clerical class where they belonged.

The mistake in classifications occurred because no one at the accountant's office understood the actual duties of the various departments involved. These mistakes could have been avoided if a representative from the manufacturer's company had been involved with the audit. The net result of all the mistakes had been a $7,500 premium overcharge, which could have been prevented by reviewing the audit and audit work papers more carefully.

## COMMON AUDIT MISTAKES

In my work consulting with employers, the mistakes I find on premium audits fall into a couple of categories:

- Mistakes in adjusting overtime
- Mistakes in assigning payroll to different classifications
- Charging for subcontractors or independent contractors who had their own insurance

When reviewing audit work papers, here's a checklist of important things to review carefully:

- Make sure you understand the overall scheme of the audit. For example, did the auditor start with total payroll numbers and then separate certain departments' payroll into other classes?
- Check the accuracy of the total payroll numbers.
- Check that overtime was adjusted back to straight time properly.
- Are limitations on executive officer payroll allowed?
- Is payroll for sole proprietors or partners excluded if they have not chosen to be covered for workers' comp?

ENTREPRENEUR MAGAZINE'S ULTIMATE GUIDE TO WORKERS' COMPENSATION INSURANCE

## Confusion with Independent Contractors

A few years ago, I was called in by an insurance agent to review the audit charges for one of his clients. The agent suspected that on prior policies, written by a different agent, the insurance company had overcharged the client, a fencing contractor. But the prior insurance company was insisting that it was too late to make any changes in those audits.

As I dug into the case, I quickly discovered that the payroll audits had been performed at the offices of the client's outside accountant—again, a red flag. In this case, the accountant worked out of his home. When I went there and reviewed the payroll records, I discovered the accountant had a computer printout of IRS 1099 payments to independent contractors. One entry on the list caught my eye: it showed payments to someone I knew was actually a partner in the business.

The accountant had never properly understood the partner's status in the company. However, the partner was listed as one of the named insureds on the contractor's workers' compensation policy. The policy read, "John Smith and Joe Jones, dba Active Fence Co." Yet payroll for "Joe Jones" was being picked up as if he were an independent contractor.

In the state where Active Fence was located, partners are not covered for workers' comp unless they choose to be. In this case, the partner had emphatically chosen to not be covered.

What went wrong here? The accountant did not properly understand his client. Also, the insur-ance company auditor did not look carefully at who was named as insured under the policy. This misunderstanding and this mistake caused Active Fence to pay significant premium overcharges for a number of years.

I also learned that a number of other independent contractors on that 1099 list were family members and friends who worked on a contract basis. However, they did not work as fencing contractors. Instead, they served as messengers and telephone solicitors for Active Fence. Their payroll belonged in the clerical class, not the fencing class. Because the accountant's records had simply listed them as independent contractors, the premium auditor had assumed they had been doing fencing work.

I also discovered that some of the other independent contractors, who actually did fencing work, carried their own workers' compensation insurance. The accountant had not known that, either.

When it all had been straightened out, I had recovered about $5,000 in overcharges—a considerable amount for a small contractor that paid only about $10,000 a year for workers' comp.

- Are there any charges for independent contractors that had their own insurance in force?
- Were any non-payroll remuneration charges picked up that shouldn't have been?
- Does assignment of particular departments within the company to particular classifications seem reasonable and appropriate for

THE PREMIUM AUDIT · 97

the work done by those departments? Did the auditor properly understand the work performed by those departments?

The fictitious audit work papers show in Figure 7-1 were adapted from real ones done for one of my clients. The names have been changed, but the format is a real one used by a real insurance company.

The first page includes a brief description of the company's operations, information about the company's ownership, and a list of factors that the auditor has reviewed in preparing the audit. For example, this audit work paper indicates that the auditor has found that overtime is not a factor for this company's payroll (Key Question #9). It also indicates that the two corporate officers have chosen to exclude themselves from coverage, so their payroll should not be included in the premium computation. It also indicates that this company does not use subcontractors, temporary employees, or leased employees.

The second page shows the detail of the payroll found in the audit. Since this audit was of a relatively small company, it lists individual names rather than listing payroll by department. A larger company's audit work papers wouldn't show payroll for each individual but would instead list it by departments.

This is a relatively simple audit, but the work paper can be used to determine exactly how the payroll was developed and enables one to identify key areas where errors might have occurred. For example, if overtime pay was actually a significant part of pay for this company, one could identify from this audit work paper that overtime had not been adjusted. If some of the individuals listed had not done masonry work but instead were employed as clerical or salespeople, this

could also be identified from the listing of the duties of individual employees.

The audit work papers used by different insurance companies will use their own format, but all can be used to double-check how the auditor has arrived at the particular payroll and classification decision that determine the audited premium. A little effort in reviewing these documents can produce significant savings.

## CORRECTING AUDIT MISTAKES

OK, let's say you've reviewed your audit and audit work papers and you feel there's an error that you need to correct. The field auditor that performed the audit should have left his or her card behind, with phone numbers and maybe an e-mail address. So as a first step, communicate to the field auditor the nature of the mistake you've found and ask that it be corrected. The auditor may be reluctant to make another trip out to your premises, so be prepared to fax or mail copies of any documentation that backs up your contention. For example, if you have certificates of insurance for subcontractors that weren't considered during the audit, send copies to the auditor.

If you don't get satisfactory results from the field auditor, contact the audit manager for the insurance company. When dealing with insurance companies, I've often found that persistence makes the difference between getting your complaint resolved and getting ignored. Given the increased workloads a lot of insurance company people are dealing with nowadays, it can take a bit of persistence to get their attention focused on solving your problem. But if you genuinely believe you're right, stick to your guns. And if you're disputing an audit that hasn't been

### Watch Payroll Allocation on Audits Carefully

One of the tricky things that an employer needs to watch carefully on a premium audit is how payroll is allocated by the auditor. Whether your company is large or small, keeping an eye on this detail can catch costly and avoidable overcharges. Consider this recent case from our files.

This Connecticut employer was in the business of landscaping and lawn maintenance. Under NCCI rules, these two types of work go into two different classifications, with the landscaping being charged at $10.45 per hundred dollars of payroll and the lawn maintenance taking a rate of only $5.29. A careful review of their audit workpapers found that some employees who belonged in the less expensive class had been assigned in the audit to the more expensive class. This detail was buried in the detail of the workpapers, but a careful review found it.

Once we were able to convince the insurance company that a mistake had been made, the premium charges were reversed, with a premium reduction to the employer of about 20 percent of the annual premium.

Taking the time to carefully review audit workpapers can require some patience and determination, but can be well worth the effort. Remember: the auditor will usually not provide a copy of the workpapers, unless you request them. If you request them, they will normally be provided without any fuss. But the employer has to remember to request them at the time the audit is done, as the insurance company may not keep them on file for too long into the future.

paid yet, you're in a relatively strong position. You probably want to pay the undisputed portion of the audit, but then you can insist that the insurance company address your concerns before you will consider paying the disputed portion.

If you can't get your problem resolved by dealing with the audit manager, you can always take your complaint to your state's department of insurance. Just make sure you can document whatever corrections you're trying to get made. With persistence and determination, you can get even overworked and unresponsive insurance company personnel to correct mistakes.

### Surviving an Extreme Audit

Sometimes an employer can be subjected to a particularly intense and strenuous payroll audit process. This is usually done when the insurance company suspects that an employer has been getting away with paying lower premiums than are really owed. Temporary agencies and employee leasing companies are favorite targets of this type of "extreme" audits, but almost any employer could be targeted for such an investigation.

The terms of the workers' compensation insurance policy give the insurance company broad latitude to examine the books and records of an employer and set no specific limits on what kind of records and documents an insurance company may insist on seeing. Sometimes employers get upset by broad demands by insurance companies for records that the employer feels are none of the insurer's business. However, by the terms of the policy, the insurance company has the right to inspect any business record that may have an impact on the premium.

If your company gets subjected to an extreme audit, resist your initial impulse to negotiate or play hardball. This will usually just make a bad situation worse. A better strategy is to cooperate as fully as possible.

Remember that if the insurance company can't get all the information and documentation they want, the manual rules allow them to estimate the premium on a "worst-case scenario" basis, and then bill you for that amount. Such worst-case-scenario premium calculations can take the breath away of an employer when they are first received, as the insurance company will typically be demanding a premium far in excess of what the employer expected.

To whatever extent possible, try to maintain a cooperative working relationship with the insurance company and the auditor. Don't take it personally. Reacting emotionally to a difficult premium audit can only create deeper suspicion on the part of the insurance company and ultimately make it more difficult to resolve any audit dispute. Remain professional in all communication with the insurance company, whether in person, over the phone, or in writing.

Work closely with the auditor, and try to understand what questions he or she may be trying to resolve with the information requests. The main issues the auditor will be focusing on will be the nature of the work done, making sure that all appropriate payroll is picked up on the audit, and ownership of the company. Some auditors may make it difficult to remain professional because

of their attitude or their demands for documents. But in the long run, employers are better served by keeping their cool and working to maintain a decent working relationship with the auditor and the insurance company.

I don't mean to make it sound like audit personnel are always unresponsive or difficult; in fact, a lot of the time they're very cooperative in fixing mistakes. But occasionally, I've encountered auditors who just didn't like to admit that a mistake had been made or who didn't want to take the time and effort to send someone back out to redo an audit. And if you should run into one of these problem situations, you'll need to be persistent to get your concerns properly addressed. But if you're in the right, stick to your guns and ultimately you should prevail.

## TIMETABLE FOR CONTROLLING WORKERS' COMP COSTS

Here's a timetable for taking action over the course of a year to control workers' comp costs.

### Nine Months Before Policy Inception

Review the incurred losses that will be reported to the rating bureau for use in the next experience modification factor. Negotiate lower claims reserves where possible.

### Two Months Before Policy Inception

Check what the appropriate rating bureaus have on file for your company regarding proper classifications and experience modification factors. Review all existing inspection reports and experience mod worksheets for errors.

| **TBV Insurance** | | | | |
|---|---|---|---|---|
| **Insured**<br>MASTERPIECE MASONRY, INC.<br>1234 PENNEY LANE<br>SOMEPLACE, IL 60232 | | **Auditor Name**<br>Will Ketchum | | |

| **Policy Number** | **Policy Period** | **Audit Period** | **File #** | **Date** |
|---|---|---|---|---|
| WC 0345622 | 03/12/2003 - 02/12/2004 | 03/12/2003 - 02/12/2004 | L03392 | 05/21/2004 |

**Description of Operations:** Provide detailed description of operations/services. Include all locations, products, or services, distribution or delivery methods, materials handled, etc.

Masonry Contractor
Bricklayer
Residential—New homes, 3 stories maximum height
No chimney or fireplaces
No casual labor or subs used this period

**List all officers, partners, or owners, their duties, remuneration, and class codes**

| **Corporation ✗** | **Individual** | **Partnership** | **Closely Held Corp.** | **LLC** | **Other** |
|---|---|---|---|---|---|

President: James Milak, Masonry, excluded per endorsement

Secretary: Laura Milak, Office, excluded per endorsement

| | **Key Questions** | **Yes** | **No** | **Other** |
|---|---|---|---|---|
| | 1. Tips included? | | | ✗ |
| **AUDIT NOTES** | 2. Severance pay excluded? | | | ✗ |
| | 3. Third-party sick pay excluded? | | | ✗ |
| Payroll up due to a very good year–per insured. | 4. Personal use of company car excluded? | | | ✗ |
| | 5. Board and lodging paid? | | | ✗ |
| | 6. Casual or contract labor? | | | ✗ |
| | 7. Aircraft operation? | | | ✗ |
| | 8. Temporary or leased employees? | | | ✗ |
| | 9. Premium portion of overtime excluded? | | | ✗ |
| | 10. Are commissions or bonuses paid? | | ✗ | |
| | 11. Are there multi-state payrolls? | | ✗ | |
| **AUDIT RECORDS** | 12. Is there a Section 125 "cafeteria" plan? | | ✗ | |
| | 13. Is there a 410(k) plan? | | ✗ | |
| Quarterly reports, 941s, U/Cs | 14. Are subcontractors used? | | ✗ | |
| | 15. Certificates current for all subs? | | ✗ | |
| | 16. All exposures/classes discussed? | ✗ | | |
| | 17. All companies accounted for? | ✗ | | |
| | 18. Was an owner or officer interviewed?<br>   Personally<br>   By telephone | ✗ | | |
| | 19. Send worksheet copy to contact? | ✗ | | |

**FIGURE 7-1.** Typical audit work paper (continued on next page)

**TBV Insurance**

| Insured | | | | | | Auditor Name | | | |
|---|---|---|---|---|---|---|---|---|---|
| MASTERPIECE MASONRY, INC.<br>1234 PENNEY LANE<br>SOMEPLACE, IL 60232 | | | | | | Will Ketchum | | | |

| Policy Number | Policy Period | | Audit Period | | | File # | | Date | |
|---|---|---|---|---|---|---|---|---|---|
| WC 0345622 | 03/12/2003 - 02/12/2004 | | 03/12/2003 - 02/12/2004 | | | L03392 | | 05/21/2004 | |

| Key | Name/Dept | Duties | Loc | St | Code | 2nd Q | 3rd Q | 4th Q | 1st Q | Gross Total |
|---|---|---|---|---|---|---|---|---|---|---|
|  | Venturelli, N. | Masonry | 001 | IL | 5022 | 10,178.00 | 10,387.00 | 11,860.00 | 7,032.00 | 39,457.00 |
|  | Teshnek, P. | Masonry | 001 | IL | 5022 | 0.00 | 6,125.00 | 11,061.00 | 4,686.00 | 21,872.00 |
|  | Adams, S. | Masonry | 001 | IL | 5022 | 5,775.00 | 7,394.00 | 7,750.00 | 1,000.00 | 21,919.00 |
|  | Booker, T. | Masonry | 001 | IL | 5022 | 5,712.00 | 4,076.00 | 6,612.00 | 3,742.00 | 20,142.00 |
| 1 | Milak, M. | Masonry | 001 | IL | Excl | 3,000.00 | 0.00 | 0.00 | 8,450.00 | 11,450.00 |
|  | Cleaver, E. | Masonry | 001 | IL | 5022 | 0.00 | 0.00 | 0.00 | 3,516.00 | 3,516.00 |
| 1 | Milak, L. | Office | 001 | IL | Excl | 0.00 | 0.00 | 0.00 | 1,808.00 | 1,808.00 |
|  | Thomas, D. | Masonry | 001 | IL | 5022 | 4,550.00 | 3,240.00 | 7,336.00 | 0.00 | 15,126.00 |
|  |  |  |  |  |  | 29,215.00 | 31,222.00 | 44,619.00 | 30,234.00 | 135,290.00 |

| Verification | |
|---|---|
| 941s | Total |
| Qtr 2 | 29,216 |
| Qtr 3 | 31,200 |
| Qtr 4 | 44,619 |
| Qtr 1 | 30,228 |
| Total | 135,263 |

FIGURE 7-1. Typical audit work paper (continued)

## Policy Inception or Renewal

Make sure all competing proposals use the same payrolls, classes, and experience mods. Keep on file a copy of the winning proposal for comparison later with the policy when it is produced.

## One Month After Renewal

Start preparing for the audit of expired policy-review payroll records to make sure the auditor will be able to break out overtime and assign proper classifications to your various departments and workers.

## During the Audit (Typically Three Months After Renewal)

Make sure someone knowledgeable about company operations is available to help the auditor. Make certain all certificates of insurance for independent contractors or subcontractors are on file and available. Request a copy of the auditor's work papers for review.

## After the Audit

Review the audit work papers carefully. Check classifications, payroll computation, overtime adjustment, and description of your operations.

## QUICK REVIEW

- Review payroll records in advance of the premium audit to make sure the records allow the auditor to give all the credits you are eligible for.
- Make sure payroll records allow overtime pay to be broken out.
- Make sure certificates of insurance are on file for all independent contractors and subcontractors.
- Always request copy of the auditor's workpapers after the audit is completed and check for problems before paying any additional premium.
- If the audit done by a third-party, such as an accountant, make sure someone knowledgeable about your operations is available to make sure the auditor does not misunderstand what is done by the company overall and by various departments.

# CHAPTER 8

# Choosing Agents and Insurers and Consultants

A S THIS IS BEING WRITTEN, THE SCANDAL uncovered by New York Attorney General Eliot Spitzer is very fresh and very big news. At the heart of the matter are the allegations that the largest insurance broker in the world, Marsh & McLennan, engaged in bid-rigging practices that improperly inflated insurance premiums for commercial policyholders. As this scandal has unfolded in both the insurance press and the general news media, the reverberations within the insurance industry have been serious. The response of the insurance industry so far has generally been to decry the particular abuses ascribed to Marsh & McLennan, but to simultaneously deny that this is more than just an isolated instance of broker misconduct. But others have suggested the matter is an indication of far deeper and more systemic problems in the way insurance is marketed. Spitzer

himself has suggested that federal regulation of insurance may be needed to address the problems he has uncovered.

Most workers' compensation coverage in the United States is sold by insurance agents or brokers. And I've found that many purchasers of insurance don't understand the role of the insurance agent or broker as well as they might, and this sometimes contributes to problems with the cost of their workers' compensation insurance. So this chapter will endeavor to explain some of the lesser-known realities about insurance agents, brokers, and the insurance companies they work with and for.

## AGENT, BROKER, OR PRODUCER— WHAT'S THE DIFFERENCE?

The terms *insurance agent* and *broker* tend to get blurred together. And the distinction can be made more difficult because the same individual or the same insurance agency may sometimes be acting as an agent of an insurance company and other times as a broker representing solely the interests of the policyholder. A newer term is used by some regulators, *insurance producer*, to reflect the fact that the distinction between insurance agent and broker can get fuzzy.

Technically speaking, an insurance agent is a licensed insurance producer who has a contract with a specific insurance company to sell its products. Some agents are tied to just one insurance company. This company is known in the insurance industry as a *direct writer*. An agent for a direct writer can only sell that particular insurer's policies. State Farm is an example of a personal-lines direct writing company. Liberty Mutual is an example of a direct writer that writes workers' compensation and other commercial lines of insurance.

An *independent agent* has contracts with multiple insurance companies and can choose which of those insurers to use for a particular client. So while an agent for Liberty Mutual could only present proposals from Liberty Mutual, an independent agent might be able to present proposals from Travelers and Fireman's Fund and CNA. An insurance broker is technically not an agent of the insurance company, but instead represents the insurance purchaser, seeking out insurance coverage on their behalf. This difference between insurance *agent* and insurance *broker* can get further complicated because some states impose stricter regulations on the status of such insurance intermediaries. In New York, for example, all insurance producers are considered to be acting as brokers on behalf of clients. In Michigan, by contrast, anyone selling

insurance has to be a licensed agent of a carrier.

In the particular instances cited by Attorney General Spitzer, Marsh & McLennan was acting as an insurance broker, seeking out insurance proposals for large corporate clients on a non-commission compensation basis. That is, Marsh was earning a fee from corporate clients for seeking out insurance proposals from various insurers. These proposals were supposed to be net of commissions, because Marsh was being paid a negotiated fee by its clients. But unbeknownst to those clients, Marsh was also receiving so-called *contingent commission* payments from insurers for placing business with them. Marsh did not disclose these contingent commissions to its clients. Worse, Marsh allegedly steered business toward those insurers on the basis of which one paid the best contingent commissions, manipulating proposals from other insurers so that the clients did not actually receive the best quotes possible. The clients could not make an informed decision about the insurance options brought to them, because the broker had decided in advance which insurer would win the account, based on contingent commission income to the broker, and then gotten the other insurers to provide inflated quotes.

Now that this has all been uncovered, insurance regulators in a number of states are tripping over themselves to address the situation. There will almost surely be new regulations in place in at least some jurisdictions to address these problems.

Direct writers of workers' compensation often stress the level of loss control and other services they can offer. Since workers' comp is their favored line of insurance, they pride themselves on providing better reports on claims and more

## My Experience as a Direct Writer

Years ago, I began my career in workers' compensation as an agent for a direct writing insurer. There came a day when a dispute arose between one of my accounts and the insurance company, regarding how an audit had been performed and the resulting premium charges.

I believed that my client was right and I argued the client's case with my manager with the district manager above him. At some point, the word came back to me, in essence, "You work for us. Shut up. We've made up our minds and that is the end of it."

I couldn't help that client, because I had no real leverage with the insurance company that employed me. That particular case stuck in my mind long after and eventually helped lead me to changing the focus of my insurance career so that I could help companies that have similar disputes with their insurance companies.

comprehensive assistance in safety engineering. They will also often be willing to write the workers' compensation insurance without also writing the other commercial lines for an insured. Another advantage of working with direct writers of workers' comp is that their personnel may be more familiar with workers' compensation insurance coverage and rating plans than the average independent agent.

The great drawback to using a direct writer, of course, is that the agent who sells its policies is an employee of the company. This may make the agent less able to represent your interests against the insurance company than an independent agent.

The direct writers of the world might well assure you that the experience cited above was an isolated case, but I don't think so. An agent for a direct writing company simply has much less leverage, on average, than an independent agent. Of course, even an independent agent has limits on what he or she can do to change the mind of insurance company underwriters and auditors. But the independent agent can always at least threaten to move the account to a different insurer, something no direct writing agent can do.

Independent insurance agents represent multiple insurance companies, so they're not tied down to just one single insurer. But independent agents don't have access to every insurance company; they typically have contracts with a limited number of insurance companies. Theoretically, an independent agent can also act as a broker—obtaining coverage for you from an insurance company that he or she doesn't have a contract with. But generally independent agents will use their contracted companies first and use other markets only when and if they absolutely must.

Sometimes an independent agent will overplay how many insurance companies he or she can access. Keep in mind that when an independent insurance agency has a contract with an insurance company, he or she has made a commitment to that insurer to place a certain volume of business with it. Meeting sales quotas and maintaining specified loss ratios can enable an agent to earn additional commissions, called *contingent commissions*. These are the commission payments that were involved in the Marsh & McLennan scandal, because these commissions allegedly were the reason Marsh steered clients to certain insurers even those insurers were not the lowest bidders for those clients.

A *broker* is an insurance producer who works solely as the representative of the policyholder and is not contracted with any insurance company as its agent. A broker may be compensated on a non-commission negotiated-fee basis or by commissions from the insurance company. Although the practice of receiving contingent commissions is under considerable scrutiny in the wake of Spitzer's revelations, as of this writing many (if not most) commercial insurance agents and brokers still receive contingent commissions. Some large brokers like Marsh have foresworn contingent commissions in penance for their alleged wrongdoing and insurance regulators are considering taking some new actions in these areas, but at the moment contingent commissions are still common in the insurance industry.

The simple truth that no attorney general or insurance commissioner can change is that human beings will always be tempted to place their own interests first. Insurance agents and brokers are susceptible to the same lapses in judgment and ethics as anyone else. So, while trust is an essential part of the insurance transaction, a wise insurance purchaser would perhaps be well advised to keep in mind an old Russian adage that President Reagan once popularized: "Trust, but verify."

In recent years, most states have deregulated workers' compensation insurance considerably, on the theory that allowing insurance companies to compete on price would foster competition and ultimately reduce costs for employers. Sometimes it's worked, sometimes it hasn't—in part because the insurance transaction is always inherently unequal. The people selling the insurance have certain advantages that deregulation

hasn't addressed—witness the problems uncovered by Attorney General Spitzer.

But insurance purchasers have certain strengths as well that can be maximized. The existence of both direct-writing and independent-agency insurance companies means that you can use them to compete against each other for your business. Just make sure that you don't let one intermediary (broker) control your access to all of the proposals from the different insurers. The kind of bid rigging alleged by Spitzer can occur only if an employer relies on one intermediary, who can then act as a gatekeeper and potentially manipulate the proposals from insurers.

Trust, but verify. So even though your broker or agent assures you that he or she can access any insurance company you want or need, make sure you protect yourself by dealing with more than one source for your insurance proposals. Not necessarily every year, but every few years you probably want to keep everybody honest by getting genuinely competitive quotes.

## Picking an Agent or Broker

So how do you pick an agent or broker to work with? It depends on your business, to some degree. A larger company may have need of greater resources from an agent. On the other hand, a smaller or medium-sized employer might not be served as well by a large agency, where your account may well end up being viewed as too small to warrant their best efforts. So try to work with insurance agencies that roughly match up with your own company's size.

Another important factor to take into account is whether a particular agent has experience with your kind of business. The insurance needs of a manufacturer can differ greatly from those of a construction company. Make sure you're dealing with an agency that has experience with your kind of business. Ask for references.

Professional designations can also be a useful method of choosing between agents. For example, to attain the designation of *Chartered Property Casualty Underwriter* (CPCU), a person must pass a series of ten examinations administered nationally, must meet certain minimum requirements for experience in the insurance industry, and must adhere to a code of ethics. Some agents may have the designation of CIC—*Certified Insurance Counselor*. Although it takes fewer examinations to attain this designation, it is also a useful benchmark in evaluating the knowledge and professionalism of agents.

Professional designations are far from the only criteria one should use, but all other things being equal, these designations should be given due consideration. They are among the few objective benchmarks in the insurance industry beyond those for salesmanship.

Don't just consider the individual agent. Find out about the agency as well, how large it is, how many accounts similar to yours it handles, how large a staff it has, and how experienced the particular people are who will be assigned to your account. You might well want to arrange a visit to their offices so you can get a feel for the agency.

One final point: make sure the agent and agency understand that they will have to make full disclosure of all commissions they would earn on any proposed program—including disclosure of all contingent commissions.

## CHOOSING AN INSURER

Once upon a time it was a lot easier to evaluate the financial stability of an insurance company. You checked its rating from A.M. Best, a worldwide insurance-rating and information agency founded in 1899; as long as an insurance company had some kind of A rating, it was probably going to be OK. But over the course of the past ten years, we've seen major insurance companies that had fine Best's ratings just before beginning a precipitous decline into liquidation. So, ratings services like A.M. Best can give a good picture of an insurer's recent past stability, but keep in mind that those ratings can have a short shelf life.

Here's a listing of the major insurance company rating services:

**A.M. Best Company**
Ambest Road
Oldwick, NJ 08858–9988
Telephone: 908 439–2200
www.ambest.com

**Standard & Poor's**
55 Water Street
New York, NY 10041
Telephone: 212 438–7200
www.standardandpoors.com

**Demotech**
2941 Donnylane Boulevard
Columbus, OH 43235–3228
Telephone: 800 354–7207
www.demotech.com

**Weiss Ratings**
15430 Endeavour Drive
Jupiter, FL 33478
Telephone: 800 289–9222
www.weissratings.com

**Moody's Investors Service**
99 Church Street
New York, NY 10007
Telephone: 212 553–1658
www.moodys.com

Generally speaking, these rating services rate insurance companies on such things as their liquidity, leverage, investments, profitability, loss ratio, and return on assets. Since the Best rating system is perhaps the most widely used, let's take a look at what the Best rating tells you.

The traditional letter ratings that Best gives insurers are called "Best's Ratings." Insurance companies that receive a letter rating have met certain criteria set by Best for quality and quantity of data. If an insurance company does not submit a sufficient quality of data, it receives instead a numerical "Financial Performance Rating." Most insurance companies rated by Best also get a rating outlook that tries to indicate the potential future direction of that company's rating. Best also shows the financial size rating for all insurance companies it reviews, based on capital, surplus, and reserve funds.

If an insurance company fails to qualify for a rating opinion, Best assigns it an "NR" or "Not Rated" classification. The highest Best ratings would be A++ and A+ (Superior). The next highest ratings are A and A- (Excellent), followed by B++ and B+ (Very Good). The ratings decline from there to C and C- (Weak), D (Poor), E (Under Regulatory Supervision), and F (In Liquidation).

Just keep in mind that the recent shift from soft market conditions to hard market conditions exposed some of the weaknesses of the insurance rating system. Some well-known insurance companies saw their Best ratings fall precipitously. One would have had to watch the insurance trade press fairly closely to track exactly how far and how fast the rating of Fremont Compensation declined in its last year or two before it was placed into liquidation.

So if the financial ratings systems have to be taken with a grain of salt, what else can you do? For one thing, it depends on what stage of the insurance cycle things are at. If you've been buying commercial insurance for a while, you know about the cycle of commercial insurance pricing. In the soft market, insurers are competing aggressively for business, mainly by discounting their prices. This typically goes on a bit too long for the good of insurance companies. Then some outside event triggers the inevitable abrupt return to hard market conditions. The last time this occurred was right around the latter part of 2001. External events such as the collapse of the dotcom stock bubble, the terrorist attack of 9/11, and record low interest rates served to shift the insurance market from soft to hard in fairly short order. And along the way, some well-known insurance companies disappeared forever. Remember Reliance Insurance? Fremont Compensation? How about Superior National?

So if the insurance market has been soft long enough that even you, as the insurance purchaser, are thinking that things are getting a little extreme, it may be the time to avoid insurance companies that are the most aggressively cutting prices. It isn't that hard to monitor the state of the insurance market nowadays. You do not have to rely on information provided by your agent or broker, although that is one source. An employer can easily access information on the commercial insurance market on the internet, where there are many free sources of insurance news. (See our list of insurance resources in Chapter 12.)

Insurance, especially workers' compensation insurance, may seem like a commodity purchase, but it isn't completely. And if your workers' compensation carrier goes under while you're relying on it, it can be a real painful experience. Even if it goes under a year or so after you leave it, you may find its liquidator aggressively seeking to reaudit your past policies to recoup premiums that they think were missed by the now-insolvent carrier.

As of this writing, however, we're not in a soft market. We're still living with a hard insurance market, although it seems ready to soften somewhat, barring further outside shocks, such as another serious terrorist attack or some unexpected financial crisis. The market has been hard long enough for just about all of the fallout from the last soft market to have passed. The insurance companies that survived the last soft market have had several years now of record high premiums and record profits, so most insurers at the moment are feeling fairly restored and reinvigorated. There are some exceptions, however, so employers should not relax their vigilance about insurer solvency and stability.

But during a hard market, employers have to be prepared to endure large jumps in insurance costs, restricted coverage, and reduced competition for their business. As the hard market matures, new players typically enter the market, attracted by the high rates the hard market allows. This has started happening already with this latest hard market.

## Using Competition to Lower Costs

Whatever the state of the insurance market,

employers can use competition for their business to hold down costs and obtain the best coverage. So long before your insurance program expires, begin the process of interviewing and selecting agents or brokers to work on your account. Begin at least six months before your current policy expires and then winnow the field down to two or at most three qualified agents or brokers, along with a direct-writing carrier. If your business is in the construction field or some other field that's somewhat more difficult to insure, it may be difficult to work with more than two independent agents or brokers and a direct writer.

## Allocate Markets

It is vital that you, as the insurance purchaser, retain control over which insurance companies may be used by which independent agent or broker. You must make sure anyone involved in the process agrees in advance to abide by your decisions regarding allocation of the insurance markets. If you do not, your incumbent agent could well "block the markets" for any other independent agent. The agent does this by making submissions to every conceivable insurance market for your account, even if that agent isn't going to seriously work with that insurer on your behalf. Once an insurance company gets a submission from one agency for your account, it cannot work with another agency to produce a quote for you.

Some years ago, I was working as an expert witness in insurance-related litigation. In the course of that work, I had access to the files of the insurance agent/broker that had written workers' compensation and other commercial insurance for a particular insured for years. While reviewing the file, I came across a document prepared by that agency. It was a form for keeping track of how effectively this agency had "blocked markets" on the account. It was titled "Market Blocking Checklist" and listed every conceivable insurance market, with spaces to indicate whether or not it had been blocked. This form wasn't for keeping track of all the markets the agency was working with in order to get the best possible deal for the client. It was designed to make sure that no viable markets were left available for any competitor agency to use.

The way market blocking works is that an agent sends in a submission with enough information to lock up that particular insurance company, but then the agent doesn't send in enough information to satisfy the underwriter or doesn't respond quickly to requests for additional information or documentation. The agent does enough to keep the insurance company tied up, but not enough to get a quote or at least not a truly competitive quote. And in the process, he or she blocks any other independent agency from using that insurance company.

I'm happy to report that the particular insurance agency involved in that market-blocking activity is no longer in business. The principal of that agency was convicted in federal court this year for misappropriating clients' premiums that were supposed to be in trust. But beware: this agency was far from being the only one to indulge in market blocking. To avoid being victimized by this tactic, allocate specific insurance markets to each independent agent working on your account. If anyone violates your allocation by approaching a market reserved for another agent, use a *broker of record letter* to assign the insurance company to a broker whom you desig-

nate and authorize to work with that company on your behalf.

If you can afford it, you may want to consider hiring an independent consultant to help you manage the process of selecting agents and agencies and allocating insurance markets among them. An independent consultant can act impartially, in your best interests, to harness the competition among agents and insurers to produce optimal results for you. Particularly if competing agents squabble over which one gets access to particular insurance markets, having an informed but independent arbitrator involved can make the process work more smoothly.

You can use the form exemplified in Figure 8-1 to help choose among competing agents or brokers on a basis other than price.

In a similar vein, you can use the profile form shown in Figure 8-2 to help in choosing between competing insurance companies on a basis other than mere price.

## Insurance Consultants

Finally, let's discuss the selection and use of people like me—insurance consultants in general and premium review consultants in particular. Insurance consultants are pretty common creatures—if for no other reason than because many agents and brokers like to call themselves "consultants." And some of them may even actually occasionally act as consultants. But one has to be careful of any consultant that also sells insurance, as it can be difficult to advise a client about what's best for the client if there is also a second agenda—selling insurance to that client.

My own clear preference is that a consultant should not be in a position to sell you insurance

Agent/Broker name: _____

Agency/Brokerage name: _____

Independent agent or captive agent: _____

Number of employees at agency/brokerage (if independent): _____

Volume of commercial insurance written by agency/brokerage annually: _____

How long has agent/broker been with this agency? _____

How long has agent/broker been in insurance business? _____

How long has agency/brokerage been in business? _____

Agent's/broker's position within agency/brokerage: _____

Professional designations of agent/broker: _____

Professional organizations that agent/broker belongs to: _____

Other clients of this agent/broker in same or similar line of work to yours: _____

Who else in agency/brokerage will be involved in servicing your account? _____

Can agent/broker offer referral to other clients for whom he or she has successfully resolved a dispute with the insurance carrier? _____

Has agent/broker ever been personally involved in changing workers' compensation classification for a client? If yes,

name of client: _____

Has agent/broker ever been involved in correcting an experience modification factor or premium audit for client? If

yes, name of client: _____

Does agency/brokerage accept contingent commissions from insurers? _____

Is agency/brokerage willing to disclose fully all compensation it will receive from insurers for writing your account? _____

**Questions for Agent/Broker References:**

How happy are they with quality of service from agent/broker and from the agency/brokerage?

_____

_____

What is reference's opinion of agent's/broker's ability to represent insured's interests with an insurer?

_____

_____

Why did reference decide to deal with this particular agent/broker and this particular agency/brokerage?

_____

_____

_____

**FIGURE 8-1.** Broker/agency profile

Insurer name: _____

Is insurer part of large group of insurance companies? _____

Is insurer direct writer or working through independent agents? _____

Current rating from A.M. Best: _____

Current rating from Standard & Poor's: _____

Is insurer able to write insurance in all states in which your company operates or is likely to operate in near future? _____

Any states where the insurer cannot write coverage: _____

How long has insurer been writing insurance in your state? _____

References of other policyholders of this insurer in your line of work: _____

Will insurer write workers' compensation insurance without also writing other lines of coverage? _____

**Questions to Ask Insurance Company References:**

How does this insurer appear to set reserves on open claims—"worst-case scenario" consistently or more reasonable and open to reconsideration? _____

Any particular problems with this insurer regarding premium audits? _____

Have loss control recommendations from this insurer been useful and practical or unreasonable and excessive and not practical to implement? _____

How long has this insurer written coverage for this reference? _____

Has this insurer been willing to stick with this reference even through occasional years of bad losses?

_____

**FIGURE 8-2.** Insurance company profile

or to be able to share in commissions behind the scenes. So in selecting someone to act as an insurance consultant, you really want to make sure there are no hidden agendas. Insist that the consultant commit in writing to you that the only compensation the consultant will accept for his or her work on your behalf is the fee you have agreed to pay the consultant.

A particular kind of insurance consultant has been emerging in recent years—the kind like the author of this book. I specialize in reviewing clients' workers' compensation insurance charges, looking to identify any overcharges due to technical mistakes in classification, experience

modifier, or premium audit. When I started this work, back in 1983, there weren't very many people doing this kind of work. Nowadays, every time I check the internet there appears to be several new companies offering to do this kind of work. And while I don't mind the competition (it keeps everyone on their toes), there have been some developments in my chosen field that concern me.

For one thing, this kind of work is unlicensed and unregulated at the moment. I've suggested to insurance regulators in my home state that this kind of work should be licensed and regulated like the sale of insurance, but they haven't been interested in taking on any new work. So even though existing regulation of insurance companies and insurance agents hasn't prevented occasional rogues and worse from plying their trade, it gives consumers some protections. The premium review business lacks even rudimentary oversight and regulation.

And that may have some positives, because insurance regulators sometimes are a little too close to the insurance industry. If the insurance industry had its way, maybe there wouldn't be any independent premium review consultants like my competitors and me.

## Problems with Consultants

But I've also learned of one or two horror stories along the way. There has been at least one outright unethical and scurrilous premium audit review firm that I know used to do major national marketing of its services. Fortunately, it appears to have gone out of business. Unfortunately, I understand that one of the principals in that firm has set up shop under a new corporate name.

That company would offer, just like my company, to review current and past workers' compensation premium charges for policyholders, recover any overcharges, and thereby earn a fee based on how much it recovers. The problem was that this company would try to obtain refunds for clients by misrepresenting the nature of the work done by those clients or by some of the clients' workers. It was essentially counseling its clients to participate in premium fraud.

As if that weren't bad enough, I learned of another way in which this competitor differed from my company: it would present its findings of (theoretical) savings, tell the client what needed to be done to recover those savings, and

then insist on payment of a fee before those savings were actually realized.

I learned of one Chicago-area company that dealt with these people, paid them a substantial fee based on a report that said the client had been misclassified, and then requested an NCCI inspection to trigger the change. However, the consultant was wrong and the NCCI inspection didn't result in a lower class—it produced a more expensive class. And it couldn't be corrected, because the higher class was really correct for this client under NCCI rules. The client was never able to recover the $20,000 it had paid this consultant for the savings that turned out to be negative.

I also learned, from contacts within the insurance industry, that this consultant often had clients write to the insurers with false information about the work done by those clients, attempting to obtain premium refunds that weren't legitimate.

Now, every other premium review company that I know of currently appears to operate ethically and legitimately. But there are some new companies out there that I know only by name or from the internet. So I don't yet know for sure if they operate ethically. What's a policyholder to do?

For one thing, never misrepresent the nature of your work or the work done by some of your employees. If any consultant suggests that you provide false or misleading information to your insurer or a rating bureau, you need to immediately stop working with that consultant and report the matter to insurance regulators in your state. Deliberate misrepresentation of information to improperly lower workers' compensation premiums is a felony in most states, and insurance companies are on the watch for it.

When considering using a premium review consulting firm, there are some important questions that need to be answered first, to make sure you're dealing with a reputable and ethical company. Here are some of those important questions (Figure 8-3).

Finally, beware of extravagant claims by premium review consultants. I've been doing this kind of work for over 20 years now, and I estimate that I find significant overcharges for clients in something like one third to one half of the programs I examine. The exact percentage fluctuates over time, but consistently ranges within these parameters. I have heard of some consultants in this field who claim to recover money for 90 percent of the clients they work with. If it's true, they're to be congratulated. But all of my experience tells me that such claims are probably greatly exaggerated. If 90 percent of all workers' compensation policies have significant overcharges, then we have an even more serious problem than I thought. It's bad enough to find overcharges one third of the time: that argues that the insurance system isn't even really trying to find and correct such mistakes on their own. But I find claims of 90 percent recovery rates to be suspect, so perhaps so should you.

By all means, *get references and check them!* You might also want to check with your state insurance regulators, to see if they have any record of complaints being filed against a company that you're considering. Remember: an ethical premium review company can do you a lot of good by finding and recovering substantial premium overcharges that your company isn't even aware have occurred. But an unethical premium review

---

How long has the company been in business? _____

Who are the principals of the company? _____

Obtain at least three references: _____

_____

What professional designations are held by the consultants who will be working with you? _____

_____

What professional insurance societies or associations does the consultant belong to? _____

_____

What is the fee basis for the consultant's work? _____

Contingent fee based on results? _____

Hourly rate? _____

Can you as the client choose the compensation method—contingent or hourly? _____

**Make clear to the consultant that you will not pay any contingent fee until you actually receive the reductions or refunds.**

Is the consultant willing to put his or her findings in writing and to communicate those findings directly to insurance company auditors and underwriters? _____

**FIGURE 8-3.** Consultant profile

company can cost you money and time pursuing bogus refunds—or, even worse, get you involved in premium fraud.

## QUICK REVIEW

- Make sure you understand what kind of insurance producer you are dealing with—independent agent, broker, or captive agent.
- Choose your insurer carefully, as well as your insurance producer. Turmoil in the industry has caused some well-known insurers to fail in recent years.
- Manage competition among insurance producers and insurance companies with a firm hand to produce best results from competitive bidding.
- Be objective in selecting the best insurance producer and agency for your company.
- Be careful in selecting insurance consultants—this area of the industry is lightly regulated, at best.

# CHAPTER 9

# Shopping for the Best Coverage at the Best Price

## HOW TO EVALUATE INSURANCE PROPOSALS

A COMMON PROBLEM IN COMPARING DIFfering insurance proposals is finding a common yardstick to measure them by. Of course, you want to obtain the best coverage at the lowest price. But anyone who's been through the process will know that it can be very difficult to figure out which proposal provides the best coverage, because often there will be significant variation in the fine details. How does one tell which differences are important and useful and which ones are not? And when it comes to cost, be careful, because sometimes the proposal with the lowest apparent cost turns out to be more expensive than some of the other quotes would have been.

Some business owners try to standardize the coverage part by telling agents and brokers to quote the insurance "apples to apples" with the expiring policies. But the problem with this approach is that the expiring policies might have serious deficiencies. It's really not in your best interest to discourage a sharp insurance agent from pointing out significant problems in your expiring coverage. But how do you tell which differences are important and which are mere nitpicking?

One approach is to develop a set of insurance specifications to be used by those bidding on the insurance. You set out a standardized schedule of coverages and make sure all proposals are consistent with this. These specifications should also spell out clearly and explicitly the basis for computing the premium, such as payrolls, sales, and experience modification factor. You can make clear that you welcome suggestions for improving coverage, but these should be shown as options with any additional cost for them broken out. This way, you can obtain competing proposals that are standardized in terms of coverage and that avoid any *lowballing* by any agents.

In insurance parlance, a lowball quote is one that seems cheap when you look at the premium dollars, but really isn't so cheap because it's based on lower payrolls or sales estimates.

In the case of workers' compensation insurance, to avoid lowballing you want to make sure that all proposals spell out in detail exactly how the estimated premiums have been calculated. This means that the proposal must show all payroll estimates in each classification, with each rate for each classification, along with the experience modification factor and any other credit or debits used to calculate the premium.

## An Example of a Lowball Proposal

How does lowballing work? It simply involves making some adjustment in the estimated payrolls or rates or modifications that affect the proposed premium and then obscuring the fact. For example, consider two proposals for workers' compensation insurance:

|  | Proposal 1 | Proposal 2 |
|---|---|---|
| Clerical Payroll | $560,000 | $560,000 |
| Shop Payroll | $1,200,000 | $1,200,000 |
| Experience Mod | 1.02 | 1.02 |
| Premium | $65,749 | $96,492 |

Now, the bottom-line premium on Proposal 1 looks clearly better. And they both use the same payroll estimates and the same experience modifier. So Proposal 1 will obviously save money, right? Not necessarily.

Notice that these proposals don't really specify what class codes and rates are being used. It turns out that Proposal 1 is using a different class code (with a lower manual rate) than is being used by Proposal 2.

Maybe the agent producing Proposal 1 thinks that a lower class really is appropriate for this policyholder and he's gotten an underwriter to issue a proposal using this lower class. For example, if Proposal 2 is using code 3632 for the shop operations, but Proposal 1 is using code 3629, there's a hidden assumption built into this proposal. Maybe this agent is particularly smart about classifications and he's figured out that this insured really does belong in a lower class. But take a look at the full details of how each proposed premium was really calculated (Figure 9-1).

If the agent is wrong in Proposal 1 about the insured being eligible for code 3629, proposal 2 would actually save money, because Proposal 1 has a ten percent schedule debit built into it, while Proposal 2 does not. Proposal 1 also does not take into account the fact that if this insured really is eligible for code 3629, the 1.02 experience modifier would be higher than 1.02, because the 1.02 mod was calculated on the basis of code 3632, not 3629. The increase in experience modifier would not offset all of the rate savings from the lower classification code, but it might well offset something like 25 percent of the rate difference.

There are all kinds of ways an agent might try to lowball a workers' comp proposal. Simply using lower estimated payrolls (and keeping the class codes the same) would give one proposal an unfair advantage that won't hold up. Remember: the actual payroll is going to be

**Proposal 1**

| Code | Payroll | Manual Rate | Premium | |
|------|---------|-------------|---------|--|
| 8810 | $560,000 | 0.5 | $2,800.00 | |
| 3629 | $1,200,000 | 4.65 | $55,800.00 | |
| | | | $58,600.00 | Manual premium |
| | | | 1.02 | Experience mod |
| | | | $59,772.00 | |
| | | | 10% | Schedule debit |
| | | | $65,749.20 | Standard premium |

**Proposal 2**

| Code | Payroll | Manual Rate | Premium | |
|------|---------|-------------|---------|--|
| 8810 | $560,000 | 0.5 | $2,800.00 | |
| 3629 | $1,200,000 | 7.65 | $91,800.00 | |
| | | | $94,600.00 | Manual premium |
| | | | 1.02 | Experience mod |
| | | | $96,492.00 | |
| | | | $65,749.20 | Standard premium |

FIGURE 8-1. Comparison of two proposals

determined with an audit, so the illusory savings produced by depressing the payroll estimate will vanish then.

To make sure you aren't being lowballed, make sure all proposals for workers' compensation insurance spell out all the following elements of the premium calculation:

- Classification description
- Code number
- Estimated payroll by classification
- Manual rate
- Experience modifier
- Scheduled credit or debit applied
- All other premium credits used
- Premium discount factor

## TYPES OF WORKERS' COMPENSATION POLICIES

And of course, all of the above elements cover only the variables of a *guaranteed-cost* proposal. If the competing plans are *loss-sensitive*, then you will also need a detailed projection of cost at various loss levels. So let's review how to compare competing loss-sensitive proposals.

Back in Chapter 2 we briefly reviewed different kinds of workers' compensation insurance policies, including the above-mentioned loss-sensitive policies. But let's get into more detail now, so we can review how to specifically compare such plans.

## RETROSPECTIVE RATING

As we had mentioned in Chapter 2, one of the most common types of loss-sensitive plan is retrospective rating (or retro, as the plans are often called). There can be great variation in retro plans, but let's start with the basics that they all have in common.

All retro plans make subsequent adjustments to standard premium, based on losses that occur during that policy. Standard premium is your regular workers' compensation insurance premium, calculated just like for a guaranteed-cost policy, but before application of a premium discount factor. So standard premium gets computed via payroll placed in specific classifications, with rates per hundred dollars of payroll, adjusted by experience modification factor and any other credits or debits that apply.

A retro plan then adjusts that standard premium according to a predetermined formula that factors in the losses that occur during the policy period. Depending on the cost of those claims, the retro premium might be less than standard premium (in which case the insurance company returns money back to you), more than standard premium (in which case the insurance company bills you for the additional premium), or it could work out to be just the same as the standard premium.

Traditionally, most retro plans used incurred losses to figure retro premiums. Incurred losses include not just the amounts the insurance company has actually paid out to date on claims, but also the reserves it's estimated for what it thinks will be the ultimate cost of those claims. Those loss reserves figure into the calculation just as much as the actual paid losses.

But there is another kind of retro, called a *paid-loss retro*, which counts only the claims costs actually paid by the insurance company. Ultimately both kinds of plans should end up at the same place, everything else being equal, but a paid-loss retro offers cash flow advantages to the policyholder. Paid-loss retro plans tend to be more available from insurers in soft insurance markets, but I've also seen companies continue to offer them to select accounts during hard markets.

Retro plans make their premium adjustments well after the policy has ended. That's why they're called retrospective rating, as they

"look back" at a prior policy period. The first retro adjustment is made using loss numbers valued six months after the policy has expired. So for a policy that ended December 31, 2004, the first retro adjustment would use loss numbers valued as of June 30, 2005. Of course, that doesn't mean that the adjustment will be calculated on June 30. It typically takes a few months more for the calculation to be made and sent out, so for this hypothetical plan the first retro adjustment might be sent to the policyholder in September 2005. After that, there will be annual subsequent recalculations, each done using revised loss numbers as of June 30 of each year. So sometime in September 2006, our hypothetical policyholder would receive a revised retro adjustment calculated using losses valued as of June 30, 2006. And the same would happen in 2007 and 2008, either until all claims are closed out and finalized or until policyholder and insurer agree on a negotiated final retro adjustment. Typically, if there are still open claims, the insurer will come up with its best projected loss numbers and propose a final retro calculation using these numbers. If the policyholder agrees, the insurer would then close out the retro so there would be no further adjustments. But if the policyholder and insurer can't agree to terms, the retro could undergo further adjustments, possibly producing significant additional premiums in future years for that policy that ended in 2004.

There's generally an accepted framework for calculating these retro premium adjustments. One element is the *basic charge*. This is a heavily discounted insurance charge. Traditionally, this has been expressed as a percentage of standard premium. Thus, a basic of .15 means that the basic premium would be 15 percent of standard premium.

The next part of the retro calculation is the losses. Remember: this could either be *incurred* losses, which means that reserves are included, or just *paid* losses. Either way, the insurance company doesn't just charge the loss number. It charges a *loss conversion factor* (LCF) to the loss numbers. The LCF is a percentage add-on to the loss numbers. So an LCF of 1.15 would mean that the loss numbers would be multiplied by 1.15—in other words, a 15 percent additional charge.

So far, we've identified two elements of a retro adjustment—the basic premium and converted losses (losses times the LCF). These get multiplied by a *tax factor*. This is a premium tax charged by the state; it varies from state to state and from year to year.

Now let's run some numbers for a hypothetical retro. For simplicity's sake, let's continue using a simplified retro formula. Under this kind of retro formula, you would add the basic charge to the converted losses and then multiply that sum by the tax factor. Let's assume, in our hypothetical retro, that there was only one state involved and the tax factor for that state was 1.07. So you would add the basic factor to the converted losses and then multiply that sum by 1.07, to get the retro premium for this simplified retro.

Let's say the standard premium for the account was $100,000. With a basic charge of .15, the basic premium would be $15,000. Now let's assume that incurred losses are $50,000. Multiplying that by the LCF of 1.15 produces converted losses of $57,500. Adding the basic, we get

$$\$15,000 + \$57,500 = \$72,500$$

Multiplying this by the tax factor we get

$$\$72,500 \times 1.07 = \$77,575$$

This would be the retro premium for this plan.

So far, we've been examining a simplified retro formula. Years ago, insurance companies actually wrote retro plans that were this simple. But over the course of the past ten or 15 years, such simple retros have been complicated by many insurers. Still, if you understand the basic retro formula as detailed above, it will help you understand some of the complications that insurers have introduced in recent years.

The older, simpler kind of retro formula served insurers and insureds pretty well for decades. But needless to say, insurers eventually decided that such simple retros needed to be made more complicated (and of course, more expensive). So they came up with ways to further inflate the loss costs that would go into the retro formula by coming up with *allocated loss adjustment expenses* and *unallocated loss adjustment expenses*. These are additional charges for certain expenses associated with handling claims. Mind you, that's what the loss conversion factor already did, but insurers wanted to be able to make additional charges for their expenses. Allocated loss adjustment expenses are loss adjustment and handling costs that can be allocated to a specific claim. So in retro plans that include this charge, the loss figure includes not just what's paid out and what's reserved, but specific handling charges for those claims as well. Unallocated loss adjustment expenses are charges for costs that aren't associated with specific claims.

Another feature of retro plans that can be added at the insured's option is a *loss limitation*. This places a cap on the amount of any single claim that gets counted in the retro calculation, so that a single very expensive claim doesn't do too much economic damage when figuring the retro premium. There is, of course, an additional charge for this limitation.

There are two other important factors in any retro calculation: the *minimum* and the *maximum* charges. The minimum charge is, as its name implies, a floor to the retro premium. It is the minimum premium that will be due under the plan, even with zero losses. Conversely, the maximum charge is the ceiling on the retro premium. It is the maximum amount that can be charged for the plan, no matter how high the losses are.

Of course, since retro plans are designed by insurance companies, the minimum and maximum premiums aren't fixed dollar amounts. Historically, they have been defined as percentages of standard premium. Remember: standard premium is the workers' comp premium developed for a company using the regular guaranteed cost rules—rates times payroll, adjusted by experience modification factor and other credits and debits, but without the premium discount factor. So a minimum premium of .30 would mean that the minimum premium would be 30 percent of standard premium and a maximum premium of 1.40 would mean that the maximum premium would be 140 percent of standard premium. And since standard premium for a policy is known only after the audit, the dollar amounts of the minimum and maximum premium charges can't really be known until the audited standard premium is known.

Remember also that as your standard premium varies significantly from what was estimated when the policy began, the basic charge may vary also. Although maximum, minimum, LCF, and other retro factors are set when the policy begins, the basic factor is actually calculated through a complicated formula that takes into account the size of the premium. If your actual standard premium is significantly lower than originally estimated, the basic factor used on the retro adjustment may be higher than originally stated. If your audited standard premium is significantly higher than originally estimated, the basic factor under the plan may be lower than originally stated.

## LRARO Rating

In 1991, NCCI started filing a new concept in its retrospective rating manual—*large-risk alternative rating option* (LRARO). Most states, but not all, have approved this change to the retrospective rating plan manual. The new sections of the manual made up only a few paragraphs, in contrast with hundreds of pages in the rest of the manual dealing with other retro options. But those few paragraphs added language to the effect that for larger policyholders the factors of a retro plan could be negotiated between the insurance carrier and the policyholder

Think about it. For decades, a manual consisting of hundreds of pages had been used to detail how retro plans worked, how factors had to be calculated. But suddenly two or three paragraphs inserted into that voluminous manual allowed insurance companies to disregard all those detailed manual rules and negotiate retro plans with larger policyholders. If you've ever purchased a large, complicated workers' compensation insurance program, you know that the negotiation is usually pretty one-sided.

Worse yet, over the years the definition of

what constitutes a "large" policyholder has been ratcheted downwards. The original rationale for these LRARO plans that was that they would offer large sophisticated insurance buyers greater flexibility in insurance pricing. But since the introduction of LRARO, the threshold for qualification has been lowered in many states, so that now these plans are being offered to policyholders with only a few hundred thousand dollars of premium, instead of the original threshold of $1,000,000.

Some policyholders have taken the advent of LRARO rating to mean that "anything goes" when it comes to workers' compensation retro plans, but this is not really true. Some states have deregulated things to the point where an insurer can literally file any kind of loss-sensitive plan and then use it shortly thereafter. But not all states have taken this approach. The state-by-state mosaic of workers' compensation insurance remains very much a patchwork of different regulatory approaches. If your company does business in a number of states, you need to be aware that sometimes insurance companies take shortcuts with the regulatory approval process. In their desire to offer multistate employers a single policy covering all (or most) states, I have seen some insurers attempt to get around state insurance regulations and offer rating programs that were not allowed in some of the states covered by the policy.

## Side Agreements

One technique used by insurers to attempt to skirt state regulations on retro rating is the use of a separate side agreement that purports to define how premiums will be calculated under the policy. But these side agreements are not part of the policy and thus really cannot alter the terms of the policy. The standard workers' compensation insurance policy makes this clear in its fine print. It states, "The only agreements relating to this insurance are stated in this policy. The terms of this policy may not be changed or waived except by endorsement issued by us to be part of this policy." Yet I have seen side agreements drafted by insurance companies that did indeed attempt to change the terms of the policy, because the side agreement would contain a formula for computing the premium that was very different from the one contained in the actual policy. The insurance company would insist that the policyholder sign the side agreement and then use that as the basis for computing premiums, even though the policy itself contained a different formula that would have produced a lower premium.

Not all side agreements attempt this insurance sleight of hand. With some policies, such as paid-loss retro plans, a side agreement may be legitimately used to contractually spell out funding agreements between the policyholder and the insurer, so that the insurance company has a guarantee that it isn't left holding the bag for claims costs under the policy. But a side agreement that changes the terms of the policy itself is not valid, per the terms of the policy itself.

Why would an insurance company go to the trouble of drafting a side agreement that differs from the terms of the policy? Why wouldn't it just endorse the policy itself to use the formula contained in the side agreement? The answer is that if the insurance company wants to use a retro formula that isn't approved in some of the states covered by the policy, it can't endorse such a retro formula onto the policy itself. So some insurance companies have chosen to attempt to sidestep the insurance regulators. They have to file the policy forms, but they don't have to file side agreements. The only problem, as noted above, is that the policy itself makes it clear that the terms of the policy can be changed only through an endorsement to the policy itself. Any attempt to make a change through any separate side agreement contradicts the terms of the policy.

If your insurance company asks you to sign a side agreement for a workers' compensation insurance policy, take a close look at it. Compare the premium computation formula in that side agreement with what's on the policy. If there is a difference between the two, you may want to carefully consider the ramifications of the (probably more expensive) formula contained in the side agreement.

## Comparing Retro Proposals

When you're comparing competing proposals of retrospective rating plans, you want to identify the key components, make sure all are using the same standard premium as a starting point, and then run each plan through hypothetical loss levels and compare the resulting retro premiums.

One thing to watch for: some retro plans being offered that utilize separate side agreements to define the retro formula define "minimum" and "maximum" differently than historically done in approved retro plans. Historically, minimum and maximum premiums in a retro were defined as percentages of standard premium. However, some side agreements instead define minimum and maximum premium as being a rate per hundred dollars of payroll. They also typically define "basic pre-

mium" as a rate per hundred dollars of payroll. So when comparing retro plans, check carefully to see exactly how each plan defines basic, minimum, and maximum.

The historic method of defining these retro factors as percentages of standard premium means that all the detailed rules and regulations that govern calculation of standard premium still have meaning. For example, in a retro that defines basic, minimum, and maximum as percentages of standard premium, the experience modification factor still affects your premium. This means that the employer has the benefit of all the rules and regulations that govern experience mods. So if you discover an error in the calculation or application of an experience mod under a traditional retro, correcting the experience mod will reduce your basic, minimum, and maximum premiums.

But under the kinds of retro formulas often used in side agreements, because basic, minimum, and maximum are no longer defined as percentages of premium, correcting an error in experience mod (or in classification code, for that matter) would no longer affect your basic, minimum, or maximum premium charge. In other words, defining basic, minimum, and maximum as merely rates times payroll deprives the policyholder of subtle but sometimes important protections against overcharges. No wonder some insurers have circumvented insurance regulators with these side agreements—it enables them to further tilt the odds in their own favor when it comes to computing premiums.

## Large-Deductible Plans

There's another kind of loss-sensitive plan that is often offered to larger employers—the large-deductible plan. This type of plan calls for the policyholder to essentially self-insure most claims. For example, a large-deductible plan with a $100,000 deductible means that the employer is responsible for reimbursing the first $100,000 of each claim to the insurance company.

We discussed these plans in Chapter 3, but let's go into a little more detail now and consider how to compare competing proposals.

Remember: in a large-deductible plan, the insurance company still is responsible for paying the claims. This is different from deductibles in other kinds of insurance. Insurance regulators wanted to make sure that the insurance companies were ultimately responsible for paying claims, regardless of the financial condition of the employer, so they made sure that workers' compensation deductibles still made the insurance company responsible for paying claims, whether the employer reimburses the insurer or fails to do so.

So large-deductible plans normally have side agreements that obligate the employer to reimburse the insurance company for the claims that fall under the deductible. And those deductible agreements normally specify a dollar amount for each claim as well as an annual aggregate amount. The aggregate amount represents the most that the employer will have to reimburse for all claims.

One tricky area is that many deductible agreements will state that the deductible amount is either the stated dollar amount or a rate per hundred dollars of payroll, whichever is higher. So if the audited payrolls are higher than the estimated payrolls, the aggregate deductible amount may well be higher than the dollar amount specified.

In addition to reimbursing the insurer for claims that fall under the deductible amounts,

the employer will also have to pay an insurance premium. This is a highly discounted premium, commensurate with the fact that the employer will actually be paying for most of the claims under the policy. The insurance premium represents what the insurance company is charging for being responsible for claims above the deductible amounts, as well as for other expenses.

When comparing large-deductible plans, compare the insurance premiums charged by each one, as well as the specific deductible limits on each. Note whether the plans call for flat dollar amounts in the deductible limits or limits that are adjustable based on payroll. If adjustable, make sure the payroll estimates used in both plans are the same and are reasonable estimates for your coming year. Lowballed payroll estimates can make a big difference not only in the insurance premium charges but also in the amount of the aggregate deductible.

Here's an example of something that went terribly wrong in one employer's large-deductible plan.

This client was a large road-construction contractor that had purchased a large-deductible policy from a very large and well-known insurer. They had used this kind of policy for several years, but had called me in to review things after they had left this insurer. The insurer was now claiming the contractor owed about $1,000,000 in additional charges, mainly for claims that had fallen under the deductible amounts in various years. In fact, the insurance company had filed suit against the contractor, seeking that million dollars.

But when I reviewed the policies and deductible billings, I found something odd: the insurer had changed the aggregate deductible amounts after the policies had begun. In one instance, it had changed the aggregate deductible amount after the policy had *expired*.

The original policies had contained endorsements clearly stating the deductible amounts as flat dollar amounts. But later endorsements changed this so that the deductible amount was either the dollar amount or a rate times payroll, whichever was greater. And since payrolls had increased from the original policy estimates, the deductible based on payroll was much higher than the flat dollar amount.

However, the state in which this contractor was located had an insurance regulation that prohibited insurers from making changes in deductibles after policy inception. And so I was able to report to my client that they didn't owe the insurance company a million dollars—and that the insurance company owed them about four million dollars back in overcharges.

And ultimately, in settlement of the litigation, the insurer paid roughly that amount, giving back about four million dollars to the contractor.

## QUICK REVIEW

- Utilize insurance specifications to minimize problems with competitive bidding on insurance.
- Watch out for "low ball" insurance proposals.
- Understand all factors of a retro-type policy before agreeing to it. A poorly designed retro can be a very expensive mistake.
- Be sure to understand how the terms of a side agreement may be an attempt to revise the terms of the policy to the advantage of the insurance company.
- Compare all loss-sensitive plans carefully and objectively. There can be many confusing details in these plans and an employer may need outside professional advice to avoid purchasing a plan that is not well-designed.

# CHAPTER 10

# Managing Workers' Comp Costs Between Renewals

S O FAR WE'VE COVERED WHAT EMPLOY-
ERS need to do when they're shopping for workers' compensation
coverage and what they need to do
when the policy ends and the audit is
being done. But in between those two
events there are many important steps that
employers also need to take to control
their workers' compensation costs and
make sure their coverage is right.

First and foremost, employers need to
be active in managing claims. Although
many larger employers have learned the
hard way about how important this can be,
it's surprising how many companies don't
take as much responsibility in this as they
could. Taking your eye off this ball can be a
very costly mistake.

First off, make sure you have procedures
in place to report all workplace injuries
promptly to your insurer. We covered this
earlier in our section on experience modifi-

cation factors, but it bears repeating: if you
don't report an incident to your insurer on
a timely basis, it can later deny responsibility for the claim. That's why it's important
to report all workplace injuries, even minor
ones, because sometimes minor injuries
develop into major claims. Remember that
under the current NCCI experience rating
formula medical-only claims are discounted by 70 percent, so minor medical-
only claims are not going to have a serious
effect on your experience mod.

Many states now have small-deductible
plans in place, so if you want to self-insure
small claims, do it the right way by endorsing the small deductible onto your policy.
That way, you can handle small claims
yourself but still be protected in case some
of them turn into something major.

Many states have enacted managed care
provisions into their workers' compensation systems, but not all states have. In

states where employees are free to choose their own treating physician, employers can still exercise some influence over where employees are treated initially. Your insurance company can probably help you identify local clinics that will provide proper medical care and attention to employees at reasonable cost. Although employees in these states will still be able to choose to see their own physician if they wish, most of your employees aren't looking to make their workplace injury some kind of lottery win. If you can get them to good and competent medical treatment quickly, with a physician or clinic that you know is not going to try to capitalize on the claim, you can go a long way toward controlling medical costs.

After a claim is turned in, don't leave everything in the hands of the insurance company. Make sure you do your own follow-up with your employee. If the employee is having difficulty with claims personnel at the insurance company, you want to know about it right away so you can intervene. A wise manager will do everything possible to make an injured employee feel that the company is on his or her side and that the employer is working with the employee to make sure the insurance company is treating both of them properly.

Do whatever you can to make sure that any difficulties or hard feelings toward the insurance company are not transferred to you, the employer. If you make the effort to help the injured employee get proper medical care and make sure the insurer pays all bills promptly, you may well ultimately reduce the cost of the claim. And remember: claims costs will ultimately greatly influence your premiums, either on the current policy if it's loss-sensitive or on future

policies through the experience rating mechanism.

It's been pretty well documented that when employees retain an attorney, the ultimate cost of the claim increases significantly. So it's in your best interests to do everything you can to make your injured employees feel that they don't need an attorney. That may mean putting pressure on an insurance company that is handling claims slowly or in a manner that is antagonizing your employee. You probably know your people better than the insurance company does, so make sure you protect your people from any problems in the insurance claims adjustment process. The more your employees perceive you as being on their side, helping them to get fair and equitable treatment from the insurer, the better the odds that your claims will not be unnecessarily inflated.

When any of your employees cannot do their regular duties due to a compensable injury, do your best to find them some alternative light duty. An employee who is sitting at home watching daytime television will see plenty of ads from attorneys who would love to take their case. Finding light-duty work wherever possible can be a very cost-effective measure to hold down the costs of workers' compensation claims.

Keep track of your company's critical date for the insurer to send loss data to the rating bureau for use in your next experience modification factor. Remember: your insurer will essentially "take a snapshot" of your loss information, including reserves, six months after policy expiration. So if your policy expires January 1, the insurer will be reporting your losses and loss reserves as of July 1. So review open claims for excessive claims well in advance of that critical date, so you can negotiate with your carrier about appropriate reserves. Once those figures get reported to the rating bureau, any lowering of reserves won't affect your next modifier, but only the one after that. So don't let that critical window of opportunity close without checking your open claims carefully to see if there are any loss reserves that may be too high.

## CERTIFICATES OF INSURANCE

Earlier in Chapter 7 we reviewed how important it is to have all your certificates of insurance on file from any subcontractors, temporary agencies, or employee-leasing companies you use. But the best time to be working on this isn't just before your audit, but rather all during the year, to make sure that those subcontractors or others that owe your company a certificate provide those certificates on a timely basis.

Remember: a certificate of insurance is a written assurance that someone else is providing workers' compensation insurance for certain workers. If you don't have a copy of the certificate, when your insurance company's auditor shows up you will be charged for those workers. So make sure you initiate proper procedures in your office to follow up with those who owe you certificates.

While you're at it, make sure you have someone on your staff who is trained to read and understand certificates properly. If some third party owes your company a certificate, there is probably some contractual basis for it; that contract should spell out the details about the insurance coverage that is required. Review the certificate carefully to make sure the insurance described matches up with the requirements of

the contract. What kind of information should be checked? The effective dates, the financial strength of the insurer, and any additional insured requirements your company may have imposed.

Keep in mind something else about certificates of insurance—they provide only the coverage that is on the policy. Certificates are normally prepared by an insurance agent. If the insurance agent puts incorrect information on the certificates, the policy isn't meeting the requirements you've set out contractually.

If you have the certificate on file for your workers' comp audit, you will make sure you aren't charged for workers who are supposed to be covered elsewhere. But if the actual policy described by the certificate is somehow inadequate or if the policy is cancelled and you're not notified, then having the certificate won't help you with any claims that the policy should have covered.

It's one of the great ironies of the insurance industry—a lot of time and effort is expended providing certificates of insurance, but only the policy itself determines the actual coverage for a claim.

So if the policy gets cancelled early for nonpayment, it won't make any difference that you have a certificate of insurance showing that coverage was in force. You probably have the basis for legal action against the party that was contractually obligated to keep the insurance in force, but that can be an expensive, time-consuming effort, with no guarantee of success. If a company couldn't afford to pay its insurance, what are the odds you can successfully recover anything through litigation?

Similarly, if the certificate states that your

company has been added as an additional insured under a subcontractor's policy, but the actual policy is not so endorsed, the certificate does not actually give you the coverage.

So what can you do? One solution is to request a copy of the policy itself or at least pertinent parts of it, showing effective date and any additional insured endorsements. This may still not completely protect you if the policy gets cancelled midterm for non-payment or other reason, but it gives you a more solid basis for verifying coverage than a certificate.

## FLUCTUATIONS IN PAYROLL

Since the payrolls (and classifications) on the policy are really only estimates, sometimes those estimates, even when made with the best effort, turn out to be off the mark. You could find yourself with actual payroll running substantially lower than the policy estimates—or substantially higher. In such cases, it may well make sense to get the policy's estimates adjusted midterm, rather than waiting for the eventual audit.

Particularly if your actual payrolls are running significantly lower than the policy estimates, your company may find it imperative to get the policy estimates adjusted downwards. But be warned: this can be a touchy negotiation with your insurer. Insurance companies hate to be left holding the bag at audit time. From hard experience, they know that sometimes it can be difficult or impossible to collect a large bill for additional premium that's been developed at the audit, so they're reluctant to be lowballed on the payroll estimates.

To get your policy's payroll estimates lowered during the course of the policy may take some

time and effort on your part. With persistence and some documentation, you should be able to get your insurer to work with you on this, but be prepared to encounter some initial resistance. You will probably have to make a convincing case for changes in business conditions since the policy estimates were made. Still, by working with your agent, you should be able to get some accommodation.

If your payrolls are running substantially higher than estimated, you may be tempted to just let things ride and take advantage of the cash flow advantage. But there can be dangers with this approach. Allowing a substantial additional premium to ride until the policy expires means that you have to be sure your company's cash flow will enable you to pay the entire additional premium at once. Endorsing the higher payrolls onto the policy midterm will space out your payment of that additional premium and help you keep current with this expense.

## TEMPS, PEO'S, AND SUBS

We've covered some of this topic already in our discussion of certificates of insurance. Remember that just because a company has contractually agreed to provide workers' comp for certain workers doesn't mean that it has actually done so. Over the course of the past five or six years, with extreme fluctuations in the state of the commercial insurance marketplace, there have been significant disruptions in the availability of workers' compensation insurance for temporary agencies, professional employer organizations (also known as employee-leasing), and some other kinds of businesses. Just a few years ago, one of the largest single PEOs in the

United States went out of business unexpectedly, in large part because of problems with obtaining workers' compensation insurance. It had contractually agreed to cover large numbers of workers at its clients' operations, but in fact it did not have coverage in place for months and months before going out of business.

If you contract with a PEO or other alternative employer (like a temp agency) that is then obligated to provide workers' comp for some workers at your business, but then something goes wrong and that other party doesn't meet that obligation, you can be assured that any injured workers will in all likelihood be able to make a claim against your workers' compensation coverage. And so your insurer will make sure to get its premium for that exposure, in spite of the fact that you have a contract saying that another party is responsible for those claims. If the other party doesn't have valid insurance, then your insurance will be picking up the exposure. And insurance companies like to get premium for exposures.

Many PEOs and temporary agencies find it difficult to obtain voluntary market workers' comp—particularly in hard insurance markets. Assigned risk plans insure many temporary agencies, but PEOs (employee-leasing companies) often don't find assigned risk coverage very conducive to their business plans. Many PEOs use lower workers' comp costs as a key selling point to prospective clients, but it's difficult to offer lower workers' comp costs if your policy is written through an assigned risk plan.

That was the dilemma facing the large PEO mentioned earlier. Although assigned risk coverage was always an option, it didn't pursue that coverage because it just would have been too expensive—the PEO couldn't offer any cost savings to its clients. So, instead it pursued all kinds of complicated strategies to try to obtain voluntary market coverage. These strategies had worked for it in the soft insurance market. But the insurance market had just recently shifted to hard conditions and the PEO's old voluntary insurer had gone into liquidation abruptly.

Currently, with hard market conditions still applying, many PEOs have had to adopt other strategies to obtain voluntary market coverage. One PEO I'm familiar with has obtained a large-deductible policy in the voluntary market, but bills clients on a guaranteed-cost basis. As long as claims are held to reasonable levels, this strategy can work. But if claims get out of control, the PEO could potentially get squeezed between fixed charges coming in from clients and escalating insurance costs owed to its carrier.

Not only that, but the clients of this PEO are generally unaware of the behind-the-scenes arrangements made by the PEO for workers' comp. They just know that the PEO has valid insurance and that the charges they receive from the PEO are lower than what they could obtain on their own. And as long as claims remain under control, this arrangement should work just fine. But if claims get out of control, it's conceivable that someday the clients of the PEO might find problems arising unexpectedly.

So when using a PEO (employee-leasing) arrangement, it's wise to ask for detailed information about exactly how the PEO has met its workers' compensation obligations. Remember: a certificate of insurance won't detail the kind of workers' compensation policy that's in place. It won't say, for example, that the policy is a large-deductible policy. So you wouldn't be able to spot a potential problem just by examining the certificate.

## FRONTING

Another practice in the insurance industry that could cause unforeseen problems is *fronting*. It's an unregulated practice; insurance commissioners are aware of it but don't know exactly how widespread it is. By its very nature it is deceptive, although legal—and practiced by many large and reputable companies. Here's how it works.

Relatively large companies can find it advantageous to use a *captive insurance company*—a company owned by the policyholder. So ABC Corp. can set up an insurance company based offshore (or even in some U.S. jurisdictions) to write its insurance. The problem is, states regulate which insurance companies can write workers' comp and captives almost always don't meet those requirements. But some creative insurance folks came up with a solution to that problem: fronting. If you can get a large and well-known insurance company to write your workers' comp policy, but then reinsure all your claims with your captive, you get the best of both worlds. The claims are actually being paid by your captive and most of the premiums are going into the captive. (The fronting insurer keeps a small cut as a "fronting fee.") But to the outside world, your workers' comp isn't written by ABC Corp. Captive but instead by Giant Well-Known Insurance, Inc.

Now technically, should the captive be unable to pay the claims, the fronting insurance company would be on the hook for the claims. But it's careful to make sure the captive meets financial standards so that is unlikely and it drafts reinsurance agreements that make it clear that the fronting carrier doesn't have to pay the claims.

Still, the practice is inherently deceptive. Your company might well have certificates of insurance that state that a large and well-known insurance company is writing the workers' compensation insurance for your subcontractor or for your PEO, but the actual responsibility for handling claims rests instead with some offshore captive insurance company located in the Cayman Islands. And you can't tell the difference.

At the moment, there isn't anything you can do about this situation. Even if you were to get a full copy of the policy from the large, well-known insurer, you wouldn't be able to tell it was a front. Will these elaborate arrangements ever create problems for the insurance system? For your company? No one really knows. Insurance regulators have considered enacting some oversight of these practices, but as of this writing no one has.

The only lesson one can draw from these practices is that even though you think that another company is responsible for the workers' comp for some of your workers, you can't assume that these arrangements are airtight. It's conceivable that you could end up paying premium charges for some workers who were supposed to be covered by a subcontractor or an independent firm you're using to provide services to your company (a janitorial service, for instance) or a temp agency or a PEO. Get certificates of insurance from these parties, by all means, and check those certificates carefully. Get copies of the actual policies, if possible, to make sure the certificates are accurate.

## TRACKING ENDORSEMENTS TO YOUR POLICY

Finally, here is one more fundamental thing that the cost-conscious employer needs to do to control workers' comp costs: carefully track all endorsements that you receive during the course of the policy. Because workers' compensation policies always start out with estimated premiums, the insurance company typically will make changes to those estimates by endorsing the policy. For example, after the audit of the prior policy is completed (typically a few months after the succeeding policy has started), the insurance company may want to endorse that succeeding policy to the same payroll and classifications as were found on that audit.

Let's say that the policy effective January 1, 2005 had the estimated premium shown in Figure 10-1. But in early March 2005, the 2004 policy is audited, resulting in the audited payrolls and premiums shown in Figure 10-2.

Typical insurance company practice, if the 2005 policy was written by the same insurer as had written the 2004 policy, would be to endorse the 2005 policy up to the same payrolls as had been found during the audit of the preceding policy. So now the 2005 policy would be endorsed as follows (Figure 10-3).

Notice that the estimated payrolls for 2005 now match what was found on the audit for the 2004 policy, but the premium is higher because the 2005 policy is using different rates for each class.

That's a fairly routine endorsement that's done to a policy. But suppose that the

increase in payrolls wasn't so incremental. Suppose that the 2004 audit had found $2,627,456 in Machine Shop payroll—but the year was up and down: during the first half of 2004 business had been really booming and then had dropped off all during the second half. If 2005 were continuing that same unfortunate trend, the audited payrolls for 2004 might be an unreasonably high estimate for 2005. If this is the case, you need to start negotiating and explaining immediately to your insurance company about why the 2005 payroll estimates should not be endorsed up to the same levels as found on the 2004 audit.

Or consider a different scenario: the 2005 pol-

| Class | Code | Payroll | Rate | Premium |
|---|---|---|---|---|
| Machine Shop (NOC)* | 3632 | $565,000 | $7.43 | $41,979.50 |
| Outside Sales | 8742 | $125,000 | $0.86 | $1,075.00 |
| Clerical | 8810 | $450,000 | $0.55 | $2,475.00 |
| | | | Manual Premium | $45,529.50 |
| | | | Experience Modifier | 0.92 |
| | | | Modified Premium | $41,887.14 |

*Not otherwise classified

**FIGURE 10-1.** Policy: estimated premium

| Class | Code | Payroll | Rate | Premium |
|---|---|---|---|---|
| Machine Shop (NOC)* | 3632 | $565,000 | $7.43 | $41,979.50 |
| Outside Sales | 8742 | $125,000 | $0.86 | $1,075.00 |
| Clerical | 8810 | $450,000 | $0.55 | $2,475.00 |
| | | | Manual Premium | $45,529.50 |
| | | | Experience Modifier | 0.92 |
| | | | Modified Premium | $41,887.14 |

*Not otherwise classified

**FIGURE 10-2.** Policy: audited premium

| Class | Code | Payroll | Rate | Premium |
|---|---|---|---|---|
| Machine Shop (NOC)* | 3632 | $627,456 | $7.43 | $46,619.98 |
| Outside Sales | 8742 | $123,554 | $0.86 | $1,062.56 |
| Clerical | 8810 | $466,789 | $0.55 | $2,567.34 |
| | | | Manual Premium | $50,249.88 |
| | | | Experience Modifier | 0.92 |
| | | | Modified Premium | $46,229.89 |

*Not otherwise classified

**FIGURE 10-3.** Policy: endorsements

icy starts out as shown above, but five months into the policy the insurer endorses the policy to use a 1.45 experience modifier in place of the .92. In Chapter 6, when we were covering experience modification factors, it was mentioned that some states place limitations on how late in the policy experience modifiers can be increased. So, depending upon the state in which this hypothetical machine shop operated, this endorsement that increases experience modifier might be acceptable or it might not. But remember: you can't rely on your insurance company to be aware of what the rules are in each state about this. It might seem like this is something it should be watching, but in my experience insurance companies do not. So to make sure you aren't overcharged because your insurance company is not following the particular rules of your state, you'll have to take an active role in protecting yourself. Even your insurance agent may well not be aware of the particular rules for your state. Your best option is to contact your state's department of insurance and review the rules in your state with a knowledgeable regulator.

If you find that your insurance company has violated the rules that pertain in a particular state, you will want to respond promptly to the endorsement in writing, pointing out exactly why this endorsement is not proper. If this doesn't get results, file a written complaint with your state insurance regulators. Nowadays, many state insurance regulators allow policyholders to file such complaints online.

There are two kinds of regulations that you may need to check to see what the rules are about experience modification increases in a particular state. One kind of regulation is contained in a state's statutory insurance code; state regulators are most familiar with this kind of regulation. The second kind of regulation that may give some help is within the manual rules of the rating bureau for that state. State insurance regulators may not be as familiar with the details of these manual rules as they are with the statutory insurance code, so you may need to consult the rating bureau as well as state insurance regulators, to learn the rules for a particular state and determine if your insurance company has violated them. In NCCI states, check the rules in the *Basic Manual* that limit how late in the policy experience modifiers can be increased. For non-NCCI states, consult the rating bureau that is used within that state, as indicated in Chapter 1.

Sometimes insurance underwriters will change classification codes mid-policy, via endorsement. If the classification change involves adding a more expensive classification that was not on the original policy, you may want to do the same kind of checking as discussed above for experience mod increases.

Some states limit when in a policy term an insurance company is allowed to add a more expensive class, but some states do not place any limits on this. Some states will allow such an endorsement to be made early in a policy term, but not later, while other states will not allow such an endorsement at all once the policy has begun.

## GET YOUR POLICY AND REVIEW IT

While we're on the subject of tracking endorsements, there is a related matter that every business owner and manager should keep in mind. It's something that drives both policyholders and insurance agents crazy sometimes—late policy production. If your policy is effective July 1, 2005, you shouldn't have to wait until April 2006 before you receive your copy of the policy. Yet such extreme delays in receiving a workers' compensation policy are not unheard of.

Sometimes this is the fault of the insurance company. Sometimes it is the fault of the insurance agent. But no matter whose fault it is, it is important to you, the policyholder, to insist that your policy be produced to you within a reasonable time—say within three months from the effective date.

If you don't have a copy of the policy in a reasonable time, it is more difficult to catch your insurance company making an improper increase in experience mod or classification. Insist on getting your policy on a timely basis. Then review it carefully to make sure it conforms to the proposal you accepted in its details. Check classifications, rates, experience modifiers, and all credits and debits to make sure they are as proposed. And if not, insist that the policy be corrected to conform to that proposal.

Here's an extreme example of what can happen when policy doesn't match proposal, from my case files.

This case occurred in the early 1990s, when I was consulting with a *Fortune* 100 manufacturer of heavy equipment. This major manufacturer had come up with an insurance program for its manufacturing suppliers—that is, smaller manufacturers that made parts for my client. My part of the program was to review workers' comp classifications, audits, and premiums for those suppliers, but the overall program actually tried to sell insurance to those suppliers as well. As it turned out, one supplier had purchased insurance through the program, only to find out that the rates on the policy weren't going to be what had been on the proposal. It turned out that the people working on the insurance program were based up in Wisconsin, but this supplier was in Illinois. The agent had somehow used Wisconsin rates in the proposal, but when it came time to issue the policy the insurance carrier balked, saying that there was no way it could use rates anywhere near what had been quoted. It was shaping up as a major problem for this fledgling insurance program, but I got to play hero for both the policyholder and the program. It turned out that the supplier had been misclassified for many years; once the classification mistake was corrected, the actual premium was even lower than in the proposal that had used Wisconsin rates.

Now, this particular problem surfaced fairly soon after the policy had begun. But sometimes insurance agents aren't so quick to own up to mistakes. Although most insurance agents are very good about checking over policies when they come in, sometimes it can be difficult to tell when the agent is being less than forthright.

Just this year, in my hometown of Chicago, an extremely well-known and well-connected insurance broker was convicted in federal court of misappropriating millions of dollars from clients. One of his schemes was to "shortstop" audits that produced return premiums for clients. The insurance company would issue the credits to the agent's account, but the agent wouldn't forward those refunds on to policyholders. And because this particular broker was extremely well connected politically, I suspect that some of those policyholders found it politic to not ask too persistently about their refunds. Eventually, the federal prosecutor asked.

But this isn't the only instance I've found over the years of such unethical and illegal behavior on the part of agents. I have seen other instances—relatively rare, thank goodness!—of agents or brokers somehow forgetting to forward return premiums that were due policyholders. And sometimes with complex accounts these "oversights" had gotten lost in the complicated insurance billings.

One of the most successful insurance salesmen I've ever known ended up also serving federal time for misappropriating clients' premium moneys. When I started in the insurance business, I was told to tag along with this guy as he made his rounds, as our manager hoped I might learn a little of whatever magic this agent seemed to possess.

I left that insurance company a few years later without ever having learned too much of

that guy's secrets—but I saw enough to know that he was very persuasive, very charming, but he also cut a lot of corners and played a lot of angles. I didn't learn exactly how many corners he was cutting until years later, when I talked with another insurance broker in downstate Illinois. I learned that this broker's agency had been in the middle of being acquired by my old "friend's" agency, until the broker discovered that moneys were being misappropriated from his agency even before the deal was finished. And that's how the one-time Golden Boy ended up going to jail.

What's a little frightening is that I was told that this was rather unusual—that this agent was sent to jail only because his offenses were so egregious. Most insurance agent infractions, so I was told, are handled more discreetly: the money is put back and everything is taken care of behind closed doors.

I thought of that as I read about the more recent scandal involving the politically connected broker, because our state's department of insurance, when it had learned of his misappropriations of funds, had merely told the broker to replace the money and then all would be forgotten. Fortunately, the newly appointed federal prosecutor here did not take the same view.

The point of all this is that, although the vast majority of insurance people are extremely ethical, conscientious, and honest, the occasional rogue can sometimes get away with a lot of financial shenanigans before getting caught. And sometimes it is the best and most persuasive salesperson who is the least ethically rigorous. So, as I stated earlier in this book, "Trust, but verify."

## QUICK REVIEW

- Stay in active communication with injured workers—don't let the insurance company monopolize all contact. You want to know if any employee is having problems with the insurer that may increase the cost of the claim.

- Remember that certificates of insurance provide only limited assurance that an independent contractor or subcontractor really has its own workers' comp insurance.

- Review payroll estimates mid-policy to make sure they are still reasonable. Adjust them if necessary to avoid large premium surprises at audit.

- Exercise care when using employee leasing or temporary agencies to make sure they have valid workers' compensation coverage for workers they provide you.

- Keep a careful eye on all endorsements to your policy during the policy period to make sure you understand why they are being made and that you receive all endorsements that are supposed to be part of policy. Also watch out for changes in classification or experience modifier that may be prohibited by your state rules.

# CHAPTER 11

# Alternative Approaches to Traditional Insurance

SO FAR, WE'VE BEEN REVIEWING INSURANCE coverage for workers' compensation exposures. Insurance is the most common way for employers to handle their workers' compensation obligations, but it's not the only way. There are a number of alternative approaches to handling this business exposure, which this chapter will discuss.

## SELF-INSURANCE

Most states give employers the option of self-insuring their workers' compensation obligations. But self-insurance is not the same thing as just not having workers' compensation insurance. Self-insurance means that the state has approved a company to take care of its workers' compensation claims itself, instead of buying an insurance policy. But since states retain their keen interest in making sure that injured workers

are going to be taken care of, they impose restrictions on employers. Essentially, a company has to be approved by state insurance regulators to be self-insured. The requirements for approval vary significantly from state to state. Only North Dakota prohibits self-insurance of workers' compensation, although Wyoming offers it on an extremely limited basis.

Harking back to our concept of workers' compensation being a state-by-state mosaic, keep in mind that to qualify as a self-insurer you have to do it state by state. In many states, self-insurance is practical only for larger employers, so self-insurance might not be practical, even for a large employer, in each state where the employer has operations. A company can qualify for self-insurance in some states, but in some others where it has smaller operations still need to purchase traditional insurance.

As an example, consider Alabama. That state's requirements for self-insurance are:

- Provide audited financial statements
- $5,000,000 minimum net worth
- Current-assets-to-current-liabilities ratio of 1.0 or greater
- Positive net income

States will typically require that a company post some kind of financial guarantee, usually a *surety bond*, to make sure that claims are paid, along with excess insurance to cover claims above the amount guaranteed.

There are companies that specialize in helping employers put together a viable self-insurance program, so you're still going to be dealing with outside insurance people. After all, with a self-insured program, you're going to need experienced people to handle the claims and you're going to need excess insurance, to limit your exposure to claims costs. If you investigate self-insurance, you'll find that, although it may have the potential to reduce your ultimate cost of workers' compensation, it will be just as complicated as negotiating a large insurance program.

To qualify as a self-insurer, you'll need to meet the particular requirements of each state you wish to be self-insured in. You'll have to provide a financial guarantee, such as a surety bond. You'll need to find and hire a third-party administrator to handle claims. You'll need to establish a funding mechanism to provide funds to pay claims as you go along. You'll need to purchase excess insurance. Fortunately, there are specialists in self-insurance that can assist you with all of these things, so you can take a one-stop-shopping approach. A good source of information about self-insurance for workers' compensation can be found on the internet at www.specandagg.com.

## GROUP SELF-INSURANCE

A more recent development in many states has been the approval of group self-insurance plans. These programs allow an employer to meet its workers' compensation obligations within a state by joining a multiple-employer program. From an employer's point of view, such programs look and feel a lot like buying traditional workers' compensation insurance. But there are very important differences that employers need to be aware of before entering such programs.

Initially, group self-insurance programs typically offer significant savings over what is available in the insurance marketplace. So the initial going-in cost can look very attractive, especially when compared with assigned risk rates.

But those same low rates can later cause problems for employers that have entered these group self-insurance programs. Because the true cost of workers' compensation claims can take years to be known, these programs can be vulnerable to being devoured by escalating costs as time goes on.

As of this writing, it's just been announced that a very large and well-known group self-insurance program in Kentucky has fallen prey to such problems. And now employers that had been members of the program are receiving very large assessments to make up the shortfalls.

That's the potential problem with such programs. All members of the group are liable not just for the cost of their own claims, but for the claims of the entire group. So if things go badly, you may receive a very large bill from the group, even if you haven't been a member for a few years.

My home state of Illinois has had similar experiences with group self-insured programs. A decade or so ago, these programs were established with great fanfare as a cost-saving alternative to traditional insurance programs. Many business groups established such plans and marketed them aggressively to their members. But regulatory oversight was not as tight as it could have been, so many of these plans have gone belly up, leaving members and past members with very large and very unexpected assessments to make up shortfalls.

Group self-insurance programs may offer short-term savings, but it can be very difficult to know if the particular program you're contemplating is going to encounter problems in future years. Being a member of a group self-insurance program that isn't charging sufficient rates is like having a ticking time bomb under your desk. Given the very mixed record of such programs, any employer that decides to become a member had better realize the potential risk it's accepting. Although rates may seem very attractive right now, the liability of members for the performance of the group as a whole can be a very unpleasant surprise further down the road.

## "VIRTUAL" WORKERS' COMP INSURANCE

Another recent development in the field is what I call "virtual" workers' compensation insurance. This approach uses separate insurance products to attempt to produce coverage for an employer that comes close to meeting workers' compensation obligations without actually using a workers' compensation insurance policy. Instead, it uses a combination of other insurance products like health insurance, disability insurance, and life insurance to cobble together a program that

provides benefits for employees that come close to those provided by a workers' compensation policy.

These programs have been developed and marketed to companies that find traditional workers' compensation insurance to be very expensive. The problem is that in many states, these "virtual" workers' compensation programs do not meet an employer's legal liability for workers' compensation under state law.

However, Alabama has recently allowed such programs to be offered to employers in that state with the approval of insurance regulators. They call them "alternative workers' compensation plans." However, even the Alabama Department of Insurance notes that this is a new provision in the workers' compensation law that is untested in the courts. The department also notes that it is unclear which *guaranty association* would guarantee such alternative coverage in the event that an insurance company becomes insolvent.

As time goes on, other states may give official approval to such alternative workers' compensation programs, but you would be well advised to check carefully with your state's insurance regulators to determine whether or not such programs have any legitimacy in your state. Some insurance agents have marketed these programs within states that have not approved them, so an employer should not assume, just because some insurance agent is offering such an alternative program, that it must be legal and legitimate within the state. Just the opposite may be true, and you could be exposing your company to fines and sanctions from insurance regulators if you have not met state requirements regarding your workers' compensation obligations.

## GOING BARE

Some small employers may be tempted to not purchase workers' compensation insurance or utilize any other approved method of meeting state-imposed obligation. They "go bare," as the saying goes. Some states allow this legally, although most do not.

Technically speaking, in most states any business that doesn't have employees (a sole proprietorship or a partnership) doesn't have to buy insurance for the sole proprietor or partners. Of course, the business has the option of buying insurance for these business owners anyway. But once a business has employees who aren't owners of the business, most states require that the business either buy insurance or meet the obligation through some other approved method (self-insurance, group self-insurance, etc.).

But some states allow very small employers to not purchase insurance. Alabama, for example, does not require insurance if the employer has four or fewer employees. Illinois does not require that commission-only salespeople be covered by workers' compensation insurance. Texas gives all employers the option of not purchasing insurance.

But keep in mind that just because the state doesn't require insurance, this doesn't mean that your business won't be liable for claims. You will indeed be held liable for workplace injuries or illness of your workers—and these liabilities can be substantial. So going bare always involves an element of risk, because you are creating significant potential liabilities for your company.

Another issue that often comes up for such small employers is when a client requires proof of workers' compensation insurance. I've often heard small employers question why their customer can require workers' compensation insurance from them when the state does not.

The answer is really pretty simple. Those customers understand that even though the state does not require a workers' compensation policy, the liabilities to injured workers still remain. And those customers understand that they could well be liable for workplace injuries of employees of companies they contract with for services. So even though a state may not require your small business to have workers' compensation insurance, your customers may well require it contractually before they will hire your company.

## PROFESSIONAL EMPLOYER ORGANIZATIONS

Another alternative to purchasing a workers' compensation policy is to utilize the services of a professional employer organization (PEO). This is also known as *employee leasing*. Under such arrangements, your employees technically become the employees of the PEO. If you enter into an agreement with a PEO, those people who may have been working directly for you for years will now receive their paychecks from the PEO, which will also provide such benefits as workers' compensation coverage.

Historically, lower workers' compensation cost has been one of the major selling points of PEOs. There is a certain logic to this, because a PEO should be able to achieve certain economies of scale and workers' compensation insurance can theoretically be purchased at a lower unit cost when the policy is larger. But there have also been some significant problems with PEOs and workers' comp insurance over the years.

The insurance industry has generally not welcomed the development of PEOs and has not been enthusiastic about underwriting such companies. Because a PEO can be a conglomeration of hundreds of different workplace exposures, it's difficult to effectively classify and underwrite a policy for a PEO.

There has been another major problem with workers' compensation insurance for PEOs—experience modification factors. Experience modification factors are designed to adjust the cost of current workers' compensation insurance based on recent past losses of a particular employer. But an employer that shifts to a PEO arrangement for its workers' compensation coverage can escape the effects of its own loss history.

Experience modification factors use the claims history of a company in calculating an adjustment factor for that company's workers' comp insurance premiums, but if an employer moves over to a PEO, that employer is now insured under a policy whose experience mod has been calculated from the loss history of that PEO and its members, not that particular employer.

For example, consider Wonder Widgets, a company that has a 1.25 experience modifier that will be effective on its workers' compensation policy effective July 1, 2005. That experience mod is based on the losses that Wonder Widget has had during its 2003-04 policy, its 2002-03 policy, and its 2001-02 policy. But if it goes with a PEO effective July 1, 2005, its insurance is now written through a policy purchased by the PEO, which has an experience mod of .98, based on the loss experience of its client companies for 2003-04, 2002-03, and 2001-02.

The concern of some insurance regulators and insurance companies is that this enables Wonder Widget to escape the financial consequences of its poor loss record. This can have the effect of reducing or eliminating the incentive to manage workplace safety.

So many states have enacted requirements that PEOs use the individual experience modifiers developed for their client companies, which has increased the complexity of workers' compensation insurance programs administered by PEOs.

The biggest risk involved with using PEOs is that, because they sometimes have difficulty finding and maintaining workers' compensation insurance (particularly in hard insurance markets), there can sometimes arise behind-the-scenes difficulties that you won't find out about until it's too late. If you're relying on a PEO for workers' comp coverage, but that PEO loses its insurance, you might end up lacking coverage you've paid for while the PEO scrambles to replace the insurance. Remember: if the PEO loses its coverage, then you're back to being responsible for your employees. If you maintain your own workers' comp policy to cover your non-leased workers (such as clerical), you might find that your audit ends up charging you for coverage you thought that the PEO was providing.

The bottom line to always remember when considering any lower-cost alternative to regular workers' compensation insurance is that there is a reason that workers' compensation insurance tends to be expensive—claims. Lower-cost alternatives may save some money in the short term, but sometimes they end up being much more expensive in the long run, when all claims costs are finally accounted for. Just ask all those Kentucky employers that are now receiving huge assessment bills for their group self-insurance program.

A guaranteed-cost assigned risk policy might seem expensive (and it often is), but in the long run it might turn out to be the most cost-effective approach. A proper workers' compensation insurance policy relieves you of all responsibility for whatever claims may arise from your workers' compensation liabilities. In spite of all the problems with this insurance product, it is a tested means of transferring these risks to a third party. Sometimes clever solutions to fundamental problems get a little too clever.

Larger employers may well have more complex alternative programs presented to them. These may well involve some form of "fronting," as discussed in Chapter 10, and may involve *captive insurance companies*, as explained in Chapter 10, or *rent-a-captive*, which is basically an arrangement to lease the services of a captive insurance company. These alternatives are probably less risky than some of the others already reviewed, but still rely on complex arrangements. When coupled with effective loss control, such programs may be able to offer some price stability over time, when compared with the fluctuations of the commercial insurance market. Typically, such programs cannot match the savings that may become available during soft market conditions, but can avoid the extreme price increases that come when the market moves to hard conditions. Additionally, these programs can provide viable coverage alternatives for employers that have difficulty finding traditional insurance at competitive rates.

## QUICK REVIEW

- An insurance policy isn't the only way most states allow an employer to meet workers' compensation obligations. Be aware of the alternatives such as self-insurance and group self-insurance.
- Beware "virtual" workers' compensation insurance programs, as only a few states recognize them as actually meeting an employer's workers' compensation obligations.
- Be aware of the potential problems of using employee leasing to solve workers' compensation obligations.
- Make sure you understand your state's requirements before going without workers' compensation coverage. Only a few states allow employers to "go bare" without insurance, although some states allow very small employers to go without insurance.
- Be aware that even if your state allows your company to operate without workers' compensation insurance, you run the risk of expensive claims from injured workers that your company would then be liable for. Being exempt from purchasing workers' compensation insurance does not shield an employer from responsibility for injured workers.

# CHAPTER 12

# Claims, Safety, and Resources

S O FAR WE HAVEN'T ADDRESSED CLAIMS costs too directly. We've reviewed how the costs of claims impact your experience modification factor and loss-sensitive plans, but we haven't really gotten into what an employer can do to control the costs of claims. But once you've mastered all the other techniques and recommendations in this book and reduced your workers' compensation costs by using them, there remains one last area where an employer can wring out unnecessary costs: claims.

Traditionally, the insurance industry tends to focus on claims first and foremost as the way to reduce workers' compensation costs. But I've held off discussing this area, because the traditional approach tends to focus almost exclusively on claims control and ignores all the important areas that we've been covering in the earlier sections of this book. Besides, I think the

insurance industry likes to focus on claims as the primary method of cost control because controlling the costs of claims also directly improves the bottom line for insurance companies.

I like to focus first on all the other ways that workers' compensation costs can be increased unnecessarily and leave claims control for the last. That way, all those other important areas aren't pushed out of the limelight. But the traditional approach has a point: the cost of claims is far and away the biggest driver of costs for workers' compensation insurance and there are things that can be done to address the issue.

If your company is one of those blessed and fortunate operations that incur few workers' compensation claims, God bless. Either you're extremely lucky or you're doing some things right. But even well-managed and safety-conscious companies can have problems with workers' compensation claims. But most companies can reduce the cost of their claims over time.

## FIRST, KNOW YOUR CLAIMS

The theme of this entire book has been "Trust, but verify." And it applies to your claims at least as much as it does to all the other areas we've been covering. Unless your company somehow has so few claims that you know each of them intimately, your first course of action is to have a full-blown review of your recent years' claims to make sure that all the claims the insurance company is saying belong to your company really do belong to your company. Occasionally, an employer will get tagged with a claim that belongs to someone else. So check into each and every claim (or at least those of any significant size) and make sure that those injured workers really belong to you. This suggestion may sound too simple to be of any use, but mistakes happen here just as they do anywhere else.

In addition, check to make sure that the insurance company shouldn't be exploring subrogation possibilities. Sometimes the circumstances of a claim are such that some third party actually is responsible, at least in part. For example, a salesman injured in an auto accident may be eligible for workers' compensation, but your workers' comp insurer may be able to subrogate that claim against the driver of the other vehicle, to recover some or all of the amount of the claim.

My company has often been involved in reviewing the claims files of insurance companies. It is not uncommon for us to find that an insurance company has not pursued obvious subrogation opportunities. You want to make sure you follow up with your insurance company so that it vigorously pursues potential subrogation for your claims.

If the insurance company succeeds in getting reimbursed by some third party, that's one of the few circumstances that enable you to get an old experience modification factor revised retroactively, to reflect that subrogation. Your insurance company typically won't file the necessary corrected unit statistical report in such cases, but if you become aware of a successful subrogation, make sure your insurer files that corrected unit stat report with the appropriate rating bureau.

Another important thing you can learn by going over your claims carefully is to identify patterns—to figure out what's causing your claims, so you can take some action to prevent such claims in the future.

Finally, examine closely all claims that have significant open reserves. Don't accept as gospel the insurance company's reserve determinations, as there is far more art than science in the way that insurers set reserves. Be as demanding and as skeptical as you can be in questioning why the insurance company sets reserve levels as high as they are. If necessary, bring in outside claims experts, either from your agent or broker or as independent consultants, to review those reserve levels.

Particularly when you are insured on a loss-sensitive plan such as a retrospective rating plan, you have a right to insist that the insurer has handled claims in a competent and professional manner. If disputes over loss-sensitive premiums end up in litigation, your insurer may have to be able to demonstrate that settlements were made in good faith and that calculations of reserves were reasonable and justifiable.

## SECOND, KNOW YOUR WORKERS

Another very effective technique to control claims costs is to utilize pre-employment physicals where possible. It's perfectly reasonable to make sure that the new employees you're hiring are physically able to perform the jobs you want to hire them to do. However, be careful to not run afoul of the Americans with Disabilities Act (ADA). The ADA impacts employers with 25 employees or more and requires that pre-employment physicals not be given to job applicants until after a conditional offer of employment has been extended. So only those potential hires who are otherwise qualified for employment may be subjected to a pre-employment physical exam.

To avoid problems, make the conditional offer of employment in writing. Set forth all conditions that a candidate will have to meet before you will actually offer employment, such as the pre-employment physical and pre-employment drug screening. Also make clear that the employment will be on an *at-will* basis.

*Return-to-work programs*, also known as *modified work* or *light duty* policies, can be an essential part of your company's claims control efforts. Some employers dislike these programs or feel that it's difficult to find appropriate light duty work for recovering employees. But these programs can reduce the cost of claims significantly. Consult with specialists at your insurer and/or your agent to implement effective return-to-work programs. And if you can't get appropriate help from these sources, consider shopping for other sources of insurance that do provide this kind of support service. If this is not practical because of the size of your company, you may well want to consider bringing in some outside assistance on your own. If your company is experiencing significant losses, you need to take action to get these under control.

## THIRD, PROMOTE SAFETY

Not only do you need to manage claims carefully to make sure the costs of those claims aren't excessively affecting your insurance cost, you also need to address the root causes of those claims. That's where loss control or safety engineering can play a vital role.

Again, there may be significant resources available from your insurance company and/or your insurance agent or broker. If not, you should seriously consider finding other sources for your insurance. This is one of those areas where the lowest-cost insurance can ultimately end up to be more expensive, if the insurer or the agency you use does not have adequate resources to help you address the safety issues that are driving your claims costs.

Here's a listing of some large and well-known independent safety consultants.

### Broadspire Services, Inc. / NATLSCO
4 Corporate Drive, Suite 100
Lake Zurich, IL 60047
847 719-5376
www.choosebroadspire.com

### Clayton Group Services
45525 Grand River Avenue, Suite 200
Novi, MI 48734
248 344-8577
www.claytongrp.com

### FARA (F.A. Richard & Associates, Inc.)
1625 W. Causeway Approach
Mandeville, LA 70471
800 259-8388
www.fara.com

**Gage-Babcock & Associates**

5175 Parkstone Drive, Suite 130

Chantilly, VA 20151-3816

703 263-7110

www.gagebabcock.com

**National Safety Council**

1121 Spring Lake Drive

Itasca, IL 60143-3201

630 285-1121

www.nsc.org

**North American Risk Management, Inc.**

100 First Avenue South, #266

St. Petersburg, FL 33701

727 287-1565

www.narm.biz

**Regional Reporting, Inc.**

40 Fulton Street, 20th Floor

New York, NY 10038

212 964-5973

www.regionalreporting.com

**Risk Consultants, Inc.**

P. O. Box 490850

Atlanta, GA 30349

770 964-1226

www.riskcon.com

**Safety Resources, LLC**

239 New Road, Building C

Parsippany, NJ 07054

973 575-0900

www.safetyresc.com

**Strategic Safety Associates, Inc.**

P.O. Box 80161

Portland, OR 97280-1161

503 977-2094

www.ssafety.net

## RESOURCES

Here's a list of internet resources that can provide valuable and useful information regarding your workers' compensation insurance and related subjects.

### www.cutcomp.com

The first one is the one closest to my heart—the web site for my own company. Here you will not only find the usual propaganda about how brilliant and wonderful my company is, but more to the point, you can find lots of useful information about workers' compensation insurance, including updated news and information about the latest developments that affect your workers' compensation insurance.

### www.ncci.com

This is the web site for the National Council on Compensation Insurance (NCCI). Although you have to pay money to get access to its online manuals (or to order hard copies), there is some useful information available from the web site at no charge.

### www.comp.state.nc.us/ncic/pages/all50.htm

Set up by the North Carolina Industrial Commission, this site has links to all the state agencies that administer workers' compensation claims matters.

### www.ultimateinsurancelinks.com

This site allows searches for listings and links to just about every insurance company, supplier, insurance organization, or industry publisher known.

### dmoz.org/Business/Human_Resources/

This is the Open Directory Project listing of Human Resources links. It offers lots of links to many sources of human resources information.

**www.hr-guide.com/**

HR-Guide.com is another large source of links to free human resources information.

**www.insurancejournal.com/**

This is the online edition of the *Insurance Journal*. The online edition is free, is updated daily, and contains valuable information on insurance-related subjects such as the current state of the insurance market, court rulings that affect insurance coverage, insurance company ratings, and more.

## TRUST, BUT VERIFY

We began this book by looking at the big picture. Then we filled in the details about how to control the cost of your company's workers' compensation insurance and how to make sure your coverage is right for your operations. Getting things right in your workers' compensation insurance can take a little effort on the part of a business owner or manager, but it definitely is worth the effort. No one else has as much incentive to make sure things are right, because ultimately it's your money. Trust, but verify.

## QUICK REVIEW

- Know thy claims—don't leave it all to your insurance company.
- If claims costs are increasing your workers' comp costs, take action. Figure out the patterns that can be observed and work to address workplace safety issues aggressively. Don't rely exclusively on your insurance company to solve this problem for you.
- Utilize return-to-work programs whenever possible for workers who can return to light duty.
- Make sure your insurer pursues subrogation possibilities for those claims that may be eligible.

# Workers' Compensation Insurance for Construction Risks

ALTHOUGH EVERYTHING THROUGH-OUT THE chapters of this *Ultimate Guide to Workers' Compensation Insurance* applies to employers in construction-related fields, there are a number of unique aspects to workers' compensation insurance for such employers. For employers in construction-related work, workers' compensation is typically even a higher priority than for other employers. Rates tend to be high and the number of insurance companies interested in writing workers' comp for these employers tends to be lower. Additionally, many customers use experience modification factors as a rough benchmark of workplace safety. Finally, there are some kinds of workers' compensation insurance policies that typically are an issue only for construction-related risks.

For instance, contractors may encounter projects where workers' compensation cov-erage is handled by separate policies that cover all the workers on that particular project. Such programs are known as *consolidated insurance programs* (CIPs) or *wrap-up insurance programs* (wrap-ups). Such insurance programs cover the project owner and all contractors and subcontractors working on the project, rather than having each party provide coverage through separate policies.

These programs have been created to resolve some of the difficulties involved with all of these parties having their own policies. Making sure that all the contractors and subcontractors have met the contractual requirements for insurance can be a major undertaking. Consolidated insurance programs eliminate this chore, as coverage for all workers on a project is provided by a single policy.

Such programs are also often known as *owner-controlled insurance programs* (OCIPs).

In theory, CIPs offer some real advantages for large projects. A CIP coordinates not only coverage, but also safety and loss control functions. In reality, though, these programs can have limitations. For instance, a contractor with effective safety and loss control programs may find that those used by the CIP are less effective.

Another issue that can arise is that, while ideally an OCIP should cover everyone involved with the project, in the real world, it usually does not. An OCIP will typically exclude suppliers, vendors of materials, hauling firms, and blasting and demolition contractors. It can be important for construction companies participating in an OCIP to have a clear listing of who is covered under the plan and who is not.

Most importantly, from a cost control standpoint, contractors participating in an OCIP need to make sure their regular workers' compensation coverage coordinates properly so that they aren't charged twice for the same payroll.

When dealing with subcontractors, an OCIP can also cause some complications. A contractor will normally have certain procedures in place for handling and verifying certificates of insurance from subcontractors. But in an OCIP, the subcontractors may be required to file certificates with the OCIP broker or administrator. To avoid problems, a contractor should arrange that copies of all certificates are forwarded to the contractor as well.

Construction-related firms also need to make sure that data from OCIPs is filed with appropriate rating bureaus so that it is included in calculating the experience modification factors for those firms. Sometimes there can be delays in getting data reported from OCIP work, which can distort your experience modi-fication factor. Remember: your company's data from OCIP work should be reported to rating bureaus for inclusion in your experience modification factor. This is different from a joint venture, which forms a business entity for which an experience modification factor will be calculated that will remain separate from your company's mod.

If you are the project owner utilizing an OCIP, you need to take steps to realize the cost-saving potential of the OCIP. For one, understand that because you as project owner are paying for the workers' compensation insurance, you have a greater need to make sure accurate payroll information is received from contractors and subcontractors. In an OCIP, the contractors and subcontractors may have less incentive to make sure records provided are accurate. So the project owner needs to pay attention to details such as the following questions:

- Has overtime pay been adjusted down to remove the premium portion?
- Have contractors and subcontractors kept adequate records so that payroll can be divided among appropriate classifications?
- Have payrolls been submitted for those exposures and operations that are excluded from the OCIP?

Project owners also need to check that proper rates have been applied in computing the premium. When the inception date of the OCIP is different from the inception date of the contractor's own workers' comp policy, you should add an *anniversary rating date* (ARD) *endorsement* to the OCIP. This endorsement splits classifications, payrolls, experience mods, and other elements of the premium into pre-ARD and post-ARD, so that proper rates are applied to each. This makes sure that increased rates that may have applied after the contractor's ARD are used only for the post-ARD component and not also to the pre-ARD component.

Whether your workers' compensation is through an OCIP or through your own policy, it is important to remember for construction-related risks that, unlike other kinds of employers, the payroll for individual employees is commonly divided among classifications—*where the payroll records allow.*

So it is vital to make sure that payroll records keep track of the exact time each employee spends at various job functions that may eligible for lower rates. If you do not keep track of the exact time spent in each job function, all of the payroll for that employee will be assigned to the classification that has the highest rate.

Another vital area of concern for construction-related risks is to make sure you receive all *contractors' premium adjustment credits* you may be eligible for. Many states have separate programs that can produce additional premium credits for construction-related companies that pay relatively high hourly wages. But the *employer* needs to apply for these credits by submitting information about average hourly wages paid. This is different from experience modification factor calculations, which are done automatically by the insurance system. Contractors' premium adjustment credits will not be computed for you if you do not submit the proper form to the rating bureau. It is not uncommon for contractors to miss out on these credits because their agent or insurer has not properly explained the process to them.

# Workers' Compensation Insurance Glossary

**Advisory organization** The new designation, recently coined by the National Association of Insurance Commissioners, for an entity formerly known as a *rating bureau* (such as the National Council on Compensation Insurance). This new term is meant to reflect more accurately the role of NCCI and other such organizations (like Insurance Services Office) that compile rating data and file policy forms for use by member insurance companies.

**Agent, insurance** An insurance producer who represents the insurer, as either an employee or an independent contractor, in negotiating, servicing, or effecting insurance policies.

**Agent of record letter** A document by which a company authorizes a designated agent to handle specified insurance business on behalf of that company.

**ALE** See *allocated loss expenses*.

**Allocated loss adjustment expenses** Loss adjustment and handling costs that can be allocated to a specific claim.

**Allocated loss expenses (ALE)** Insurance company costs for adjusting and settling claims that can be identified with a specific claim. The ALE are often then included in the claims costs used to adjust premium in some loss-sensitive premium adjustment types of workers' compensation policies, such as *sliding-scale dividend plans* or some *retrospective rating plans* or *retention plans*.

**Alternative employer** A company that provides workers for a third party and maintains an employer relationship with them, such as a temporary employment agency, a professional employer organization (PEO), or an employee-leasing company.

**Alternative employer endorsement** A written amendment to an insurance policy that extends coverage for people who work for a company while employed by another, such as workers from a temporary agency or an employee-leasing company.

**Anniversary rating date (ARD)** The month and day when manual rules and rates and the experience rating modification factor apply to a workers' compensation policy. This is usually the date on which the policy becomes effective and each anniversary of that date.

**Anniversary rating date endorsement** A written amendment to an insurance policy that advises the insured company that the premium, rates, and experience rating modification factor may change on the *anniversary rating date.*

**ARAP** In all states but Massachusetts, *assigned risk adjustment program*—an additional debit charge placed on assigned risk policies (in *National Council on Compensation Insurance* jurisdictions) with experience modification factors higher than 1.00. In Massachusetts, *all risk adjustment program*, a surcharge to adjust for reported losses greater than expected under the experience rating plan, in addition to the *experience modification factor*, a surcharge for which every employer, whether in the *assigned risk pool* or the *voluntary market*, is eligible.

**Assigned risk adjustment program (ARAP)** An additional debit charge placed on assigned risk policies (in *National Council on Compensation Insurance* jurisdictions) with experience modification factors higher than 1.00.

**Assigned risk plan** A mechanism established by individual states to make sure that employers can obtain workers' compensation insurance even if insurance companies are not willing to write such insurance on a voluntary basis.

Assigned risk plans in many states carry higher rates than the *voluntary market*. Also known as an *assigned risk pool*, the *involuntary market*, or the *residual market*.

**At-will employment** Employment that is presumed to be voluntary and indefinite for both the employee and the employer: the employee may quit the job at any time, for any or no reason, and the employer may discharge the employee at any time, for any or no reasons, even unfair reasons, with certain exceptions.

**Audit** A review of the financial records of an insured company conducted by the insurer, for the purpose of adjusting the premium paid. An audit is usually performed annually, after the policy period ends and when the items to be audited are assumed to be final. If it is determined that the premium was too low, the insurer will assess an additional premium. If it is determined that the premium was too high, the insurer will issue a return on the premium.

**Audited premium** The final premium for the policy term, produced by auditing actual payroll exposures.

**Audit work papers** Worksheet prepared by the premium auditor, can be either hand-written or computerized, showing how the auditor arrived at the payroll numbers that are used to determine the audited premium.

**Basic charge** A factor used in calculating the premium for a *retrospective rating plan*, a percentage of the standard premium.

**Basic Manual** *The Scopes® of Basic Manual Classifications,* produced by the *National Council on Compensation Insurance*, a guide that details which kinds of workplace exposures belong in particular workers' compensation classification codes. Also known as the Scopes® Manual.

**Broker, insurance** An insurance producer who works solely as the representative of the policyholder, to seek out insurance coverage, and is not contracted as an agent of any insurance company.

**Broker of record letter** A document by which a company authorizes a designated broker to handle specified insurance business on behalf of that company.

**Captive** See *captive insurer.*

**Captive agent** An insurance producer who represents only one insurance company and cannot by agreement submit any business to any other company unless the company that he or she represents has rejected it. A captive agent is not employed by the company, but usually receives financial assistance for office expenses and some employee benefits.

**Captive insurer** An insurance company organized and owned by a business entity for the purpose of providing the entity with insurance at lower rates. It is usually not authorized by the state's insurance department to do business in that state, but it has the right to reinsure with an insurer that is so authorized, under special circumstances.

**Certificate of insurance** Written evidence of an insurance policy, indicating both the types of coverage and the amounts. It provides legal assurance that a company is providing workers' compensation insurance for certain workers. If a company uses contract or leased workers and it does not have a copy of a certificate of insurance, it may be charged for covering those workers if audited.

**Certified Insurance Counselor (CIC)** Designation granted by the National Alliance for Insurance Education and Research. To attain this designation, a person must take five CIC courses and pass the examinations.

**Chartered Property Casualty Underwriter (CPCU)** Designation granted by the Insurance Institute of America. To attain this designation, a person must pass a series of ten examinations administered nationally, meet certain minimum requirements for experience in the insurance industry, and adhere to a code of ethics.

**CIC** See *Certified Insurance Counselor.*

**Classification code** An identification of activities that is used to place an insured organization into underwriting and rating groups as a basis for computing premiums. Also known as *class code.*

**Classification, governing** See *governing classification.*

**Consolidated insurance program (CIP)** Insurance for a large construction project that the owner or general contractor arranges to combine the interests of the owner, the general contractor, subcontractors, architects, engineers, surveyors, and any others involved in the project and cover them under one policy with a single insurer. A CIP always includes workers' compensation and usually also general liability, umbrella liability, and builders' risk insurance. Also known as *owner-controlled insurance program* (OCIP) and *wrap-up insurance program* (wrap-up).

**Contingent commission** An incentive paid by an insurance company, in addition to the regular or ordinary commissions received for selling policies. Contingent commissions may be based on a certain volume of business, an increase in business, the profitability of the policies, or any combination.

**Contractors' premium adjustment credits** Credits available for a qualifying workers' compensation insurance policy that contains one or more contracting classifications and has a specified minimum of its exposure or premium in the contracting classifications.

**Converted losses** A loss factor used in retrospective rating plans calculated by multiplying incurred losses by a *loss conversion factor*.

**CPCU** See *Chartered Property Casualty Underwriter*.

**Credit modifier** An *experience modification factor* adjusted *downward* to reflect a history of reported past losses lower than average.

**D-ratio** See *discount ratio*.

**Debit modifier** An *experience modification factor* adjusted *upward* to reflect a history of reported past losses higher than average.

**Deductible plans** A form of loss-sensitive workers' compensation insurance. The employer accepts responsibility for reimbursing the insurer for claims that fall within a specified deductible amount and, in return, gets a discount on the premiums. Deductible plans come in two basic types: *small-deductible* plans, where the amount per claim is relatively low, such as $1,000, and *large-deductible* plans, where the amount per claim is typically $25,000 or more.

**Direct writer** An insurance company that does not work through independent insurance agents. Agents for direct writers are employees of the insurance company. The largest direct writer of workers' compensation insurance is Liberty Mutual.

**Discount ratio** In the experience modification rating formula, a factor that is applied to expected losses to determine what percentage of those expected losses should be considered primary *losses* and what should be considered *excess losses*.

**Dividend** A return of premium, calculated after policy expiration, based on the overall performance of the insurance company or of a group of insureds. Dividends cannot be guaranteed in advance, although they may be shown on proposals for insurance estimates.

**Dividend plans** Insurance policies that return some portion of a guaranteed-cost premium to the employer based on loss experience. Dividend plans used to be much more common, but have been largely supplanted by other types of loss-sensitive plans, such as *sliding-scale dividend plans*.

**Employee leasing** An arrangement by which a *professional employer organization* provides employees to client companies for a fee. Some leasing companies hire the employees of their client companies and then lease them back to those companies. The leasing companies handle payroll and tax reports and provide workers' compensation and employee benefit coverages for the employees.

**Employers' liability** Insurance that covers an employer's liability for bodily injury to employees occurring within the scope of their employment when that liability is not covered by the statutory workers' compensation provisions of the state, in Part Two of the standard workers' compensation insurance policy, with a dollar limit for the coverage.

**Employers' liability coverage endorsement (stopgap)** A written amendment to an insurance policy that provides employers' liability coverage for employees in a monopoly state. Monopoly state funds do not provide the employers' liability coverage provided by Part Two of the standard workers' compensation policy, so this endorsement extends Part Two coverage to employees covered under such monopoly fund programs.

**EMR** Experience modification rating. See *experience modification factor*.

**Endorsement** A written amendment to an insurance policy. Although the standard workers' compensation policy tends to provide very broad coverage, some endorsements are commonly used to extend or restrict coverage in certain situations: *alternative employer endorsement; employers' liability coverage endorsement (stopgap); foreign voluntary compensation endorsement; joint venture as insured endorsement; medical benefits exclusion endorsement; partners, officers, and others exclusion endorsement; sole proprietors, partners, officers, and others coverage endorsement; voluntary compensation and employers' liability coverage endorsement; and waiver of our right to recover from others endorsement.*

**Exception, standard** See *standard exception*.

**Excess liability coverage** Insurance that provides coverage beyond the limits of primary insurance, providing catastrophe coverage.

**Excess loss** In the *experience modification factor*, the amount of any single claim that exceeds $5,000 (under the *National Council on Compensation Insurance* rating formula).

**Expected loss ratio (ELR)** A number calculated by averaging the losses of all businesses in a specific classification in a state per hundred dollars of payroll.

**Expected losses** Projections of expenses from losses and based on actuarial probability calculations.

**Experience modification factor** An adjustment to *manual premium*, calculated by an *advisory organization* (also known as a *rating bureau*) such as the *National Council on Compensation Insurance*, based on historic loss and payroll data of a particular insured. Also known as a *modifier (mod)*, this is a multiplier that is based on a company's reported workers' compensation losses. If the losses are lower than average, it might earn a *credit modifier*. If the past losses are higher than average, it will probably get a *debit modifier*.

**Experience modification rating (EMR)** See *experience modification factor*.

**Experience modifier** See *experience modification factor*.

**Experience period** The window of time from which loss and payroll data is used to calculate an experience modification factor for an employer. Normally this window is a three-year period, starting four years prior to the effective date of the experience modifier. However, rating bureaus do not wait until three full years of data are in the experience period before producing an experience rating for an employer. If an employer reaches a certain, relatively low threshold of workers' compensation insurance premiums in any one of the three years in the experience period window, this will make that employer eligible for experience rating.

**Experience rating** The most widely applied

adjustment for the *manual premium,* using the *experience modification factor.*

**Foreign voluntary compensation endorsement** A written amendment to an insurance policy that extends coverage to employees who are working outside the country for an extended period. Importantly, this also can include repatriation expense, which can be a significant expense for injured workers who are out of the country.

**Fronting** An arrangement between two insurance companies to produce an insurance policy (usually workers' compensation) for a third party wherein one insurance company produces the official policy (for a fee) but cedes all losses from that policy to the other insurer. This kind of arrangement is used in situations where the insurer writing the risk is not an admitted company in a state in which the coverage must be written by an admitted carrier. In order to meet the statutory requirements, the first insurer pays a second (admitted) insurer to "front" the policy, even though the first insurer remains responsible for paying all losses arising under the policy. This kind of arrangement is often used by *captive insurers* when they are not admitted carriers in a particular state.

**Governing classification** The classification code on an employer's workers' compensation insurance policy that generates the most payroll, the primary classification, aside from standard exception classifications such as clerical or outside sales (unless there is no other workplace classification applicable other than a standard exception).

**Guaranteed-cost plan** A workers' compensation insurance policy that is not subject to adjustment due to losses that occur during the policy term. In a guaranteed-cost policy, the only variable affecting the premium that should change between policy inception and audit is payroll: the premium is adjusted based only on payroll fluctuations, not on the cost of claims incurred or paid out under the policy. This is in contrast to the various kinds of *loss-sensitive plans,* such as *retrospective rating plans, retention plans,* or *sliding-scale dividend plans,* where the premium is adjusted based on losses incurred during the policy term.

**Guaranty association** An organization in a state that is composed of all the insurance companies providing a specific type of policies within that state, whose purpose is to protect the policy owners of any of its member companies against any losses suffered if their companies become insolvent.

**Incidental exposure** Liability incurred away from the work site or outside the state of coverage when employees are not engaged in their usual work activities, but are traveling or performing work-related activities.

**Inclusion, standard** See *standard inclusion.*

**Incurred losses** *Paid losses* plus loss reserves for estimated future claims costs. Many loss-sensitive insurance policies adjust premiums based on incurred losses rather than just on paid losses.

**Independent agent** An insurance agent who has contracts with multiple insurance companies and can choose which of those insurers to use for a particular client.

**Insurance producer** See *producer, insurance.*

**Interstate rating** An experience modification factor that applies across more than one state.

Interstate ratings are calculated by the *National Council on Compensation Insurance* for employers whose past workers compensation insurance policies show payroll in more than one state. Most, but not all states, participate in the interstate rating system. A few states, such as Michigan, Pennsylvania, and Delaware, do not participate in interstate rating, but instead continue to calculate separate experience ratings for employers who operate in their jurisdictions, even if those employers also qualify for interstate rating. Those employers thus have one experience modifier applying to their operations in most states but a separate modifier calculated by the stand-alone state rating bureau. The separate stand-alone modifier would apply only to workers compensation insurance premiums developed for the employer's operations in that stand-alone state.

**Involuntary market** See *residual market.*

**Joint underwriting association** An organization of insurance companies that is formed with statutory approval to provide a specific type of insurance, usually because the *voluntary market* is not meeting a need. Regulators generally permit joint underwriting associations to develop their own policy forms and set their own rates.

**Joint venture as insured endorsement** A written amendment to an insurance policy that is used when the named insured on the policy is a joint venture. It clarifies that coverage extends to the members of the joint venture, but only regarding their capacity as members of the joint venture. If you also have other business enterprises separate from the joint venture, you will need separate workers' compensation coverage.

**Large-risk alternative rating option (LRARO)** A provision of retrospective rating plans developed by the *National Council on Compensation Insurance* and approved by most states that allows companies with an annual estimated workers' compensation standard premium above a certain amount to negotiate the factors of their retro plans with the insurance company.

**LCF** See *loss conversion factor.*

**Letter of credit** A financial instrument issued by a bank for a customer that backs payment up to a specified amount, as a guarantee to a creditor, such as an insurance company.

**Loss conversion factor (LCF)** A number that is multiplied by *incurred losses* to calculate *converted losses,* often used in calculating *retrospective rating plans,* to cover the expenses of claim adjustments and claim service.

**Loss limitation** An option in retrospective rating plans that allows the insured—for an additional charge—to place a cap on the amount of any single claim that gets counted in the retro calculation, so that a single very expensive claim doesn't do too much to raise the retro premium.

**Loss-sensitive plan** Any of various workers' compensation policies that adjust the premium based on losses incurred or paid out under the policy. Loss-sensitive plans use the rate times hundred dollars of payroll to calculate premiums, but then make further adjustments based on the losses under the policy. These adjustments may lower premiums if losses are low or may raise premiums even higher than the *guaranteed-cost* premium would have been if losses are high. The common types of loss-sensitive plans are the *retrospective rating plan*, the *retention plan*, the *sliding-scale dividend plan,* and *deductible plans.*

**LRARO** See *large-risk alternative rating option.*

**Manual premium** A workers' compensation premium calculated by multiplying payrolls by appropriate *manual rates*, before applying an *experience modifier*, a *schedule credit*, or a *premium discount.*

**Manual rate** An insurance rate contained in a manual published by an insurance company or a rating bureau for a unit of insurance. The manual rate for a workers' compensation plan is the rate that the insurance company applies to all insureds in a state for a particular classification. The manual rate is a starting point for calculating premiums, before any adjustments.

**Maximum premium factor** A ceiling set on the premium for *retrospective rating plans,* usually as a percentage of the standard premium, to limit exposure no matter how high the claims cost ultimately go.

**Medical benefits exclusion endorsement** A written amendment to an insurance policy that is used in states that allow employers to pay medical benefits directly, instead of through a workers' compensation policy. This endorsement excludes medical benefits for specified states and makes the employer responsible for payment of these benefits.

**Medical-only claims** Claims for which the only cost is medical care, without any lost-time benefits being paid.

**Merit rating** A premium adjustment used in some *National Council on Compensation Insurance* states for employers too small to qualify for an *experience modification factor.* Based on prior claims (or lack of claims), it provides either a *credit* to adjust the premium downward or a *debit* to adjust the premium upward.

**Minimum premium factor** A floor set on the premium for *retrospective rating plans,* usually as a percentage of the standard premium, no matter how low the claims cost may be.

**Modified premium** Workers' compensation premium calculated after the application of an *experience modification factor.* It is similar to *standard premium,* but it does not reflect any *schedule credits or debits.*

**Modifier (mod)** See *experience modification factor.*

**Monopoly/monopolistic state** A state that requires all workers' compensation insurance to be placed with its state fund and does not allow any private insurer to write workers' compensation coverage. Monopoly state funds do not provide the employers' liability coverage provided by Part Two of the standard workers' compensation policy, so an employers' liability coverage endorsement (stopgap) extends Part Two coverage to employees covered under such monopoly fund programs.

**Named insured** An individual or entity that is specified by name in the declarations of a policy as insured by that policy. The named insured is responsible for paying the premium.

**National Council on Compensation Insurance (NCCI)** The organization responsible in many states for determining proper workers' compensation classifications, calculating *experience modification factors,* and collecting data used for ratemaking. NCCI also writes the manuals used in many states to calculate workers' compensation premiums, and also administers the *assigned risk plan* in many jurisdictions. NCCI is a private organization, not connected with government, although it is often mistakenly thought to be a governmental agency.

**NCCI** See *National Council on Compensation Insurance.*

**NOC** Not otherwise classified, a term used in the classifications section of workers' compensation rating manuals, to indicate a classification to be used if a company cannot be classified more specifically.

**OCIP** See *owner-controlled insurance program.*

**Other states insurance** Coverage of the insured company if it expands its operations into states not declared when the policy was issued or renewed. If the company elects this coverage and then begins operating in a state listed under "other states," the insurer provides the same coverage as if the state had been declared in the policy when it was issued.

**Owner-controlled insurance program (OCIP)** See *consolidated insurance program.*

**Paid-loss retrospective plan** A retrospective rating plan for which the premium is calculated based on *paid losses* (the losses ultimately paid under that policy), not *incurred losses* (paid losses plus loss reserves for estimated future claims costs).

**Paid losses** Losses ultimately paid under a policy, in contrast with *incurred losses,* which also include loss reserves for estimated future claims costs.

**Partners, officers, and others exclusion endorsement** A written amendment to a insurance policy that is used when partners and executive officers wish to exclude themselves from coverage and thus exclude their remuneration from premium computation.

**PEO** See *professional employer organization.*

**Pool** See *assigned risk plan.*

**Premium auditor** Someone who is responsible for determining actual exposure (remuneration) for a policy period, in order to determine the final audited premium. The auditor typically works either directly for the insurance company or for a third-party company retained by the insurance company.

**Premium discount** A premium credit, based on size of the premium paid. It is normally given automatically on voluntary market policies, although *retrospective rating plans* and *sliding-scale dividend plans* usually do not have a premium discount. Also known as *sliding-scale discount.*

**Primary loss** In the experience modification factor, the first $5,000 of any single loss (under the *National Council on Compensation Insurance* rating formula).

**Producer, insurance** An *agent,* a *broker,* or any other person who is directly involved in the sale of insurance.

**Professional employer organization** A company that contractually assumes many of the rights, responsibilities, and risks of an employer—payroll management, benefits, unemployment insurance, and workers' compensation administration.

**Rate** The cost per unit of coverage that is applied to the rating basis (e.g., payroll) to determine the premium for the policy period.

**Rating bureau** An organization formed to collect actuarial data, survey risks, and develop rates. See *National Council on Compensation Insurance*. Some states maintain their own separate rating bureaus, although these often follow NCCI rules and use NCCI manuals. Currently, California, Delaware, Indiana, Massachusetts, Michigan, Minnesota, New Jersey, New York, North Carolina, and Pennsylvania operate their own non-NCCI rating bureaus. Many of these largely follow NCCI rules for computing premiums and classifications, but California, Delaware, Texas, and Pennsylvania are notably different from NCCI in some aspects of classification and premium computation. See *advisory organization*.

**Remuneration** The basis for calculating a workers' compensation premium. Remuneration is primarily payroll, but may also include other forms of employee compensation. Workers' compensation premiums are computed by applying varying rates (for different classifications) per hundred dollars of remuneration.

**Rent-a-captive** An arrangement by which an organization obtains the benefits of a captive insurance company, without the upfront costs and capital investment required to form its own captive, by leasing the capital base of a captive insurer. Also known as *non-owned captive*.

**Reserves** Funds that an insurance company sets aside to ensure that it can cover its estimate of the ultimate cost of claims.

**Residual market** Any insurance mechanism designed to assume risks that are considered generally unacceptable in the normal insurance market, such as *assigned risk plans* and government insurance programs.

**Residual market system** The particular mechanism that a state uses to make sure that all employers can get workers' compensation coverage, usually an *assigned risk plan*.

**Retention plan** Similar to a *retrospective rating plan*, a workers' compensation policy format that adjusts the premium up or down, based on losses (and associated costs) that occur during the policy period.

**Retrospective rating plan** A workers' compensation insurance policy that makes a subsequent adjustment to premium, after policy expiration, based on losses generated during the policy period. The adjustment can go up or down, within set parameters, based on those losses.

**Return-to-work program** A system of getting an injured worker back in action as soon as possible, either to his or her original job, with some restrictions according to the injury, or to a temporary alternate job that accommodates the injury. Also known as *modified work* or *light duty* policies.

**Schedule credit or debit** A discretionary premium adjustment (credit, downward; debit, upward) based on underwriters' evaluation of special characteristics of a risk not reflected in the *experience modifier*.

**Scopes® Manual** *The Scopes® of Basic Manual Classifications*, produced by the *National Council on Compensation Insurance*, a guide that details which kinds of workplace exposures belong in particular workers' compensation classification codes. Also known as the *Basic Manual*.

**Short rate penalty** A penalty applied by insurers when a workers' compensation insurance policy is cancelled by the insured before the expiration date of the policy. This penalty is steep in the early days of the policy and gradually tapers off the closer the policy gets to the expiration date.

**Single enterprise rule** A principle of classifying employers that states that it is the overall business of the employer that is classified, not necessarily each and every job function done there.

**Sliding-scale discount** See *premium discount.*

**Sliding-scale dividend plan** A workers' compensation plan that provides a return of premium, after policy expiration, based on the actual loss experience of the insured business. The size of the dividend, generally expressed as a percentage of the premium, varies with the actual loss ratio of the insured business.

**Sole proprietors, partners, officers, and others coverage endorsement** A written amendment to an insurance policy that extends coverage to sole proprietors, partners, and officers who are not required to be covered but who choose to extend coverage on themselves.

**Standard exception** A classification of employees that is normally not included in the governing classification. Standard exceptions include clerical, outside sales, and often (but not always) drivers.

**Standard inclusion** A type of activity work that is not broken out into a separate classification, under *National Council on Compensation Insurance* rules. For example, maintenance people in a manufacturing plant would not be broken out into a separate classification but would be included in the manufacturing classification that applies.

**Standard premium** The premium after application of the *experience modifier* and any *schedule credit or debit*, but before the *premium discount.*

**Subrogation** The action of an insurance company, after paying a claim for an insured company, to recoup all or some of the amount paid by making its own claim against one or more third parties that may have caused the loss or contributed to it.

**Surety bond** A guarantee by a corporate insurer to pay if the company that purchases the bond defaults on its obligation to cover claims.

**Tax factor** A factor applied in retrospective rating plans to cover the insurer's costs for licenses, fees, assessments, and taxes that it must pay on the premiums that it collects. The factor varies by state and is sometimes a composite of two or more state factors. States also charge taxes on premiums for guaranteed-cost policies, but insurers build these taxes into their rates for guaranteed-cost policies, rather than calculating them separately as for retro policies. Also known as a *tax multiplier.*

**Third-party administrator** A claims administrator or insurance company that processes workers' compensation claims on behalf of a self-insured organization.

**Umbrella liability coverage** An insurance policy that supplements a primary or underlying liability policy by providing high excess coverage over the primary or underlying policy, broader coverages than the primary policy, and automatic replacement of coverage provided by underlying policies in case their coverage is reduced or depleted by losses.

**Unallocated loss adjustment expenses** Charges for costs that are not associated with specific claims.

**Unit statistical report (unit stat report)** A printed form or electronic file for each employer by the

*National Council on Compensation Insurance* or a state workers' compensation rating bureau that contains all the information (payroll and claims) necessary for calculating a workers' compensation experience modification factor for that employer. Also known as a *unit statistical filing.*

**Voluntary compensation and employers' liability coverage endorsement** A written amendment to an insurance policy that extends coverage to certain employees who are not required to be covered for workers' compensation benefits in a state, such as domestic or farm workers and commission-only salespeople. This endorsement obligates the insurance company to pay, on behalf of the insured, compensation benefits equal to those to which those employees would be entitled if they were covered by the workers' compensation law of that state.

**Voluntary market** The world of insurance in which companies are free to select insurance providers and negotiate plans and in which insurance providers are free to deny coverage, in contrast with an *assigned risk plan,* in which a state ensures coverage of companies unable to secure coverage in the voluntary market.

**Waiver of our right to recover from others endorsement** A written amendment to an insurance policy that stipulates that the insurance company waives its right of subrogation against third parties who may be responsible for some losses under the policy. This endorsement should name the particular parties who are covered by this waiver.

**Workers' compensation insurance** Insurance that covers an employer's responsibility to compensate employees for injuries, illnesses, disabilities, or death, as prescribed by the workers' compensation laws of the specific state.

# State-by-State Residual Market Systems

A RESIDUAL MARKET SYSTEM IS THE PARTICular mechanism that a state uses to make sure that all employers can get workers' compensation coverage. Most states use an assigned risk pool mechanism, but some states use their state fund as the insurer of last resort for workers' compensation. Here's a state-by-state rundown.

The following states use an *assigned risk pooling system*:

Alabama
Alaska
Arizona
Arkansas
Connecticut
Delaware
District of Columbia
Georgia
Hawaii
Idaho
Illinois
Indiana
Iowa
Kansas
Massachusetts
Michigan
Minnesota
Mississippi
Missouri
Nebraska
Nevada
New Hampshire
New Jersey
New Mexico
North Carolina
Oregon
South Carolina
South Dakota
Tennessee
Vermont
Virginia
Wisconsin

The following states use a state fund as the workers' comp insurer of last resort:

California

Colorado
Kentucky
Louisiana
Maine
Maryland
Montana
New York
North Dakota
Ohio
Oklahoma

Pennsylvania
Rhode Island
Texas
Utah
Washington
West Virginia
Wyoming

Finally, Florida uses a *joint underwriting association.*

# State-by-State Information:
## Requirements for Workers' Compensation Insurance

| State | Workers' Compensation Required for |
|---|---|
| Alabama | all employers with 5 or more employees |
| Alaska | all employers with 1 or more employees |
| Arizona | all employers, including sole proprietors |
| Arkansas | all employers with 3 or more employees |
| California | all employers and all employees |
| Colorado | all employers with 1 or more employees |
| Connecticut | all employers and all employees |
| Delaware | all employers and all employees |
| District of Columbia | all employers and all employees |
| Florida | all employers with 4 or more employees (1 or more employees for construction companies) |
| Georgia | all employers with 3 or more employees |
| Hawaii | all employers with 1 or more employees |
| Idaho | all employers and all employees |
| Illinois | all employers and all employees (except commission-only sales-people) |
| Indiana | all employers and all employees |
| Iowa | all employers |
| Kansas | all employers (except employers with less than $20,000 payroll) |

| Kentucky | all employers with 1 or more employees |
| Louisiana | all employers with 1 or more employees |
| Maine | all employers and all employees |
| Maryland | all employers with 1 or more employees |
| Massachusetts | all employers with 1 or more employees |

| **State** | **Workers' Compensation Required for** |
| --- | --- |
| Michigan | all employers with 3 or more employees (or fewer if third employee works 33 hours per week for 13 weeks for same employer) |
| Minnesota | all employers and all employees |
| Mississippi | all employers with 5 or more employees |
| Missouri | all employers with 5 or more employees (construction companies with 1 or more employees) |
| Montana | all employers and all employees |
| Nebraska | all employers with 1 or more employees |
| Nevada | all employers and all employees |
| New Hampshire | all employers with 1 or more employees |
| New Jersey | all employers (sole proprietors, partners, and LLCs are exempt if no employees) |
| New Mexico | all employers with 3 or more employees (1or more employees for construction companies) |
| New York | all employers with 1 or more employees |
| North Carolina | all employers with 3 or more employees (but all that expose workers to radiation) |
| North Dakota | all employers and all employees |
| Ohio | all employers with 1 or more employees |
| Oklahoma | all employers and all employees |
| Oregon | all employers with 1 or more employees (sole proprietors and partners exempt unless in construction) |
| Pennsylvania | all employers and all employees |
| Rhode Island | all employers with 1 or more employees |
| South Carolina | all employers with 4 or more employees |
| South Dakota | all employers and all employees |
| Tennessee | all employers with 5 or more employees (1 or more employees if in coal production) |
| Texas | not required—employers can choose to go without WC insurance |
| Utah | all employers with 1 or more employees |

| | |
|---|---|
| Vermont | all employers and all employees |
| Virginia | all employers with 3 or more employees |
| Washington | all employers and all employees |
| West Virginia | all employers with 1 or more employees |
| Wisconsin | all employers that pay wages of $500 or more in a quarter |
| Wyoming | all employers defined as "extra-hazardous," which means most employers in the state |

# Dealing with Insurance Companies

IF AND WHEN YOU DO IDENTIFY SOME ERROR IN computing your company's workers' compensation insurance charges, you'll need to work with your insurance company to get it corrected. This can be a process somewhat analogous to Alexander the Great and the Gordian Knot. You may be tempted to consider Alexander's solution to the problem, which was just to slash the knot with his sword, but you will probably find that insurance disputes can often be resolved without resort to cutlery. Here are some tactical suggestions, gleaned from years of experience in dealing with insurance companies on behalf of clients.

## DOCUMENT EVERYTHING

Put as much of your communication with the insurer in writing as is possible. Keep everything in one single file where you can keep it all together, separate from other insurance documents. If you communicate by e-mail, print out all such electronic communications and any responses and keep these hard copies in the file. If you have phone conversations with insurance personnel, document these in detail by writing down who you spoke with, when it took place, and what was said. Make sure you get the names of everyone you speak with and put it in the file.

## PAY THE UNDISPUTED PORTION OF THE PREMIUM

If you feel an error in computation has increased the premium improperly and there is additional premium due on the audit, calculate how much of the additional premium is undisputed (if any) and pay that amount. Doing this puts you in a much stronger position to avoid having the insurance company try to cancel your current coverage (and use this as leverage to win the dispute).

## KEEP THE AGENT/BROKER IN THE LOOP

Assuming that the agent or broker for the disputed policy is still your agent, you want to keep him or her informed of everything you do. The agent or broker may want you to leave everything to him or her, and this can be useful to a point. But if the agent or broker cannot get the insurance company to revise the audit, and you still feel you are correct, don't just accept the agent's or broker's assurances that he or she has done everything that can be done. You have the right to deal with the insurance company's audit personnel directly if you need to in order to resolve such disputes, so be prepared to do so when necessary. But keep all communications with auditors professional, no matter how tempting it may be to get upset and level accusations of wrongdoing or incompetence.

## SOMETIMES ALEXANDER'S APPROACH CAN WORK

If patient and professional discussion and communication just don't make any difference to your insurance company, yet you're convinced you're right, it may be time to stop trying to unravel the knot and pull out your sword. You can do this by filing a complaint with your state insurance regulators. Every state insurance regulatory agency has a way for insurance consumers to file formal complaints with them about premium charges by an insurance company. Take a look at the web site for your state insurance reg-

ulators to see what procedure they have in place. If you can't get satisfaction there, but are still convinced your insurance company is doing something wrong, you may want to contact an independent consultant specializing in handling such disputes. You may also want to consult with an attorney (particularly if there are significant sums of money at stake).

## IF A COLLECTION AGENCY GETS INVOLVED

Often, the staff of an insurance company will forward disputed audits to outside collection agencies once they perceive that they're not being paid what they think they're owed in a reasonable amount of time. And collection agencies get paid for being fairly tough in handling collections. But in my experience, even tough collection agencies respect legitimate audit disputes, if you send documentation to them that the matter has been sent for review to a legitimate third party such as an insurance regulatory agency or a rating bureau (like NCCI). So if your account gets turned over to a collection agency, send the agency copies of all correspondence to the insurer and to third parties, and ask them to suspend taking further action until the dispute is resolved. In my experience, collection agencies will respect such requests.

## PURSUE APPEALS

As you may have noticed from reading some of the case histories included in this book, it can sometimes take a very persistent approach to finally resolve a premium dispute successfully. Often, we've seen clients who were turned down in the initial stages of a dispute, only to ultimately prevail by continuing to pursue the matter higher up the regulatory food chain. So just because an NCCI inspector doesn't agree with you, don't necessarily roll over and pay the bill. Do your homework and gather your documentation if needed, but if you're still sure you're right then spend the time and effort to take the matter to the next level. Often, such efforts pay off.

# The Annotated Workers' Compensation Insurance Policy

O N THE FOLLOWING PAGES YOU WILL FIND a copy of the standard workers' compensation insurance policy currently in use in U.S. jurisdictions. This is the 1992 policy version, drafted by NCCI but used in all states that allow private insurance, even the non-NCCI states. This is the oft-cited "fine print" that sets out the terms and conditions under which an insurance company insures an employer's workers' compensation obligations.

Of course, every employer that purchases workers' compensation insurance has a copy of this document. Few of them have probably actually read it. For the layperson, it can be a daunting task to try to read through such dense and legal language, even though this latest version of the policy has been made easier to read than earlier incarnations.

So here is a brief guide to some of the most important provisions of the policy, with explanations of what exactly is being promised by this contract.

We've talked a fair bit about *proper classification* earlier in this book. To see what the policy says about this, take a look under "Part Five—Premiums," section B, "Classifications." This policy section states:

Item 4 of the Information Page shows the rate and premium basis for certain business or work classifications. These classifications were assigned based on an estimate of the exposures you would have during the policy period. If your actual exposures are not properly described by those classifications, we will assign proper classifications, rates and premium basis by endorsement to this policy.

The "we" in this section refers to the insurance company. So notice that the policy does not state that "we" (the insurance company) will "attempt to use the correct classification" or that "we will use the classification we think is right." It says that if the classifications shown on the policy don't describe your actual exposures, then the insurance company "will assign proper classifications". This is an unambiguous promise by the insurance company that it will ultimately use the correct classification to determine your premiums, even if the classification used in the Information Page to develop estimated premium is something different.

Remember that the workers' compensation insurance policy is what the lawyers call "a contract of adhesion." It's a unilateral contract, drafted by the insurance company. The only choice the employer gets is whether or not to accept the terms of this contract that was drafted by the other party, the insurance company. As the employer, you don't get to negotiate the terms of this policy; it's take it or leave it. This means that legally, any ambiguity is supposed to be resolved in favor of the employer. But there really isn't anything very ambiguous about this particular section of the policy. The insurance company contractually agrees that it will use the correct classification to determine the premiums for the policy.

Sometimes insurance companies need to be reminded about this contractual obligation, because in practice some of their people sometimes get a little sloppy about using correct classifications. As the policyholder, you have the right to insist that the insurance company live up to the terms of the contract that it drafted.

But how does one know what the "correct classification" really is for a particular employer? That's actually addressed in the preceding section of "Part Five—Premium," section A, "Our Manuals," reads:

All premium for this policy will be determined by our manuals of rules, rates, rating plans and classifications. We may change our manuals and apply the changes to this policy if authorized by law or a governmental agency regulating this insurance.

Now, this might appear to give the insurance company carte blanche to write its own rules. But this isn't quite so. Because even though an insurance company could theoretically write its own manual of rules about all of these things, in actual practice they don't. The manuals of rules, rates, rating plans and classifications that are referred to here are actually the manuals written by NCCI or other rating bureaus. Insurance companies don't want to take the time and effort to create their own manuals of rules. They use the manuals created by NCCI (or other rating bureaus in the non-NCCI states) because those manuals are well understood and familiar by insurance company personnel and are submitted to and approved by state insurance regulators. So this section of the policy commits the insurance company to following the manuals of rules and regulations that have been approved by state regulators for workers' compensation insurance. That means that "proper classifications" are defined by the manuals of rules written by NCCI or other rating bureaus, as approved by state regulators. So the insurance company is required, by the terms of the contract, to use the proper classification and other rating elements for your business according to the detailed manuals of rules filed with regulators. The company can't just make it up as it goes, much as it might like to sometimes. There are detailed manuals of rules that govern the details of how the insurance company is supposed to compute the premium for workers' compensation insurance.

NCCI produces the following manuals that set out in excruciating detail different aspects of how premiums are to be calculated. These are:

*The Basic Manual for Workers' Compensation and Employers' Liability Insurance.* This manual lays out the general rules for premium computation, coverage, classifications, payroll, rates, cancellation, endorsements, and many other aspects of the Workers Compensation policy.

*The Scopes® of Basic Manual Classifications.* This manual gives the details of what is intended to be covered by each of its NCCI's classification codes (including state special classifications).

*The Experience Rating Plan Manual.* This gives the detailed rules on how experience modification factors are to be computed and applied to policies.

*The Retrospective Rating Plan Manual for Workers' Compensation and Employers' Liability Insurance.* This manual contains the detailed rules that govern retrospective rating plans (a particular kind of loss-sensitive plan) in NCCI states.

Remember that in states that don't use the NCCI system, the independent rating bureaus for those states produce their own sets of manuals that govern policies covering those states.

This same policy section means that the insurance company has to follow the manual rules about things like experience modification factors and other credits and adjustments to the policy.

There is another important section on page 5 of the policy. Take a look at "section G, Audit." This policy provision states:

You will let us examine and audit all your records that relate to this policy. These records include ledgers, journals, registers, vouchers, contracts, tax reports, payroll and disbursement records, and programs for storing and retrieving data.

"All your records that relate to your policy"— that's a pretty broad description and it covers a lot of territory. The specific documents named in the following sentence do not limit the insurance company to just "ledgers, journals, registers …," etc., but rather these are just offered as examples. The insurance company, per the terms of the contract, has the right to examine "all your records that relate to your policy." This question often comes up when an employer is in the middle of an audit, particularly an "extreme audit," when the records demands of an insurer may seem a bit onerous. So keep in mind that, when push comes to shove, the policy gives the insurance company the right to examine any record of yours that relates to the policy. So any record that relates to anything affecting coverage or premium computation is fair game.

Another important part of this contract is found at the end of page 4 and spills over to the start of page 5. It is headed "Part Four: Your Duties If Injury Occurs" and reads:

Tell us at once if injury occurs that may be covered by this policy. Your other duties are listed here.

Provide for immediate medical care and other services required by the workers' compensation law.

Give us or our agent the names and addresses of the injured persons and of witnesses, and other information we may need.

Promptly give us all notices, demands, and legal papers related to the injury, claim proceeding or suit.

Cooperate with us and assist us, as we may request, in the investigation, settlement or defense of any claim, proceeding or suit.

Do nothing after an injury occurs that would interfere with our right to recover from others.

Do not voluntarily make payments, assume obligations or incur expenses, except at your own cost.

Pay particular attention to the part that says the employer must tell the insurance company at once if injury occurs that may be covered by this policy. If the employer fails to notify the insurance company in a timely manner about an injury the insurance company can decline coverage. So anytime an employer attempts to handle some apparently minor injury on its own (to hold down the costs that will be used to figure future premiums), the employer runs the risk of the insurance company being able to later deny coverage if that claim develops into something more serious and expensive. And make no mistake about it, sometimes injuries that seem to be minor later turn out to have complications that cost a lot of money. Or maybe someone just alleges that it had expensive complications—which from your point of view, can be just as serious. Investigating such allegations and defending yourself against even spurious allegations like this can be very expensive. If you report them promptly to your insurance company, all those expenses become someone else's headache. And that's what you're paying all that premium for—to make these matters are someone else's

responsibility.

There's another section of the standard policy that has occasionally figured into some cases we've worked on, so I recommend that all employers be aware of it. This provision is right at the beginning of the policy, right at the top of page 1, in the "General Section," headed "A. The Policy," and it reads as follows:

> This policy includes at its effective date the Information Page and all endorsements and schedules listed there. It is a contract of insurance between you (the employer named in Item 1 of the Information Page) and us (the insurer named on the Information Page). *The only agreements relating to this insurance are stated in this policy. The terms of this policy may not be changed or waived except by endorsement issued by us to be part of this policy.*

I've placed the last two sentences of this provision in italics (even though the policy itself does not) because these sentences actually set forth a part of this contract that is very important and one that is sometimes deliberately contravened by some insurance companies. In the section of this book about loss-sensitive rating plans, we reviewed how some insurance companies have issued separate side agreements that change the way the premium is computed. If these side agreements contain provisions that change what the policy itself says about the computation of premiums, and if those side agreements are not actually endorsed onto the policy itself, then the insurance company has violated this provision of the policy.

If the terms of the side agreement produce higher premiums than those called for under the terms of the policy itself, and if such a side agreement is not actually endorsed onto the policy, you as the policyholder have the right to insist that the insurance company compute your premiums per the terms of the policy itself. Of course, your insurance company may well not be too happy about such an insistence, so you may need to reserve such insistence only for circumstances when you are prepared to end your relationship with that insurer. In the end, you may need to file a complaint with your state insurance regulator or even go to court, to insist that your premium be computed per the terms of the policy. The insurance company will, in all likelihood, assert that you entered into a separate contract (the side agreement) that they have a right to enforce. So this isn't an argument that you want to get into lightly. To avoid such disputes, you may want to make sure that any separate agreement your insurance company wants you to sign is in fact consistent with the terms of the policy and is endorsed onto the policy itself. If your insurer is not willing to comply, it may well be a warning sign that your insurance company is trying to sell you a rating plan that has not actually been authorized by regulators.

These aren't the only important sections of the workers' compensation policy, of course. Each and every provision of the policy can be important. But the sections annotated above are those that are often the subject of questions by employers or disputes between employers and insurers. The entire standard six-page workers' compensation insurance policy is reproduced on the following pages, for your review and reference.

# WORKERS' COMPENSATION AND EMPLOYER'S LIABILITY INSURANCE POLICY

In return for the payment of the premium and subject to all terms of this policy, we agree with you as follows:

## GENERAL SECTION

### A. The Policy

This policy includes at its effective date the Information Page and all endorsements and schedules listed there. It is a contract of insurance between you (the employer named in Item 1 of the Information Page) and us (the insurer named on the Information Page). The only agreements relating to this insurance are stated in this policy. The terms of this policy may not be changed or waived except by endorsement issued by us to be part of this policy.

### B. Who Is Insured

You are insured if you are an employer named in Item 1 of the Information Page. If that employer is a partnership, and if you are one of its partners, you are insured, but only in your capacity as an employer of the partnership's employees.

### C. Workers' Compensation Law

Workers' Compensation Law means the workers or workmen's compensation law and occupational disease law of each state or territory named in Item 3.A. of the Information Page. It includes any amendments to that law which are in effect during the policy period. It does not include any federal workers or workmen's compensation law, any federal occupational disease law or the provisions of any law that provide nonoccupational disability benefits.

### D. State

State means any state of the United States of America, and the District of Columbia.

### E. Locations

This policy covers all of your workplaces listed in Items 1 or 4 of the Information Page; and it covers all other workplaces in Item 3.A. states unless you have other insurance or are self-insured for such workplaces.

## PART ONE
## WORKERS COMPENSATION INSURANCE

### A. How This Insurance Applies

This workers compensation insurance applies to bodily injury by accident or bodily injury by disease. Bodily injury includes resulting death.

1. Bodily injury by accident must occur during the policy period.
2. Bodily injury by disease must be caused or aggravated by the conditions of your employment. The employee's last day of last exposure to the conditions causing or aggravating such bodily injury by disease must occur during the policy period.

### B. We Will Pay

We will pay promptly when due the benefits required of you by the workers' compensation law.

### C. We Will Defend

We have the right and duty to defend at our expense any claim, proceeding or Suit against you for benefits payable by this insurance. We have the right to investigate and settle these claims, proceedings or suits.

We have no duty to defend a claim, proceeding or suit that is not covered by this insurance.

### D. We Will Also Pay

We will also pay these costs, in addition to other amounts payable under this insurance, as part of any claim, proceeding or suit we defend:

1. reasonable expenses incurred at our request, but not loss of earnings;
2. premiums for bonds to release attachments and for appeal bonds in bond amounts up to the amount payable under this insurance;

3. litigation costs taxed against you;

4. interest on a judgment as required by law until we offer the amount due under this insurance; and

5. expenses we incur.

### E. Other Insurance

We will not pay more than our share of benefits and costs covered by this insurance and other insurance or self-insurance. Subject to any limits of liability that may apply, all shares will be equal until the loss is paid. If any insurance or self-insurance is exhausted, the shares of all remaining insurance will be equal until the loss is paid.

### F. Payments You Must Make

You are responsible for any payments in excess of the benefits regularly provided by the workers' compensation law including those required because:

1. of your serious and willful misconduct;

2. you knowingly employ an employee in violation of law;

3. you fail to comply with a health or safety law or regulation; or

4. you discharge, coerce or otherwise discriminate against any employee in violation of the workers' compensation law.

If we make any payments in excess of the benefits regularly provided by the workers' compensation law on your behalf, you will reimburse us promptly.

### G. Recovery From Others

We have your rights, and the rights of persons entitled to the benefits of this insurance, to recover our payments from anyone liable for the injury. You will do everything necessary to protect those rights for us and to help us enforce them.

### H. Statutory Provisions

These statements apply where they are required by law.

1. As between an injured worker and us, we have notice of the injury when you have notice.

2. Your default or the bankruptcy or insolvency of you or your estate will not relieve us of our duties under this insurance after an injury occurs.

3. We are directly and primarily liable to any person entitled to the benefits payable by this insurance. Those persons may enforce our duties; so may an agency authorized by law. Enforcement may be against us or against you and us.

4. Jurisdiction over you is jurisdiction over us for purposes of the workers' compensation law. We are bound by decisions against you under that law, subject to the provisions of this policy that are not In conflict with that law.

5. This insurance conforms to the parts of the workers' compensation law that apply to:

   a. benefits payable by this insurance;

   b. special taxes, payments Into security or other special funds, and assessments payable by us under that law,

6. Terms of this insurance that conflict with the workers' compensation law are changed by this statement to conform to that law.

Nothing in these paragraphs relieves you of your duties under this policy.

### PART TWO
### EMPLOYERS' LIABILITY INSURANCE
### A. How This Insurance Applies

This employers' liability insurance applies to bodily injury by accident or bodily injury by disease. Bodily injury includes resulting death.

1. The bodily injury must arise out of and in the course of the injured employee's employment by you.

2. The employment must be necessary or incidental to your work in a state or territory listed in Item 3.A. of the Information Page.

3. Bodily injury by accident must occur during the policy period.

4. Bodily injury by disease must be caused or aggravated by the conditions of your employment. The employee's last day of last exposure to the conditions causing or aggravating such bodily injury by disease must occur during the policy period.

5. If you are sued, the original suit and any related legal actions for damages for bodily injury by accident or by disease must be brought in the United States of America, its territories or possessions, or Canada.

## B. We Will Pay

We will pay all sums you legally must pay as damages because of bodily injury to your employees, provided the bodily injury is covered by this Employers' Liability Insurance.

The damages we will pay, where recovery is permitted by law, include damages:

1. for which you are liable to a third party by reason of a claim or suit against you by that third party to recover the damages claimed against such third party as a result of injury to your employee;

2. for care and loss of services; and

3. for consequential bodily injury to a spouse, child, parent, brother or sister of the injured employee; provided that these damages are the direct consequence of bodily injury that arises out of and in the course of the injured employee's employment by you: and

4. because of bodily injury to your employee that arises out of and in the course of employment, claimed against you in a capacity other than as employer.

## C. Exclusions

This insurance does not cover:

1. liability assumed under a contract. This exclusion does not apply to a warranty that your work will be done in a workmanlike manner;

2. punitive or exemplary damages because of bodily injury to an employee employed in violation of law;

3. bodily injury to an employee while employed in violation of law with your actual knowledge or the actual knowledge of any of your executive officers;

4. any obligation imposed by a workers' compensation, occupational disease, unemployment compensation, or disability benefits law, or any similar law;

5. bodily injury intentionally caused or aggravated by you;

6. bodily injury occurring outside the United States of America, its territories or possessions, and Canada. This exclusion does not apply to bodily injury to a citizen or resident of the United States of America or Canada who is temporarily outside these countries;

7. damages arising out of coercion, criticism, demotion, evaluation, reassignment, discipline, defamation, harassment, humiliation, discrimination against or termination of any employee, or any personnel practices, policies, acts or omissions;

8. bodily injury to any person in work subject to the Longshore and Harbor Workers' Compensation Act (33 USC Sections 901–950), the Nonappropriated Fund Instrumentalities Act (5 USC Sections 8171–8173), the Outer Continental Shelf Lands Act (43 USC Sections 1331–1356), the Defense Base Act (42 USC Sections 1651–1654), the Federal Coal Mine Health and Safety Act of 1969 (30 USC Sections 901–942), any other federal workers' or workmen's compensation law or other federal occupational disease law, or any amendments to these laws;

9. bodily injury to any person in work subject to the

Federal Employers' Liability Act (45 USC Sections 51–60), any other federal laws obligating an employer to pay damages to an employee due to bodily injury arising out of or in the course of employment, or any amendments to those laws;

10. bodily injury to a master or member of the crew of any vessel;

11. fines or penalties imposed for violation of federal or state law;

12. damages payable under the Migrant and Seasonal Agricultural Worker Protection Act (29 USC Sections 1801–1872) and under any other federal law awarding damages for violation of those laws or regulations issued thereunder, and any amendments to those laws.

## D. We Will Defend

We have the right and duty to defend, at our expense, any claim, proceeding or suit against you for damages payable by this insurance. We have the right to investigate and settle these claims, proceedings and suits.

We have no duty to defend a claim, proceeding or suit that is not covered by this insurance. We have no duty to defend or continue defending after we have paid our applicable limit of liability under this insurance.

## E. We Will Also Pay

We will also pay these costs, in addition to other amounts payable under this insurance, as part of any claim, proceeding or suit we defend:

1. reasonable expenses incurred at our request, but not loss of earnings;

2. premiums for bonds to release attachments and for appeal bonds in bond amounts up to the limit of our liability under this insurance;

3. litigation costs taxed against you;

4. interest on a judgment as required by law until we offer the amount due under this insurance;

and

5. expenses we incur.

## F. Other Insurance

We will not pay more than our share of damages and costs covered by this insurance and other insurance or self-insurance. Subject to any limits of liability that apply, all shares will be equal until the loss is paid. If any insurance or self-insurance is exhausted, the shares of all remaining insurance and self-insurance will be equal until the loss is paid.

## G. Limits of Liability

Our liability to pay for damages is limited. Our limits of liability are shown in Item 3,B. of the Information Page. They apply as explained below.

1. Bodily Injury by Accident. The limit shown for "bodily injury by accident–each accident" is the most we will pay for all damages covered by this insurance because of bodily injury to one or more employees in any one accident. A disease is not bodily injury by accident unless it results directly from bodily injury by accident.

2. Bodily Injury by Disease. The limit shown for "bodily injury by disease–policy limit" is the most we will pay for all damages covered by this insurance and arising out of bodily injury by disease, regardless of the number of employees who sustain bodily injury by disease. The limit shown for "bodily injury by disease–each employee" is the most we will pay for all damages because of bodily injury by disease to any one employee. Bodily injury by disease does not include disease that results directly from a bodily injury by accident.

3. We will not pay any claims for damages after we have paid the applicable limit of our liability under this insurance.

## H. Recovery From Others

We have your rights to recover our payment from anyone liable for an injury covered by this insurance.

You will do everything necessary to protect those rights for us and to help us enforce them.

### I. Actions Against Us

There will be no right of action against us under this insurance unless:

1. You have complied with all the terms of this policy; and
2. The amount you owe has been determined with our consent or by actual trial and final judgment.

This insurance does not give anyone the right to add us as a defendant in an action against you to determine your liability. The bankruptcy or insol~ vency of you or your estate will not relieve us of our obligations under this Part.

## PART THREE
## OTHER STATES INSURANCE

### A. How This Insurance Applies

1. This other states insurance applies only if one or more states are shown in Item 3.0. of the Information Page.
2. IF you begin work in any one of those states after the effective date of this policy and are not insured or are not self-insured for such work, all provisions of the policy will apply as though that state were listed in Item 3.A. of the Information Page.
3. We will reimburse you for the benefits required by the workers' compensation law of that state if we are not permitted to pay the benefits directly to persons entitled to them.
4. If you have work on the effective date of this policy in any state not listed in Item 3.A. of the Information Page, coverage will not be afforded for that state unless we are notified within thirty days.

### B. Notice

Tell us at once if you begin work in any state listed in Item 3.C. of the Information Page.

## PART FOUR
## YOUR DUTIES IF INJURY OCCURS

Tell us at once if injury occurs that may be covered by this policy. Your other duties are listed here.

1. Provlde for Immediate medical and other services required by the workers' compensation law.
2. Give us or our agent the names and addresses of the injured persons and of witnesses, and other information we may need.
3. Promptly give us all notices, demands and legal papers related to the injury, claim, proceeding or suit.
4. Cooperate with us and assist us, as we may request, in the investigation, settlement, or defense of any claim, proceeding or suit.
5. Do nothing after an injury occurs that would interfere with our right to recover from others.
6. Do not voluntarily make payments, assume obligations or incur expenses, except at your own cost.

## PART FIVE–PREMIUM

### A. Our Manuals

All premium for this policy will be determined by our manuals of rules, rates, rating plans and classifications. We may change our manuals and apply the changes to this policy if authorized by law or a governmental agency regulating this insurance.

### B. Classifications

Item 4 of the Information Page shows the rate and premium basis for certain business or work classifications. These classifications were assigned based on an estimate of the exposures you would have during the policy period. If your actual exposures are not properly described by those classifications, we will assign proper classifications, rates and premium basis by endorsement to this policy.

### C. Remuneration

Premium for each work classification is determined by multiplying a rate times a premium basis.

Remuneration is the most common premium basis. This premium basis includes payroll and all other remuneration paid or payable during the policy period for the services of:

1. all your officers and employees engaged in work covered by this policy; and
2. all other persons engaged in work that could make us liable under Part One (workers' compensation Insurance) of this policy. If you do not have payroll records for these persons, the contract price for their services and materials may be used as the premium basis. This paragraph 2 will not apply if you give us proof that the employers of these persons lawfully secured their workers' compensation obligations.

### D. Premium Payments

You will pay all premium when due. You will pay the premium even if part or all of a workers' compensation law is not valid.

### E. Final Premium

The premium shown on the Information Page, schedules, and endorsements is an estimate. The final premium will be determined after this policy ends by using the actual, not the estimated, premium basis and the proper classifications and rates that lawfully apply to the business and work covered by this policy. If the final premium is more than the premium you paid to us, you must pay us the balance. If it is less, we will refund the balance to you. The final premium will not be less than the highest minimum premium for the classifications covered by this policy.

If this policy is canceled, final premium will be determined in the following way unless our manuals provide otherwise:

1. If we cancel, final premium will be calculated pro rata based on the time this policy was in force. Final premium will not be less than the pro rata share of the minimum premium.

2. If you cancel, final premium will be more than pro rata; it will be based on the time this policy was in force, and increased by our short-rate cancelation table and procedure. Final premium will not be less than the minimum premium.

### F. Records

You will keep records of information needed to compute premium. You will provide us with copies of those records when we ask for them.

### G. Audit

You will let us examine and audit all your records that relate to this policy. These records include ledgers, journals, registers, vouchers, contracts, tax reports, payroll and disbursement records, and programs for storing and retrieving data. We may conduct the audits during regular business hours during the policy period and within three years after the policy period ends. Information developed by audit will be used to determine final premium. Insurance rate service organizations have the same rights we have under this provision.

### PART SIX—CONDITIONS

### A. Inspection

We have the right, but are not obliged to inspect your workplaces at any time. Our inspections are not safety inspections. They relate only to the insurability of the workplaces and the premiums to be charged. We may give you reports on the conditions we find. We may also recommend changes. While they may help reduce losses, we do not undertake to perform the duty of any person to provide for the health or safety of your employees or the public. We do not warrant that your workplaces are safe or healthful or that they comply with laws, regulations, codes or standards. Insurance rate service organizations have the same rights we have under this provision.

### B. Long-Term Policy

If the policy period is longer than one year and sixteen days, all provisions of this policy will apply as though a new policy were issued on each annual anniversary that this policy is in force.

### C. Transfer of Your Rights and Duties

Your rights or duties under this policy may not be transferred without our written consent.

If you die and we receive notice within thirty days after your death, we will cover your legal representative as insured.

### D. Cancelation

1. You may cancel this policy. You must mail or deliver advance written notice to us stating when the cancelation is to take effect.
2. We may cancel this policy. We must mail or deliver to you not less than ten days' advance written notice stating when the cancelation is to take effect. Mailing that notice to you at your mailing address shown in Item 1 of the Information Page will be sufficient to prove notice.
3. The policy period will end on the day and hour stated in the cancelation notice.
4. Any of these provisions that conflict with a law that controls the cancelation of the insurance in this policy is changed by this statement to comply with the law.

### E. Sole Representative

The insured first named in Item 1 of the Information Page will act on behalf of all insureds to change this policy, receive return premium, and give or receive notice of cancellation.

# Tips for Large Employers to Control Workers' Comp Costs

ERE ARE SOME PARTICULAR AREAS WHERE large employers want to particularly focus to make sure their workers' compensation insurance costs aren't out of control.

**Use Competitive Bidding to Keep Your Agent or Broker Competitive.** An independent agent or broker may make the argument that he or she can access a large number of insurance companies, so there is no need to bring in competitive brokers. But the fallacy of this has been exposed by New York Attorney General Eliot Spitzer, who found large agents and brokers engaging in anti-competitive practices behind the scenes, increasing costs for employers. An effective way to prevent such practices is to divide available insurance markets among several independent agents or brokers.

**Review Common Ownership with Other Entities.** Make sure the experience modifi-cation factor used on your policies has been calculated using data from all commonly owned entities, to make sure your experience mod benefits from loss and payroll data from the other firms.

**Read Any Side Agreement for a Loss-Sensitive Plan Carefully.** As detailed earlier, some insurers now offer large employers loss-sensitive plans for which the final premium calculation is contained in a separate written agreement that is not actually part of the policy. This is done because the particular rating plan in such agreements has not been filed with and approved by state regulators, and in fact conflicts with the terms of the policy. Such agreements in loss-sensitive plans can turn very expensive if losses are not favorable—sometimes to the point where the employer would have been better off in the assigned risk plan.

**Make Sure You Understand the Details of Any Loss-Sensitive Plan.** Some of these plans can get extremely complex and difficult to understand. If you are not sure you fully and truly understand the fine details of a proposed loss-sensitive plan (and insurers often will offer such plans to large employers), you may be well advised to hire an independent consultant to review the plan and offer an analysis about whether this plan truly makes sense for your company.

**Keep a Careful Eye on Loss Reserves.** Many large employers are on loss-sensitive plans that charge for loss reserves just the same as actual paid-out claims. If that's the case, the insurance company has less incentive to keep claims reserves reasonable. An employer can't dictate reserves to an insurer, but you may be able to negotiate on some of them. So don't just let the insurance company handle things as it chooses. Not only may this inflate future premiums via the experience rating mechanism, it can also inflate current premiums on many loss-sensitive plans that have been sold to large employers.

# Tips for Small Employers to Control Workers' Comp Costs

ERE ARE SOME PARTICULAR AREAS WHERE small employers want to particularly focus to make sure their workers' compensation insurance costs aren't out of control.

**Determine if You're in an Assigned Risk Plan.** Sometimes an insurance agent handling the workers' compensation insurance for a small employer doesn't make it clear that the policy procured is an assigned risk policy. And in many states, the rates and premium for an assigned risk policy are much, much higher than for the same policy written through the voluntary market." An assigned risk policy doesn't look different from any other workers' comp policy, except for some subtle differences. So make it a point to insist on knowing if your policy has been written through an assigned risk plan.

If you are in an assigned risk plan, check with your state's insurance regula-

tors to see if assigned risk policies in your state have higher rates and premiums. If this is the case, then do everything in your power to find coverage outside the assigned risk plan. Talk with other agents, talk with direct-writing insurance companies, talk with employee leasing companies, investigate group self-insurance programs available in your state—but don't let it be your agent's responsibility to get you out of the assigned risk plan. Your agent just may not have a viable alternative for you, but that doesn't mean that such an alternative doesn't exist.

**Check What Credits May Be Available to You in Your State.** If you're not in an assigned risk plan, make sure your policy gives you whatever credits you might be eligible for in your state. If your state offers credits for drug- and alcohol-free workplace, find out if you are eligible. If your state offers merit rating, see if you are eligible for that from an insurer. If your premium is appropriate, make sure you are getting the proper experience modification factor. If your state offers a small-deductible credit, look into obtaining this.

### Insist on Getting Audit Workpapers After Any Audit.

If the insurance company sends out an auditor to determine your final premium, make sure to request a copy of the audit work papers so you can review them carefully and make sure payroll computation adjusts overtime properly and allocates payroll of different employees correctly.

### Check into Alternative Sources of Workers' Compensation Insurance.

Many business and trade associations sponsor insurance programs that include workers' compensation insurance. Check into all organizations to which you belong or that you might be eligible to join; they may offer sponsored insurance programs that could reduce your rates or premium.

# Reporting Changes in Ownership

UNDER THE RULES DEVELOPED BY NCCI and most other rating bureaus, separate business entities that share a sufficient degree of ownership are supposed to be combined together for computing an experience modification factor.

Employers need to be careful about this point, because the insurance system often doesn't catch changes in ownership, so this particular monkey rests squarely on the back of the policyholder. That is, responsibility for reporting common ownership lies with the employer, even though the employer may not realize how such ownership can impact the experience modifier (and thus premiums).

NCCI and most other rating bureaus ask that employers complete a form known as an ERM-14. (It's called ERM because the form is part of the Experience Rating Manual published by NCCI.)

Employers need to be aware of how ownership can affect experience mods, because if the information used to calculate your modifier is out of date you might end up with a modifier higher than it really should be and thus end up paying premiums higher than you really need to.

An employer could also unintentionally leave the company open to a charge of deliberate insurance fraud, if someone decides that the employer knowingly concealed ownership information that would have impacted the modifier in such a way as to increase premiums. In other words, if an employer doesn't report ownership changes and this results in a modifier lower than the rules call for, an insurance company could seek criminal charges for insurance fraud against that employer.

Increasingly, insurance companies are exercising this option when they feel an employer has not acted in good faith.

Certainly, the threat of seeking criminal charges can be a powerful tactic if a dispute arises between your company and your insurance company over proper premiums. So by all means, do not think that reporting accurate ownership information is a trivial matter, one that you can neglect in order to reduce premiums. The rules obligate an employer to report accurate information about common ownership with other entities.

But keep in mind that reporting accurate information can also be beneficial, as reporting accurate information may well result in a lower experience modifier.

Because the insurance system relies on employers to report changes in ownership, and many employers are unaware of this obligation or of how such common ownership can impact experience modifiers, mistakes in this area are not uncommon.

The NCCI rules regarding combination of entities are as follows.

Business entities are supposed to be combined for purposes of experience rating if they have more than 50 percent common ownership. That is, if the same person, group of people, or corporation owns *more than 50 percent* of each of the business entities in question, then those entities should have a common experience modification factor calculated that applies to all of them. Such a modifier will be based upon the combined prior loss and payroll data of all the entities.

Entities are also supposed to be combined if one entity owns more than 50 percent of another entity, that in turn owns more than 50 percent of another entity. In such a case, all of these business entities are combinable.

Now, many years ago, NCCI rules stated that when the ownership of a company changed, the experience modifier would reset back to 1.00 while the loss and payroll data of the new company accumulated to the point where a modifier could be calculated. But this was changed a long time ago, in response to what NCCI and insurers perceived as abuses on the part of some employers. Nowadays, the modifier resets only if there is a change in ownership and the operations of the company change to such a degree that the governing classification changes. This is relatively rare.

But keep in mind that when one entity is acquired by some other entity that already has a modifier calculated for it, this situation calls for a change in modifier, because now the rules call for a modifier to be calculated based on the new combined entity.

For example, if Midwest Masonry* has an experience modifier of 1.04, but gets purchased by a larger company known as Aggregate Construction Enterprises* that has a modifier of .93, then under the rules a new modifier should be calculated that would apply to both companies, even if they are on separate policies with different insurance companies. This new modifier would be calculated based on the combined past loss and payroll information of the two companies, so it might come out to something like a .94. It depends to a great degree on the relative size of the two companies. If Aggregate Construction Enterprises is a lot larger than Midwest Masonry, the loss and payroll information for the former will predominate in the calculation because of the larger payrolls that presumably were reported by past insurers. In such a case, the relatively poor loss information that produced a 1.04 modifier for Midwest Masonry would now be part of a much larger calculation, so the effect on the modifier for Aggregate would be proportionally small.

Most but not all entities that have common ownership get combined for experience rating. A joint venture, for instance, doesn't impact the experience modifiers of the members of the joint venture, but a separate modifier is calculated for the joint venture based on the modifiers of the members of the joint venture. So if Midwest Masonry and Aggregate Construction Enterprises instead set up a joint venture called Builders Two, the modifier used on the policy for Builders Two would be calculated by combining loss and payroll data for Midwest Masonry and Aggregate. But the losses that happen under the separate policy for Builders Two would not be used on future modifiers for Midwest Masonry or Aggregate.

Also, keep in mind that a few states don't combine data for experience rating. California, Delaware, Michigan, New Jersey, and Pennsylvania calculate "stand-alone" modifiers for companies that work within their borders.

So let's say that Midwest Masonry does get acquired by Aggregate Construction Enterprises, but Midwest Masonry works only in Michigan, while Aggregate works in California, Arizona, Washington (the state, not D.C.), New York, and Illinois.

In this instance, Midwest Masonry would continue to have its own separate Michigan modifier, calculated by the Michigan rating bureau, based solely on prior policy loss and payroll data. As long as Midwest operates only in Michigan, its loss and payroll data won't impact the modifier for Aggregate because of the "stand-alone" nature of Michigan.

Aggregate would have a separate California modifier calculated just for its California operations, and a separate interstate modifier calculated by NCCI based on data from past policies covering Arizona, New York and Illinois. Arizona and Illinois are both NCCI states and New York shares data with NCCI even though New York operates its own independent rating bureau. Because Washington state is a state-run monopoly fund, loss and payroll data from operations in that state would also be segregated and apply only to the fund charges of that state.

Just to complicate matters further, sometimes NCCI will combine entities even though they don't actually meet the common ownership requirements spelled out in the Experience Rating Manual. That's because NCCI rules also allow for combination of entities that share common "physical assets," although the manual does not spell out exactly what constitutes such physical assets. So sometimes disputes can arise over whether or not entities really should be combined. NCCI in the past has tended to define "assets" very broadly, to include such things as customers and employees, so if your company gets caught in such a dispute it may be worthwhile to pursue the dispute through the appeals process offered by your state's insurance regulators.

*This is a fictitious entity used only for illustrative purposes, not intended to represent any actual company.

# State-by-State Directory of Agencies Responsible for Workers' Comp Claims and Benefits

THIS IS A DIFFERENT STATE-BY-STATE DIRECTORY than the one in Chapter 1. That earlier directory listed the state agencies that regulate workers' compensation insurance. This directory instead lists those state agencies that are responsible for benefits and claims from injured workers.

## Alabama

State of Alabama—www.al.gov
Department of Industrial Relations—
 dir.alabama.gov/
Workers' Compensation Division—
 dir.alabama.gov/wc
Industrial Relations Building
649 Monroe Street
Montgomery, AL 36131
800 528-5166, 334 242-2868; Fax: 334
 353-8262

## Alaska

State of Alaska—www.state.ak.us
Department of Labor and Workforce
 Development—
 www.labor.state.ak.us/home.htm
Divsion of Workers' Compensation—
 www.labor.state.ak.us/wc/wc.ht
P. O. Box 25512
 Juneau, AK 99802-5512
 907 465-2790; Fax: 907 465-2797
Workers' Compensation Board—
 www.gov.state.ak.us/boards/factsheet/
 fact110.html
Department of Labor
P. O. Box 25512, M/S 0700
Juneau, AK 99802-5512
907 465-2790, Fax: 907 465-2797

## Arizona

State of Arizona—www.state.az.us
Industrial Commission of Arizona—

This Workers' Compensation Administrators Directory was compiled by Robert W. McDowell for the North Carolina Industrial Commission, 4340 Mail Service Center, Raleigh, North Carolina 27699-4340.

www.ica.state.az.us
800 West Washington
Phoenix, AZ 85007
   or
P. O. Box 19070
Phoenix, Arizona 85005-9070
602 542-4411, Fax: 602 542-7889;
Ombudsman: 602 542-4538, Fax: 602 542-4350
Download free fillable PDF versions of Arizona
   workers' compensation forms courtesy of
   Interface Technologies—
   www.interfacetec.com/
Industrial Commission Review Board
State Compensation Fund of Arizona—
www.statefund.com/
3031 North Second Street
Phoenix, AZ 85012
602 631-2000; Fax: 602 631-2213

## Arkansas

State of Arkansas—www.state.ar.us
Workers' Compensation Commission—
   www.awcc.state.ar.us/
Street Address:
324 Spring Street
Little Rock, AR 72203
Mailing Address:
P. O. Box 950
Little Rock, AR 72203-0950
800 622-4472, 501 682-3930; Fax: 501 682-
   2777; Legal Advisor Direct: 800 250-2511;
   Arkansas Relay System TDD: 800 285-1131

## California

State of California—www.ca.gov
Department of Industrial Relations—
   www.dir.ca.gov/
Commission on Health and Safety and
   Workers'

Compensation—www.dir.ca.gov/CHSWC
455 Golden Gate Avenue, 10th Floor
San Francisco, CA 94102
415 557-1304, Fax: 415 703-4234
E-mail: chswc@hq.dir.ca.gov
1515 Clay Street, Room 901
Oakland, CA 94612
510 622-3959, Fax: 510 622-3265
Division of Workers' Compensation —
   www.dir.ca.gov/dwc
Street Address:
455 Golden Gate Avenue, 9th Floor
San Francisco, CA 94102-3660
Mailing Address:
P. O. Box 420603
San Francisco, CA 94142
415 703-4600 ; Fax: 415 703-3971
E-mail: dwc@dir.ca.gov
Download free fillable PDF versions of
   California workers' compensation forms
   courtesy of Interface Technologies—
   www.interfacetec.com/
Workers' Compensation Appeals Board—
   www.dir.ca.gov/WCAB/
Street Address:
455 Golden Gate Avenue, Suite 9328
San Francisco, CA 94102-3660
Mailing Address:
P. O. Box 429459
San Francisco, CA 94142-9459
415 703-4580
Division of Workers' Compensation Medical
   Board—www.dir.ca.gov/IMC
P. O. Box 8888
San Francisco, CA 994128-8888
800 794-6900 (in California), 650 737-2000
Self-Insurance Plans (SIP)—
   www.dir.ca.gov/SIP

2265 Watt Avenue, Suite 1
Sacramento, CA 95825
916 483-3392; Fax: 916 483-1535
E-mail: SIP@dir.ca.gov
State Compensation Insurance Fund—
www.scif.com
1275 Market Street
San Francisco, CA 94103
415 565-1234, Claims Reporting Service (toll-free): 888 222-3211

## Colorado

State of Colorado—www.state.co.us
Department of Labor and Employment—
www.coworkforce.com/
Division of Workers' Compensation—
www.coworkforce.com/DWC
633 17th Street, Suite 400
Denver, CO 80202-3660
888 390-7936 (English), 800 685-0891
(Spanish), 303 318-8700, Fax: 303 318-8710,
E-mail: workers.comp@state.co.us
Download free fillable PDF versions of
Colorado workers' compensation forms
courtesy of Interface Technologies—
www.interfacetec.com
Industrial Claims Appeals Office
Workers' Compensation: 303 318-8131
Unemployment Insurance: 303 318-8133
2151 East 12th Avenue
Denver, COo 80203
303 318-8133

## Connecticut

State of Connecticut—www.ct.gov
Workers' Compensation Commission—
wcc.state.ct.us
Capitol Place
21 Oak Street, Fourth Floor

Hartford, CT 06106
860 493-1500, Fax: 860 247-1361
Download free fillable PDF versions of
Connecticut workers' compensation forms
courtesy of Interface Technologies—
www.interfacetec.com
Compensation Review Board—
wcc.state.ct.us/wcc/crn.htm
Capitol Place
21 Oak Street, Fourth Floor
Hartford, CT 06106
203 493-1500, Fax: 203 247-1361

## Delaware

State of Delaware—www.delaware.gov
Department of Labor—
www.delawareworks.com
4425 North Market Street
Wilmington, DE 19802
Division of Industrial Affairs—www.delaware-
works. com/divisions/industrialaffairs/diain-
dex.html
4425 North Market Street, 3rd Fl
Wilmington, DE 19802
Office of Workers' Compensation—
www.delawareworks.com/divisions/industaff
airs/services/workers.comp.shtml
State Office Building, Sixth Floor
4425 North Market Street, 3rd Fl
Wilmington, DE 19802
302 761-8200

## District of Columbia

District of Columbia—www.dc.gov
Department of Employment Services—
does.dc.gov
Government of the District of Columbia
64 New York Avenue, N.E.

Washington, DC 20002

202 724-7000, Fax: 202 724-5683, TDD/TYY: 202 673-6994

E-mail: does@dc.gov

Office of Workers' Compensation—
www.does.dc.gov/does/cwp/view.asp?a=1232&Q=537428

Mailing Address:

P. O. Box 56098

Washington, DC 20002

Street Address:

64 New York Avenue, N.E., Room 2909

Washington, DC 20002

202 671-1000, Fax: 202 671-1929

Office of Hearings and Adjudication—
www.does.dc.gov/does/cwp/view.asp?a=1232&Q=537904

64 New York Avenue, N.E., Room 2011

Washington, DC 20002

202 671-2233, Fax: 202 673-6938

## Florida

State of Florida—www.myflorida.com/

Florida Department of Financial Services—
www.fldfs.com/

Division of Workers' Compensation—
www.fldfs.com/WC

301 Forrest Building

2728 Centerview Drive

Tallahassee, FL 32399-0680

850 921-6966; Fax: 850 922-6779; Fraud: 800 742-2214 (in Florida)

Department of Insurance, Bureau of Workers' Compensation Fraud: 850 413-3116; Safety: 800 367-4378 (in Florida), 850 488-3044

E-mail: WorkCompCusServ@dfs.state.fl.us

Download free fillable PDF versions of Florida workers' compensation forms courtesy of Interface Technologies—

www.interfacetec.com

Workers' Compensation Oversight Board—
www.doi.state.fl.us/wc/pdf/2kAR_OversightBoard. PDF

100 Marathon Building

2574 Seagate Drive

Tallahassee, FL 32399-2152

850 487-2613, Fax: 850 487-3232

Florida Division of Administrative Hearings—
www.doah.state.fl.us/internet

Office of Judges of Compensation Claims—
www.jcc.state.fl.us/jcc/default.cfm

Petition for Benefits:

P. O. Box 8000

Tallahassee, FL 32314-8000

Filing:

P. O. Box 6350

Tallahassee, FL 32314-6350

Request for Assignment of Case Number:

P. O. Box 6410

Tallahassee, FL 32314-6410

850 487-1911

## Georgia

State of Georgia—georgia.gov

Georgia State Board of Workers' Compensation—sbwc.georgia.gov

270 Peachtree Street, NW

Atlanta, GA 30303-1299

800 533-0682, 404 656-3875, Fax: 404 656-7768, Enforcement Division: 404 657-1391, Safety Library: 404 656-9057

Download free fillable PDF versions of Georgia workers' compensation forms courtesy of Interface Technologies—
www.interfacetec.com

Georgia Subsequent Injury Trust Fund—
stif.georgia.gov

Suite 500, North Tower

1720 Peachtree Street, NW
Atlanta, GA 30309-2462
404 206-6360, Fax: 404 206-6363, TDD: 404
206-5053

## Hawaii

State of Hawaii—www.hawaii.gov
Department of Labor and Industrial
Relations—dlir.state.hi.us
Disability Compensation Division
830 Punchbowl Street, Room 209
Honolulu, HI 96813
808 586-9174, Fax: 808 586-9219
E-mail: pstanley@pixi.com
Labor and Industrial Relations Appeals Board
888 Mililani Street, Room 400
Honolulu, HI 96813
808 586-8600, Fax: 586-8613
E-mail: pstanley@pixi.com

## Idaho

State of Idaho—www2.state.id.us
Industrial Commission—
www.state.id.us/iic/index.htm
317 Main Street
P. O. Box 83720
Boise, ID 83720-0041
800 950-2110, 208 334-6000; Fax: 208 334-
2321; TDD: 800 950-2110
State Insurance Fund—
www.state.id.us/isif/index.htm
1215 West State Street
P. O. Box 83720
Boise, ID 83720-0044
800 334-2370, 208 334-2370 (in the Boise area);
Fax: 208 334-2262 (Policyholder Services,
Administration, Management Services,
Legal), 208 334-3253 (Claims), 208 334-3254
(Underwriting); Fraud: 800 448-ISIF (4743)

## Illinois

State of Illinois—www.il.gov
Illinois Workers' Compensation Commission—
www.iwcc.il.gov
100 West Randolph Street, Suite 8-200
Chicago, IL 60601
866 352-3033 (toll free statewide), 312 814-
6611, Fax: 312 814-6523, TDD: 312 814-2959
E-mail: iicoperations@mail.state.il.us
Download free fillable PDF versions of Illinois
workers' compensation forms courtesy of
Interface Technologies—
www.interfacetec.com
Office of Self-Insurance Administration
701 South Second Street
Springfield, IL 62704
217 785-7084, Fax: 217 785-6557

## Indiana

State of Indiana—www.in.gov
Workers' Compensation Board of Indiana—
www.in.gov/workcomp
Government Center South
402 West Washington Street, Room W-196
Indianapolis, IN 46204
317 232-3808; Claims/Statistics: 317 233-4930;
Fax: 317 233-5493; Insurance: 317 233-3910;
Ombudsman: 800 824-COMP (2667), 317
232-5922
Download free fillable PDF versions of Indiana
workers' compensation forms courtesy of
Interface Technologies—
www.interfacetec.com

## Iowa

State of Iowa—www.state.ia.us
Iowa Workforce Development—www.iowa-
workforce.org
1000 East Grand Avenue

Des Moines, IA 50319-0209
800 JOB-IOWA, 515 281-5387
Iowa Division of Workers' Compensation—
www.iowaworkforce.org/wc
1000 East Grand Avenue
Des Moines, IA 50319-0209
800 JOB-IOWA (562-4692), 515 281-5387; Fax:
515 281-6501, TTD: 515 281-4748
E-mail: IWD.DWC@iwd.state.ia.us

**Kansas**
State of Kansas—www.state.ks.us
Department of Human Resources—
www.hr.state.ks.us
Kansas Workers' Compensation—
www.hr.state.ks.us/wc/html/wc.htm
800 SW Jackson, Suite 600
Topeka, KS 66612-1227
800 332-0353, 785 296-3441; Fax: 785 296-
0839; Fraud: 800 332-0353, 785 296-6392;
Industrial Safety & Health: 800 332-0353,
785 296-4386; Ombudsman: 800 332-0353,
785 296-2996

**Kentucky**
Commonwealth of Kentucky—kentucky.gov
Kentucky Department of Labor—labor.ky.gov
1047 U.S. 127S, Suite 4
Frankfort, Kentucky 40601
502 564-3070
Office of Workers' Claims—labor.ky.gov/dwc
657 Chamberlin Avenue
Frankfort, KY 40601
502 564-5550 (Administrative Services, Open
Records); Fax: 502 564-8250 (Administrative
Services), 502 564-9533 (Ombudsman), 502
564-5732 (Open Records), 502 564-0916
(Security and Compliance); Ombudsman:
800 554-8601 (Frankfort), 800 554-8603
(Paducah), 800 554-8602 (Pikeville);

Security and Compliance: 502 564-5550
E-mail: kywc.ombudsman@mail.state.ky.us
Download free fillable PDF versions of
Kentucky workers' compensation forms
courtesy of Interface Technologies—
www.interfacetec.com
Workers' Compensation Board
Division of Workers' Compensation Funds
1047 U.S. 127 South, Suite 4
Frankfort, KY 40601
502 564-3070, ext. 391
Workers' Compensation Funding Commission
#42 Millcreek Park
P. O. Box 1220
Frankfort, KY 40602-1220
502 573-3505, Fax: 502 573-4923
Kentucky Workers' Compensation Law (via
CompEd, Inc.)—www.comped.net/

**Louisiana**
State of Louisiana—
www.louisiana.gov/wps/portal
Department of Labor—www.laworks.net
Mailing Address:
P. O. Box 94094
Baton Rouge, LA 70804-9094
Street Address:
1001 North 23rd Street
Baton Rouge, LA 70804-9094
225 342-3111, TDD: 800 259-5154
Office of Workers' Compensation
Administration—
www.laworks.net/wrk_owca.asp
Mailing Address:
P. O. Box 94040
Baton Rouge, LA 70804-9040
Street Address:
1001 North 23rd Street
Baton Rouge, LA 70802-9094

225 342-7555, Fax: 225 342-5665, Fraud: 800
  201-3362 or WCFraud@ldol.state.la.us,
  Safety: 800 201-2497
E-mail: OWCA@ldol.state.la.us

## Maine
State of Maine—www.maine.gov
Workers' Compensation Board—
  www.maine.gov/wcb
27 State House Station
Augusta, ME 04333-0027
207 287-3751; Fax: 207 287-7198
Download free fillable PDF versions of Maine
  workers' compensation forms courtesy of
  Interface Technologies—
  www.interfacetec.com

## Maryland
State of Maryland—www.state.md.us
Maryland Workers' Compensation
  Commission—www.charm.net/~wcc
10 East Baltimore Street
Baltimore, MD 21202
800 492-0479, 410 864-5100; Fax: 410 333-8122
Download free fillable PDF versions of
  Maryland workers' compensation forms
  courtesy of Interface Technologies—
  www.interfacetec.com
Insured Workers' Insurance Fund—
  www.iwif.com
8722 Loch Raven Boulevard
Towson, MD 21286-2235
800 492-0197, 410 494-2200 Fax: 410 494-2001

## Massachusetts
Commonwealth of Massachusetts—
  www.mass.gov
Department of Industrial Accidents—
  www.mass.gov/dia
600 Washington Street, Seventh Floor

Boston, MA 02111
800 323-3249, 617 727-4900; Fax: 617 727-
  6477; TTY: 800 224-6196
Download free fillable PDF versions of
  Massachusetts workers' compensation forms
  courtesy of Interface Technologies—
  www.interfacetec.com
Massachusetts Workers' Compensation
  Advisory Council—www.mass.gov/wcac
600 Washington Street, Seventh Floor
Boston, MA 02111
617 727-4900, ext. 378; Fax: 617 727-7122
Workers' Compensation Rating and Inspection
  Bureau of Massachusetts—
  www.wcribma.org/mass
101 Arch Street
Boston, MA 02110
617 439-9030, Fax: 617 439-6055

## Michigan
State of Michigan—
  www.migov.state.mi.us/MichiganGovernor.
  htm
Department of Labor & Economic Growth—
  www.michigan.gov/cis
Street Address:
611 W. Ottawa
Lansing, MI 48909
Mailing Address:
P. O. Box 30004
Lansing, MI 48909
517 373-1820, Fax: 517 373-2129
Workers' Compensation Agency—www.michi-
  gan.gov/wca
Street Address:
State Secondary Complex
General Office Building
7150 Harris Drive, First Floor, B-Wing
Lansing, MI 48913

Mailing Address:

P. O. Box 30016

Lansing, MI 48909

888 396-5041, 517 322-1296, Fax: 517 322-1808, TDD in Lansing: 517 322-5987

Download free fillable PDF versions of Michigan workers' compensation forms courtesy of Interface Technologies—www.interfacetec.com/

Board of Magistrates—www.michigan.gov/wca/0,1607,7-191-26919—-,00.html

P. O. Box 30016

Lansing, MI 48909

517 241-9380, Fax: 517 241-9379, TDD in Lansing: 517 322-5987

Workers' Compensation Appellate Commission—www.cis.state.mi.us/wkr-comp/wcac/home.htm

Victor Office Center, Third Floor

201 North Washington Square

P. O. Box 30468

Lansing, MI 48909-7968

517 335-5828, Fax: 517 335-5829

Michigan Economic Development Corporation—medc.michigan.org/

300 North Washington Square

Lansing, MI 48913

517 373-9808

Michigan Business Guide to Workers' Compensation

medc.michigan.org/services/workerscomp

Compensation Cost Control Service

Victor Office Center, Fourth Floor

201 North Washington Square

Lansing, MI 48909-7968

517 373-9809, Fax: 517 241-3689

**Minnesota**

State of Minnesota—www.state.mn.us

Department of Labor and Industry—www.doli.state.mn.us

443 Lafayette Road North

St. Paul, MN 55155-4307

800 DIAL-DLI (342-5354), 651 284-5005; TTY: 651 297-4198

Workers' Compensation Division—www.doli.state.mn.us/workcomp.html

443 Lafayette Road North

St. Paul, MN 55155

800 DIAL-DLI (342-5354) in Greater Minnesota, 651 284-5005 in the St. Paul area, 800 365-4584 or 218 733-7810 in the Duluth area; Fax: 651 284-5727

E-mail: DLI.Workcomp@state.mn.us

Download free fillable PDF versions of Minnesota workers' compensation forms courtesy of Interface Technologies—www.interfacetec.com

Workers' Compensation Court of Appeals—www.workerscomp.state.mn.us

405 Minnesota Judicial Center

25 Dr. Martin Luther King Jr. Boulevard

St. Paul, MN 55155

651 296-6526, Fax: 651 297-2520, TTY/TDD: 800 627-3529

**Mississippi**

State of Mississippi—www.state.ms.us/its/msportal.nsf?Open

Mississippi Workers' Compensation Commission—www.mwcc.state.ms.us

Street Address:

1428 Lakeland Drive

Jackson, MS 39216

Mailing Address:

P. O. Box 5300

Jackson, MS 39296-5300

   601 987-4200, Fraud: 601 359-4250

## Missouri

State of Missouri—www.state.mo.us

Department of Labor and Industrial
   Relations—
   www.dolir.missouri.gov/index.htm

Street Address:

3315 West Truman Boulevard, Room 213

Jefferson City, MO 65102

Mailing Address:

P. O. Box 504

Jefferson City, MO 65102-0504

   573 751-9691, Fax: 573 751-4135

Division of Workers' Compensation—
   www.dolir.state.mo.us/wc/index.htm

Street Address:

3315 West Truman Boulevard, Room 131

Jefferson City, MO 65102

Mailing Address:

P. O. Box 58

Jefferson City, MO 65102-0058

   573 751-4231, Fax: 573 751-2012, Employee
   Hotline: 800 775-2667, Employer Hotline:
   888 837-6069, Fraud and Noncompliance:
   800-592-6003, 573-526-6630, Workers' Safety
   Program: 573 526-3504

E-mail: Workerscomp@dolir.mo.gov

Download free fillable PDF versions of
   Missouri workers' compensation forms
   courtesy of Interface Technologies—
   www.interfacetec.com

Labor and Industrial Relations Commission—
   www.dolir.state.mo.us/lirc/index.htm

3315 West Truman Boulevard

Jefferson City, MO 65102

   or

P. O. Box 599

Jefferson City, MO 65102-0599

   573 751-2461, Fax: 573 751-7806

## Montana

State of Montana—www.state.mt.us

Montana State Fund—www.montanastate-
   fund.com

Street Address:

5 South Last Chance Gulch

Helena, MT 59601

Mailing Address:

P. O. Box 4759

Helena, MT 59604-4759

406 444-6500, Claim Reporting/Customer
   Service: 800 332-6102, Fraud Reporting: 888
   682-7463

Workers' Compensation Court—
   wcc.dli.state.mt.us

1625 11th Avenue

Helena, Montana

   or

P. O. Box 537

Helena, MT 59624-0537

406 444-7794, Fax: 406 444-7798

E-mail: pkessner@state.mt.us

Employment Relations Division—
   erd.dli.state.mt.us

Department of Labor & Industry—
   dli.state.mt.us

P. O. Box 8011

Helena, MT 59624

406 444-6530, Fax: 406 444-4140, Fraud: 800
   922-2873

Self Insurers' Guaranty Fund

P. O. Box 4133

Missoula, MT 59806

406 549-8849

## Nebraska

State of Nebraska—www.state.ne.us

Workers' Compensation Court—
www.nol.org/home/WC
State House, 13th Floor
P. O. Box 98908
Lincoln, NE 68509-8908
800 599-5155 (in Nebraska only), 402 471-6468
(Lincoln and out of state), Fax: 402 471-2700

## Nevada

State of Nevada—www.nv.gov
Department of Business & Industry—
dbi.state.nv.us
In Northern Nevada:
788 Fairview Avenue, Suite 100
Carson City, NV 89701-5491
775 687-4250, Fax: 775 687-4266
E-Mail: biinfo@dbi.state.nv.us
In Southern Nevada:
555 E. Washington Avenue, Suite 4900
Las Vegas, NV 89101
702 486-2750, Fax: 702 486-2758
E-Mail: biinfo@dbi.state.nv.us
Division of Industrial Relations—
dirweb.state.nv.us
400 West King Street, Suite 400
Carson City, NV 89703
775 684-7260, Fax: 775 687-6305
Industrial Insurance Regulation Section—
dirweb.state.nv.us/iirs.htm
400 West King Street, Suite 400
Carson City, NV 89703
775 684-7270, Fax: 775 687-6305
1301 North Green Valley Parkway, Suite 200
Henderson, NV 89014
702 486-9080, Fax: 702 990-0364
Nevada Attorney for Injured Workers—
naiw.nv.gov
555 E. Washington Avenue, Suite 4800
Las Vegas, NV 89101

702 486-2830, Fax: 702 486-2844
E-mail: NAIW@govmail.state.nv.us
1000 East William Street, Suite 213
Carson City, NV 89710
775 687-4076, Fax: 775 687-4134
E-mail: NAIW@govmail.state.nv.us
Employers Insurance Company of Nevada—
www.employersinsco.com
9790 Gateway Drive, Suite 100
Reno, NV 89521
2550 Paseo Verde Parkway
Henderson, NV 89074-7117
888 682-6671; Claim Reporting: 888 900-1455,
Fax: 888 527-3422; Underwriting/Insurance
Services: 888 682-6671
E-mail: info@eigwc.com

## New Hampshire

State of New Hampshire—www.state.nh.us
Department of Labor—
www.state.nh.us/dol/index.html
95 Pleasant Street
Concord, NH 03301
603 271-3177
Workers' Compensation Division—
www.state.nh.us/dol/wc/index.html
95 Pleasant Street
Concord, NH 03301
603 271-3174 (claims), 603 271-2042 (coverage), 603 271-6172 (self-insurance), 603 271-
3328 (vocational rehabilitation)
Download free fillable PDF versions of New
Hampshire workers' compensation forms
courtesy of Interface Technologies—
www.interfacetec.com

## New Jersey

State of New Jersey—www.state.nj.us
Department of Labor—www.state.nj.us/labor
John Fitch Plaza

P. O. Box 110
Trenton, NJ 08625
609 292-2323, Fax: 609 633-9271
Division of Workers' Compensation—
www.nj.gov/labor/wc/wcindex.html
P. O. Box 381
Trenton, NJ 08625-0381
609 292-2515, Fax: 609 984-2515
E-mail: dwc@dol.state.nj.us
Download free fillable PDF versions of New
Jersey workers' compensation forms courtesy
of Interface Technologies—www.inter-
facetec.com
N.J. Compensation Rating and Inspection
Bureau—www.njcrib.com
60 Park Place
Newark, NJ 07102
973 622-6014, Fax: 973 622-6110

## New Mexico

State of New Mexico—www.state.nm.us
Workers' Compensation Administration—
www.state.nm.us/wca
P. O. Box 27198
Albuquerque, NM 87125-7198
E-mail: WCAHotline@state.nm.us
800 255-7965, 505 841-6000, Fax: 505 841-
6009, Help Line/Hot Line: 866 WORKOMP
(967-5667)

## New York

State of New York—www.state.ny.us
New York State Workers' Compensation
Board—www.wcb.state.ny.us
100 Broadway-Menands
Albany, NY 12241
518 474-6670, Fax: 518 473-1415
Download free fillable PDF versions of New
York workers' compensation forms courtesy
of Interface Technologies—www.inter-

facetec.com
New York State Insurance Fund—
www.nysif.com
199 Church Street
New York, NY 10007
212 312-9000, Fax: 212 385-2073

## North Carolina

State of North Carolina—www.sips.state.nc.us
Department of Commerce—
www.nccommerce.com
Mailing Address:
4301 Mail Service Center
Raleigh, NC 27699-4301
Street Address:
301 North Wilmington Street
Raleigh, NC 27020-0571
919 733-4151
E-mail: info@mail.commerce.state.nc.us
North Carolina Industrial Commission—
www.comp.state.nc.us
Mailing Address:
4319 Mail Service Center
Raleigh, NC 27699-4319
Street Address:
Dobbs Building (sixth floor)
430 North Salisbury Street
Raleigh, NC 27603-5937
919 807-2500, Fax: 919 715-0282
Fraud Investigations Section: 888 891-4895 in
North Carolina)—
www.comp.state.nc.us/ncic/pages/fraud.htm
Ombudsman Section: 800 688-8349—
www.comp.state.nc.us/ncic/pages/ombudsmn.
htm
Safety Education Section: 919 807-2603—
www.comp.state.nc.us/ncic/pages/safety.htm
Download free fillable PDF versions of North
Carolina workers' compensation forms cour-

tesy of Interface Technologies—www.inter-
facetec.com

### North Dakota

State of North Dakota—discovernd.com

Workforce Safety & Insurance—
www.WorkforceSafety.com

1600 East Century Avenue, Suite One

Bismarck, ND 58506-5585

800 777-5033, 701 328-3800; Fax: 701 328-
3820; Fraud: 800 243-3331; Safety and Loss
Prevention: 701 328-3886; TDD: 701 328-
3786

E-mail: WorkforceSafety@wcb.state.nd.us

Workforce Safety & Insurance Board of
Directors

P. O. Box 2174

Bismarck, ND 58502-2174

### Ohio

State of Ohio—www.state.oh.us

Ohio Bureau of Workers' Compensation—
www.ohiobwc.com

30 West Spring Street

Columbus, OH 43215-2256

E-mail: Feedback@bwc.state.oh.us

800 OHIOBWC, 614 644-6292, Fax: 614 752-
9021

Download free fillable PDF versions of Ohio
workers' compensation forms courtesy of
Interface Technologies—
www.interfacetec.com

Industrial Commission of Ohio—
www.ohioic.com/index.jsp

30 West Spring Street

Columbus, OH 43215-2256

800 521-2691, 614 466-6136, Fax: 614 752-
8304

### Oklahoma

State of Oklahoma—www.state.ok.us

Department of Labor—www.okdol.state.ok.us

4001 North Lincoln Boulevard

Oklahoma City, OK 73105-5212

888 269-5353, 405 528-1500 Fax: 405 528-5751

Workers' Enforcement Compensation
Division—www.okdol.state.ok.us/work-
comp/index.htm

Oklahoma Workers' Compensation Court—
www.owcc.state.ok.us

Denver N. Davison Court Building

1915 North Stiles

Oklahoma City, OK 73105

800 522-8210 (statewide), 405 522-8600, Fax:
405 522-8687 (administration), 405 522-
8683 (2nd floor offices), 405 522-8651
(records department)

CompSource Oklahoma—
www.compsourceok.com
(formerly the Oklahoma State Insurance
Fund)

Mailing Address:

P. O. Box 53505

Oklahoma City, OK 73152-3505

Street Addresses:

(Administration, Claims, Financial Services,
Special Investigations)

1901 North Walnut Avenue

Oklahoma City, OK 73105

(Policyholder Services, Information Systems)

410 North Walnut Avenue

Oklahoma City, OK 73104

800 872-7015 (Report an Injury), 405 232-
7663, Fax: 405 552-5800, Fraud: 800 899-
1847

## Oregon

State of Oregon—www.state.or.us

Department of Consumer & Business
Services—www.cbs.state.or.us
350 Winter Street NE
Salem, OR 97301-3878
503 378-4100, Fax: 503 378-6444

Workers' Compensation Division—wcd.oregon.gov
350 Winter Street NE, Room 27
Salem, OR 97301-3879
800 452-0288 (Workers' Compensation
Infoline); 503 947-7810, Fax: 503 947-7514;
TTY: 503 947-7993; Fraud Hotline: 800 422-8778 (in Oregon); Small Business
Ombudsman: 503 378-4209, Fax: 503 373-7639; Ombudsman for Injured Workers: 800
927-1271, 503 378-3351, Fax: 503 373-7639

Workers' Compensation Board—
www.cbs.state.or.us/wcb
2601 25th Street SE, Suite 150
Salem, OR 97302-1282
503 378-3308

Workers' Compensation Management-Labor
Advisory Committee—
www.cbs.state.or.us/mlac

Department of Consumer & Business Services
350 Winter Street, Room 200
Salem, OR 97301-3878
503 947-7867; Fax: 503 378-6444

Ombudsman for Injured Workers—
www.cbs.state.or.us/external/wco/index.html
350 Winter Street NE, Room 160
Salem, OR 97310
800 927-1271, 503 378-3351

Ombudsman for Small Business—
www.cbs.state.or.us/external/sbo/index.html
350 Winter Street NE

Salem, OR 97301-3878
503 378-4209, V/TTY: 503 378-4100

SAIF Corporation—www.saif.com
400 High Street SE
Salem, OR 97312-1000
800 285-8525, 503 373-8000

## Pennsylvania

State of Pennsylvania—www.state.pa.us/

Department of Labor and Industry—
www.dli.state.pa.us/
Labor & Industry Building
Room 1700
7th and Forster Streets
Harrisburg, PA 17120
717 787-5279

Bureau of Workers' Compensation—
www.dli.state.pa.us/landi/cwp/view.asp?a=13
8&Q=58929&landiPNav=|#1026
1171 South Cameron Street, Room 324
Harrisburg, PA 17104-2501
800 482-2383 (inside Pennsylvania), 717 772-4447 (local/out of state), TTY: 800 362-4228
(for hearing and speech impaired only)
E-mail: ra-li-bwc-helpline@state.pa.us
Download free fillable PDF versions of
Pennsylvania workers' compensation forms
courtesy of Interface Technologies—
www.interfacetec.com/

State Workers' Insurance Fund—
www.dli.state.pa.us/landi/cwp/view.asp?a=15
1&Q=58236&landiNavDLTEST=|852|1065|2
548|
100 Lackawanna Avenue
Scranton, PA 18503
570 963-4635

Workers' Compensation Appeal Board
1171 South Cameron Street, Room 305
Harrisburg, PA 17104-2511
717 783-7838

## Rhode Island

State of Rhode Island—www.state.ri.us
Workers' Compensation Court—
www.courts.state.ri.us/workers/defaultnew-
workers.htm
One Dorrance Plaza
Providence, RI 02903
401 458-5000, Fax: 401 222-3121
Department of Labor and Training—
www.dlt.ri.gov
1511 Pontiac Avenue
Cranston, RI 02920-4407
401 462-8000
Workers' Compensation Division—
www.dlt.ri.gov/wc
Street Address:
1511 Pontiac Avenue, Building 69, Second
Floor
Cranston, RI 02920-0942
Mailing Address:
P. O. Box 20190
Cranston, RI 02920-0190
401 462-8100, Fax: 401 462-8105, TDD: 401
462-8006
Download free fillable PDF versions of Rhode
Island workers' compensation forms cour-
tesy of Interface Technologies—www.inter-
facetec.com

## South Carolina

State of South Carolina—www.myscgov.com
Workers' Compensation Commission—
www.wcc.state.sc.us
Street Address:
1612 Marion Street
Columbia, SC 29201
Mailing Address:
P. O. Box 1715
Columbia, SC 29202-1715

803 737-5700, Fax: 803 737-5768
Download free fillable PDF versions of South
Carolina workers' compensation forms cour-
tesy of Interface Technologies—www.inter-
facetec.com
South Carolina State Accident Fund—
www.myscgov.com/scoa
Street Address:
800 Dutch Square Boulevard
Columbia, SC 29221
Mailing Address:
P. O. Box 102100
Columbia, SC 29221-5000
800 521-6576, 803 896-5800
South Carolina Second Injury Fund
22 Koger Center
Winthrop Building, Suite 119220
Executive Center Drive
Columbia, SC 29210
803 798-2722, Fax: 803 798-5290
South Carolina Workers' Compensation
Uninsured Employers' Fund
22 Koger Center
Winthrop Building, Suite 119220
Executive Center Drive
Columbia, SC 29210
803 798-2722, Fax: 803 798-5290

## South Dakota

State of South Dakota—www.state.sd.us
Department of Labor—
www.state.sd.us/dol/dol.asp
Division of Labor and Management—
www.state.sd.us/dol/dlm/dlm-home.htm
Kneip Building, Third Floor
700 Governors Drive
Pierre, SD 57501-2291
E-mail: labor@dol-pr.state.sd.us
605 773-3681, Fax: 605 773-4211

## Tennessee

State of Tennessee—www.state.tn.us

Department of Labor and Workforce
  Development—www.state.tn.us/labor-wfd

Workers' Compensation Division—
  www.state.tn.us/labor-wfd/wcomp.html

710 James Robertson Parkway

Gateway Plaza, Second Floor

Nashville, TN 37243-0665

800 332-2667 (within Tennessee), 615 532-
  4812, Fax: 615 532-1468

Download free fillable PDF versions of
  Tennessee workers' compensation forms
  courtesy of Interface Technologies—
  www.interfacetec.com

## Texas

State of Texas—www.state.tx.us

Texas Workers' Compensation Commission
  (TWCC)—www.twcc.state.tx.us

7551 Metro Center Drive, Suite 100

Austin, TX 78744-1609

512 804-4000, Commissioners: 512 804-4435
  fax: 512 804-4431, Customer
  Relations/Services: 512 804-4100 or 804-
  4636, Fax: 512 804-4001, Fraud Hotline: 512
  804-4703, Injured Worker
  Hotline/Ombudsman: 800 252-7031, Safety
  Violations Hotline: 800 452-9595

Download free fillable PDF versions of Texas
  workers' compensation forms courtesy of
  Interface Technologies—
  www.interfacetec.com

## Utah

State of Utah—www.state.ut.us

Industrial Commission of Utah—www.ind-
  com.state.ut.us

Industrial Accidents Division—www.ind-

com.state.ut.us/indacc.htm

P. O. Box 146610

Salt Lake City, UT 84114-6610

801 530-6800, Fax: 801 530-6804

Workers' Compensation Fund of Utah—
  www.wcf-utah.com

Salt Lake City Office

392 East 6400 South

Murray, UT 84107

800 446-2667

## Vermont

State of Vermont—www.state.vt.us

Department of Labor & Industry—
  www.state.vt.us/labind

National Life Building

Drawer 20

Montpelier, VT 05620-3401

802 828-2288, Fax: 802 828-2195

Workers' Compensation Division—
  www.state.vt.us/labind/wcindex.htm

National Life Building

Drawer 20

Montpelier, VT 05620-3401

802 828-2286, Fax: 802 828-2195

Download free fillable PDF versions of
  Vermont workers' compensation forms courtesy of Interface Technologies—www.inter-
  facetec.com

## Virginia

Commonwealth of Virginia—
  www.virginia.gov/cmsportal

Virginia Workers' Compensation
  Commission—www.vwc.state.va.us

1000 DMV Drive

Richmond, VA 23220
  877 664-2566, Fax: 804 367-9740, TDD: 804
  367-8600

E-mail: Questions@vwc.state.va.us

Download free fillable PDF versions of Virginia workers' compensation forms courtesy of Interface Technologies— www.interfacetec.com

## Washington

State of Washington—access.wa.gov

Department of Labor and Industries— www.lni.wa.gov

Labor and Industries Building

P. O. Box 44001

Olympia, WA 98504-4001
800 547-8367, 360 902-4200, Fax: 360 902-4202

Board of Industrial Insurance Appeals— www.biia.wa.gov

Street Address:

2430 Chandler Court, SW

Olympia, WA 98504-2401

Mailing Address:

P. O. Box 42401

Olympia, WA 98504-2401

800 442-0447, 360 753-9646, Fax: 360 586-5611

Download free fillable PDF versions of Washington workers' compensation forms courtesy of Interface Technologies— www.interfacetec.com

Workers' Compensation Information— www.lni.wa.gov/ClaimsInsurance/ClaimsAppeals/GetClaimInfo/default.asp

## West Virginia

West Virginia—www.wv.gov

Workers' Compensation Commission— www.wvwcc.org

Mailing Address:

P. O. Box 3824

Charleston, WV 25338-3824

Street Address:

4700 MacCorkle Avenue, SE

Charleston, WV 25304
800 628-4265, 304 926-5060, Fax: 304 926-5372, Fraud: 800 779-6853 or lprater@wvbep.org

Workers' Compensation Commission Board of Managers

Workers' Compensation Office of Judges— www.wvwcc.org/ooj

Mailing Address:

P. O. Box 2233

Charleston WV 25328-2233

Street Address:

One Players Club Drive

Charleston West Virginia 25311

304 558-1686, Fax: 304 558-1021

Workers' Compensation Board of Review— www.state.wv.us/bep/AppBd

Mailing Address:

P. O. Box 2628

Charleston, WV 25329-2628

Street Address:

104 Dee Drive

Charleston, WV 25301

304 558-5230, Fax: 304 558-1322

## Wisconsin

State of Wisconsin— www.wisconsin.gov/state/home

Department of Workforce Development— www.dwd.state.wi.us

Workers' Compensation Division— www.dwd.state.wi.us/wc/default.htm

Mailing Address:

P. O. Box 7901

Madison, Wisconsin 53707-7901

Street Address:

Room C100

201 East Washington Avenue

Madison, WI 53703

608 266-1340; Fax: 608 267-0394; Fraud 608
  261-8486

Download free fillable PDF versions of
  Wisconsin workers' compensation forms
  courtesy of Interface Technologies—
  www.interfacetec.com

Workers' Compensation Advisory Council—
  www.dwd.state.wi.us/notespub/wcadvcou

608 266-6841

Wisconsin Compensation Rating Bureau—
  www.wcrb.org

Mailing Address:

P. O. Box 3080

Milwaukee, WI 53201-3080

Street Address:

20700 Swenson Drive, Suite 100

Waukesha, Wisconsin 53186

262 796-4540, Fax: 262 796-4400

Wisconsin Labor and Industry Review
  Commission—www.dwd.state.wi.us/lirc

Mailing Address:

P. O. Box 8126

Madison, WI 53708-8126

Street Address:

Wisconsin Public Broadcasting Building

3319 West Beltline Highway

Madison, WI 53713

608 266-9850 Fax: 608 267-4409

E-mail: dwdlirc@dwd.state.wi.us

**Wyoming**

State of Wyoming—www.state.wy.us

Department of Employment—
  wydoe.state.wy.us

Cheyenne Business Center

1510 East Pershing Boulevard

Cheyenne, WY 82002

307 777-7672, Fax: 307 777-5805

 Cindy Pomeroy, Director, 307 777-5960,
  CPOMER@state.wy.us

Charles Rando, Administrator, 307 777-6370,
  CRANDO@state.wy.us

Workers' Safety and Compensation Division—
  wydoe.state.wy.us/doe.asp?ID=9

Cheyenne Business Center

1510 East Pershing Boulevard

Cheyenne, WY 82002

307 777-7159, Fax: 307 777-5524.

To Report an Injury: 800 870-8883 or 307 777-
  7441, Fax: 307 777-6552.

To Report Fraud: 888 996-9226 or 307 777-
  6552, Fax: 307 777-3581.

Gary Child, Administrator, 307 777-7159, Fax:
  307 777-5524, GCHILD@state.wy.us

Employment Tax Division—
  wydoe.state.wy.us/doe.asp?ID=10

P. O. Box 2760

Casper, WY 82602-2760

307 235-3201 (Casper) or 307 777-7471
  (Cheyenne)

# Major Insurance Company Rating Services

**A.M. Best Company**
Ambest Road
Oldwick, NY 08858-9988
Telephone: 908 439-2200
www.ambest.com

**Demotech**
2941 Donnylane Boulevard
Columbus, OH 43235-3228
Telephone: 800 354-7207
www.demotech.com

**Moody's Investors Service**
99 Church Street
New York, NY 10007
Telephone: 212 553-1658
www.moodys.com

**Standard & Poor's**
55 Water Street
New York, NY 10041
Telephone: 212 438-7200
www.standardandpoors.com

**Weiss Ratings**
15430 Endeavour Drive
Jupiter, FL 33478
Telephone: 800 289-9222
www.weissratings.com

## Independent Safety Consultants

**Broadspire Services, Inc./NATLSCO**
4 Corporate Drive, Suite 100
Lake Zurich, IL 60047
Telephone: 847 719-5376
www.choosebroadspire.com

**Clayton Group Services**
45525 Grand River Avenue, Suite 200
Novi, MI 48734
Telephone: 248 344-8577
www.claytongrp.com

**FARA (F.A. Richard & Associates, Inc.)**
1625 W. Causeway Approach
Mandeville, LA 70471

Telephone: 800 259-8388
www.fara.com

**Gage-Babcock & Associates**
5175 Parkstone Drive, Suite 130
Chantilly, VA 20151-3816
Telephone: 703 263-7110
www.gagebabcock.com

**National Safety Council**
1121 Spring Lake Drive
Itasca, IL 60143-3201
Telephone: 630 285-1121
www.nsc.org

**North American Risk Management, Inc.**
100 First Avenue South, #266
St. Petersburg, FL 33701
Telephone: 727 287-1565
www.narm.biz

**Regional Reporting, Inc.**
40 Fulton Street, 20th Floor
New York, NY 10038
Telephone: 212 964-5973
www.regionalreporting.com

**Risk Consultants, Inc.**
PO Box 490850
Atlanta, GA 30349
Telephone: 770 964-1226
www.riskcon.com

**Safety Resources, LLC**
239 New Road, Building C
Parsippany, NJ 07054
Telephone: 973 575-0900
www.safetyresc.com

**Strategic Safety Associates, Inc.**
PO Box 80161
Portland, OR 97280-1161

Telephone: 503 977-2094
www.ssafety.net

## Government Resources

**American Federation of Labor-Congress of Industrial Organizations (AFL-CIO)**
815 16th St., N.W.
Washington, D.C. 20006
www.aflcio.org

**American Insurance Association**
1130 Connecticut Ave, NW, Ste. 1000
Washington, DC 20036
Telephone: 202 828-7100
Fax: 202 293-1219
www.aiadc.org

**Bureau of Labor Statistics**
2 Massachusetts Ave., NE
Washington, DC 20212-0001
Telephone: 202 691-5200
Fax-on-demand: 202 691-6325
www.bls.gov

**Centers for Disease Control and Prevention**
1600 Clifton Rd
Atlanta, GA 30333
Telephone: 404 639-3311
Public Inquiries: 404 639-3534
www.cdc.gov

**The Center to Protect Workers' Rights**
8484 Georgia Avenue, Suite 1000
Silver Spring, MD 20910
Telephone: 301 578-8500
Fax:301 578-8572
www.cpwr.com

**The Injured Workers' Alliance**
9205 SE Clackamas Rd, PMB 6

Clackamas, Oregon 97015-9657
www.injuredworker.org

**The Insurance Information Institute**
110 William Street
New York, NY 10038
Telephone: 212 346-5500
www.iii.org

**International Association of Industrial Accident Boards and Commissions**
5610 Medical Circle, Suite 24
Madison, Wisconsin 53719
Telephone : 608 663-6355
Fax : 608 663-1546
www.iaiabc.org

**National Academy of Social Insurance**
1776 Massachusetts Avenue, NW
Suite 615
Washington, DC 20036
Telephone: 202 452-8097
Fax: 202 452-8111
www.nasi.org

**National Association of Insurance Commissioners**
2301 McGee Street
Suite 800
Kansas City, MO 64108-2662
Telephone: 816 842-3600
Fax: 816 783-8175
www.naic.org

**National Institute for Occupational Safety and Health**
Hubert H. Humphrey Bldg.
200 Independence Ave., SW
Room 715H
Washington, DC 20201
Telephone: 800-35-NIOSH (800-356-4674)
Fax-on-demand: 888 232-3299

www.cdc.gov/niosh/

**Occupational Safety and Health Administration**
200 Constitution Avenue, NW
Washington, DC 20210
www.osha.gov

**Strategic Services on Unemployment and Workers' Compensation**
1331 Pennsylvania Avenue NW
Suite 600
Washington, D.C. 20004
Telephone: 202 637-3463
www.UWCstrategy.org

**U.S. Census Bureau**
4700 Silver Hill Road
Washington, DC 20233-0001
www.census.gov

## Internet Resources

**www.abanet.org/disability**
American Bar Association Disability Web Board

**www.comp.state.nc.us/ncic/pages/all50.htm**
Includes links to all state agencies that administer workers' compensation claims matters.

**www.cutcomp.com**
Includes updated news and information about the latest developments that affect your workers' compensation insurance.

**dmoz.org/Business/Human_Resources/**
The Open Directory Project listing of Human Resources links.

**www.dol.gov/esa/regs/statutes/owcp/stwclaw/stw claw.htm**
State workers' compensation benefit tables from the Department of Labor.

# Avoiding Criminal Liability

THERE IS A GROWING TREND IN MANY U.S. jurisdictions to seek criminal prosecutions over what amount to disputes about workers' compensation coverage and premium. Employers (and even insurance producers) need to be aware of these evolving standards. Behavior that might once have been considered to be just "standard business practice" could now expose you to criminal charges.

If you do an internet search for news relating to workers' compensation insurance, as I do every day, you will see an increasing number of stories concerning prosecutions of business owners over workers' compensation insurance. As someone who often serves as an expert witness in court cases on this subject, I supposed I should be grateful for the job security that this trend may represent. But in all seriousness, this is an area where employers and even agents need to review

their usual business practices because prosecutors now see behavior that was once just between an employer, the agent, and the insurer as potentially criminal in nature.

States are becoming more vigilant about discovering and punishing employers that should be purchasing workers' compensation insurance but aren't. Once upon a time this may have been viewed in many jurisdictions as a relatively low-priority matter, but this is definitely changing in states like California and Florida, among others. States have become very concerned that employers who don't carry workers' compensation insurance (but should under the applicable state laws) are enjoying a significant unfair advantage over their competitors who play by the rules. Such delinquencies are also leaving workers exposed to workplace risks without insurance coverage. And so enforcement activities are up dramatically in recent years.

More than ever, employers need to know if their state requires them to have workers' compensation insurance in place and if so to make sure there is valid coverage in place. Otherwise, the state may shut down the company's operations, levy fines and penalties, or (in high profile egregious cases) press criminal charges.

Even if you have workers' compensation insurance, you need to make sure it covers all states where you have operations. Florida officials in particular are very vigilant about making sure construction-related companies have workers' compensation insurance that specifically covers their state.

## INFORMATION PROVIDED TO INSURANCE COMPANIES

Employers also need to be very careful about what information they provide to the insurance company or the rating bureau about their workplace operations and payroll estimates. If an insurance company feels that any information was deliberately and fraudulently misleading, it might refer the matter for criminal prosecution. And prosecutors are increasingly interested in pursuing such charges.

In the past, some employers apparently have felt it was acceptable to be less than exact when describing the work done by some of their employees or how their payroll is distributed over various kinds of work. Once upon a time, this might have been viewed by some as just sharp business practice, doing unto the insurance companies what many employers always suspected the insurance companies did to them. Fudging some information to insurance companies to hold down insurance costs is a fairly

widespread practice, according to some insurance industry estimates. Maybe someone you know has reduced auto insurance premiums for their kid by claiming that a car that's really drive by the younger driver is really driven most of the time by someone else in the family. Or maybe you've downplayed the miles driven for work when your insurance agent asks.

Practicing similar dishonest behavior when it comes to workers' compensation insurance has been a long-standing tool of some business people, I fear, but it's one that runs an increasing chance of creating serious legal problems for them. Worse, innocent employers may get caught up by the increased enforcement activities and find themselves facing potential criminal liability over bad estimates of payroll or sloppy information about the work being done.

## FRAUD AND THE POSSIBILITY OF PROSECUTION

Earlier sections of this book have detailed how workers' compensation insurance premiums are based on particular classifications that carry rates per hundred dollars of payroll. Since the actual payrolls that will be paid during a future year can't be known in advance but only projected and estimated, the going-in premium for workers' compensation insurance is always an estimate, subject to later revision by audit. But suppose your estimate of exposures is severely off the mark, so that the insurance company feels you're trying to cheat. Not only may the company file civil suit to recover money it believes is owed, the company just might try to get criminal charges filed against you for what some prosecutors feel is fraud.

In just about every state, workers' compensation fraud is now a felony. And workers' compensation insurance fraud isn't just the filing of false claims by workers—it's also any deliberate action by an employer to deceive its insurer about the facts that determine workers' compensation insurance premiums. Sometimes even innocent errors on the part of an employer can be seen by others as a deliberate attempt to provide false information—in other words, fraud.

If your company is of a sort that the insurance industry views with suspicion from the outset, such as a temporary agency or an employee leasing company, innocent errors on your part may be more likely interpreted as deliberate fraud. However, any employer can have exposure to this problem. So it pays to be very careful and exacting when providing information to your insurance company and/or rating bureau that acts in its stead.

When estimating payrolls and classifications on an insurance application, always review recent past years' audits to make sure your estimates are consistent with these. If you really feel that your estimates need to be different from these, make sure you explain fully why these changes are reasonable. Keep your own file with documentation about the basis of your estimates. Then, if a question arises years later, you can provide credible answers about the process you went through.

Do not let your insurance agent or broker complete the application for you, or at least review what has been put down very carefully before signing. Any shortcuts or unreasonable estimates that the agent or broker includes on your application may later be held against you.

If your company does work with governmental entities, use particular care and caution. A prosecutor seeking to work his or her way up the food chain to get a high-profile political target might decide to try to further that agenda by charging a private firm that is viewed as being "politically connected."

To protect yourself and your firm from such accusations, be thorough in presenting information to your insurance company about the nature of your work, your payrolls, and anything else that they feel is pertinent to calculating your workers' compensation premiums. Document your cooperation with any requests for information or access to company personnel.

Remember, if a prosecutor decides to seek criminal charges against you regarding workers' compensation premiums, everyday acts of normal business can be construed as being violations of the law. Sending information via fax, for instance, that is alleged to be deliberately inaccurate can be characterized as wire fraud. Providing inaccurate estimates of payrolls or classifications on the insurance application that is mailed to the insurance company can be alleged to be mail fraud.

Today, fortunately, most employers will never have to worry about these matters. Inaccuracies in estimating payrolls or classifications are routinely caught and corrected by the insurance industry. Sometimes insurers make their own mistakes in these areas, because of the complexities of the system. But most of the time, the insurance industry is very vigilant about catching mistakes that cost them money, though not always.

The key elements that an employer needs to be careful about are:

- Reasonable payroll projections and estimates
- Accurate descriptions of your operations

that affect the classifications and rates used

- Accurate and complete information about ownership of your company that may affect experience rating that applies
- Timely notification to the insurer about changes in operations, ownership, or payrolls

## USE OF CONSULTANTS

Much of the focus of this book has been to educate employers about how they can protect themselves against insurance industry mistakes that increase premiums. And certainly employers need to be very vigilant about this, as my experience in the field has proven that such mistakes are common and costly. But employers also need to be wary of pursuing any premium reductions or refunds that aren't truly warranted. The field I work in, workers' compensation premium review, is unlicensed and unregulated at the moment. A good consultant may well save you thousands of dollars. An unscrupulous or unethical consultant might end up involving your firm in what some would view as premium fraud. Fortunately, most practitioners in this field that I know of are ethical and honest. But there have been instances of some consulting firms seeking refunds that were not truly warranted under the rules. So employers would be well advised to check references and credentials carefully when hiring a consultant to review workers' compensation premiums to make sure they are dealing with an experienced and ethical expert.

## COMPETITIVE BIDS

When dealing with competitive bids from differ-

ent insurance agents or brokers, an employer now has an added incentive to uncover any "low-ball" quotes, as potentially an insurer could later claim that an employer colluded with the agent/broker to defraud the insurer by providing fraudulent information about operations, classifications, or payrolls. So in competitive bidding situations, an employer should carefully review the underlying basis for any proposed workers' compensation insurance premiums to make sure the estimated payrolls, classifications, and experience modifiers are consistent with what's used on other proposals. You should carefully review radical deviations in any of these. You don't want to penalize an agent or broker who has figured out a legitimate change that reduces premiums, but you also don't want to be dealing with someone who is trying to game the system to get your business.

## THIS IS SERIOUS STUFF

If your initial response to this subject is to dismiss it as not being a reasonable concern, I would urge you to reconsider. I have personally seen people whom I believe to be innocent nonetheless found guilty in court of charges of perpetrating fraud by misrepresenting classifications and payrolls used to figure workers' compensation insurance premiums. The consequences of such a prosecution, whether those accused are found guilty or innocent, can be devastating. And having seen at close range how actions that were (I believe) innocent can be presented as being part of a criminal conspiracy, I would urge every employer and every insurance producer to look carefully at their own practices to make sure they are not leaving themselves open to similar legal problems.

# New Approaches in Workers' Compensation Insurance

IN RECENT YEARS, SOME INSURANCE COMPANIES have been getting creative in coming up with new ways of computing workers' compensation insurance premiums, particularly for larger employers. There can be advantages for employers in some of these programs, but also hidden potential pitfalls. Employers should always enter into these policies with their eyes wide open, at least as far as it is possible in the insurance relationship.

After all, buying insurance is never really done on a level playing field. The people selling the insurance almost always know the field better than even experienced and well-informed insurance purchasers. And so the relationship between buyer and seller is never one of equals— the seller almost invariably has significantly greater information than the purchaser about the product being sold.

## LARGE DEDUCTIBLES AND OTHER APPROACHES

In recent years many insurance companies have developed ways of computing workers' compensation insurance premiums that find ways to circumvent many of the traditional features of workers' compensation insurance pricing. They have done so by utilizing relatively new kinds of policies developed originally for use only with very large employers: large deductible plans and Large Risk Alternative Rating Options, or LRARO rating.

As mentioned earlier, large deductible plans establish that the employer is responsible for paying all claims up to certain set amount, such as $250,000. (The actual amount of the deductible can be lower or higher than this—this is just an example of a deductible limit.) And in return for accepting this deductible amount, the rates and premiums charged are heavily discounted.

However, some insurance companies have begun using these large deductible policies in a creative way to "emulate" guaranteed-cost policies that come up with pricing and rating formulas that don't follow the traditional rules. For example, I have seen some plans that use a large deductible policy but then sell the employer a separate policy that "buys back" the deductible for a specified rate times hundred dollars of payroll. Because such a 'buy back' policy is not technically a workers' compensation insurance policy, the insurer is free to come up with a rate and pricing formula that can radically differ from those approved for workers' compensation insurance policies.

For example, an employer operating in multiple states would normally be faced with different rates for each kind of work, and different rates for each state as well. It can get a little complex to project what your cost of workers' compensation insurance will be, as changes in the kind of work done or where it's done will alter the average rate of such a policy. The rate for widget manufacturing in Iowa might be $5.33 per hundred dollars of payroll, while the rate for the same work in Nebraska might be $4.21. And each of those rates would be adjusted by the experience modification factor and premium discount and schedule credits and debits, so that figuring out what your net rate actually is per hundred dollars of payroll can be tricky.

But by using the large deductible buy-back approach, an insurer can offer a very simple-to-understand composite net rate that applies no matter what kind of work is done, no matter what state it's done in. Under such a plan, an employer could know that workers compensa-

tion insurance will be billed at a rate of $5.25 per hundred dollars of payroll, and it doesn't matter what state the work is done in, nor whether the work falls under widget manufacturing, outside sales, clerical, or something else. It offers an employer a simple way of projecting what actual workers' compensation cost will be. And this can have powerful appeal to an employer that is tired of the complexities of traditional workers' compensation pricing.

But there is a price to be paid for such simplicity. These plans typically deprive an employer of some of the protections that have been developed over time for traditional workers' compensation insurance. For example, the "large deductible buy back" approach described above means that correcting mistakes in classification or experience modifier will no longer enable the employer to reduce premiums. Since the insurer has come up with a separate policy that really isn't a workers' compensation insurance policy as defined by regulators, the premium for that separate policy isn't regulated by the traditional rules and regulations.

Under such a plan, the insurance company has set a rate for your company based on certain projections about losses, payrolls, and classifications, but even if those assumptions are wrong the employer may have no recourse to reduce premiums. The upside to this situation is that the insurer doesn't have the ability to increase the rate either, but that is a limited benefit to the employer, as the insurance company will have been sure to build in an ample margin of error for itself in setting the rate. So the insurer is very confident of making a profit on the account, and the employer is deprived of important consumer protections that apply to the rates and premium of traditional workers' compensation insurance.

My advice to employers is to look long and hard at all alternatives available to such programs before accepting one. Remember the story Ronald Reagan used to tell about being wary of anyone who says, "We're from the government and we're here to help"? Well, I think similar advice needs to apply to commercial insurance as well. Always be careful when someone says, "We're from the insurance company and we have a great deal for you."

Another worrying aspect of these types of programs is that originally they were approved only for use by very large employers. But over time, the insurance industry has been steadily ratcheting downwards the size of employers who can be underwritten with these programs. So where once an employer needed to be running a million dollars or more of workers' compensation insurance premium before these plans could be offered, nowadays employers paying just several hundred thousand dollars of premium may be eligible in many states. The original theory was that these plans should be offered only to employers who were so large that they had considerable expertise and experience with workers' compensation insurance. That theory was always flawed of course, because even large employers are in an unequal contest with insurance companies and brokers, but it becomes even more suspect when these plans are being offered to much smaller employers.

So if your company is offered coverage through some complicated program using large deductibles or LRARO rating, a plan that involves multiple policies or side agreements, I strongly suggest you do a careful analysis of exactly how the pricing of the proposed plan

compares to that of a more traditional policy. You might even want to discuss the situation with your state's insurance regulators, and share a copy of the proposal with them before agreeing to it. It is not unheard of for an insurance company or broker to be offering an employer a plan of workers' compensation insurance that has not actually been approved for use in a particular state. There's a reason why the insurance company might be taking regulatory shortcuts, and it usually means that their rating plan has some feature to it that deprives an employer of some potential protections about how the premiums are calculated.

If what's being offered to you hasn't been approved, it doesn't mean that the coverage you would purchase would be invalid—the insurance companies are always careful to issue an actual policy that does conform to the rules. But it means that the insurance company may be figuring the premiums in a way that could work to your detriment, and you'll never even realize that you've been skinned.

## THE IDEA AND THE REALITY

The theory behind much of these new developments in workers compensation pricing is that competition will serve to hold down costs more effectively than old-fashioned regulation could. But that theory presupposes a market that is operating fairly efficiently and transparently, with both sides in the transaction having approximately equal information and bargaining position. Unfortunately, in the real world, those conditions just don't often apply when it comes to purchasing workers' compensation insurance.

For many employers, these nontraditional

premium plans are presented as a take-it-or-leave it proposition, with the only alternative being the assigned risk plan (which nowadays is particular unattractive for larger employers). The amount of genuine competition in the workers' compensation marketplace is greatly diminished because of recent mergers and the demise of a number of carriers who specialized in workers' compensation insurance.

The recent revelations about misconduct on the part of insurance brokers has also demonstrated that an employer may not be wise to rely on the advice of an insurance broker or insurance agent as being that of an impartial professional advisor. Even if a well known brokerage firm recommends a plan of insurance as being the best option for an employer, it may not be wise to accept that recommendation at face value.

Insurance regulators opened a Pandora's box when they started relying overmuch on market forces to control the cost of workers' compensation insurance. It's been a slippery slope, and now increasing numbers of employers may be offered workers' compensation programs that appear simple and straightforward when it comes to premiums, but that in fact deprive the employer of important protections that derive from some of the complex aspects of traditional workers' compensation rating rules. More than ever, the workers' compensation insurance buyer may want to beware apparently attractive shortcuts in pricing.

# Handling Workers' Compensation Injuries

**Make sure your supervisory people know what needs to be done when a workplace injury is reported to them**

- Aid the injured party. If the injury is serious, gets medical help as quickly as possible. Calls an ambulance if necessary. Make sure your people know what medical care providers are closest for emergency response. For less-urgent situations, work with your insurer to identify preferred local providers of medical care and make sure your people have this information.
- Accompany injured worker to medical treatment facility.
- Notify family of injured worker if injury is serious.
- Report incident to appropriate parties within your company.
- Assign responsible person within your company to follow up on claim.
- Reassure injured worker and family that proper insurance coverage is in place and that your firm will make sure that the insurance company responds appropriately to take care of worker. Let employee and family know who they should contact at your firm if there are any problems in dealing with the insurance company.
- Immediately complete an Employer's First Report of Injury or Illness. Make sure notice is provided to insurer on a timely basis.
- Take written statements from any witnesses to the injury and establish a file to maintain this documentation for later use by insurer.
- Determine if any other workers may have been exposed to blood or other bodily fluids due to workplace injury of another. Document this at time of occurrence and determine what state laws may apply regarding this workplace exposure and

any notification or testing requirements for these exposed workers. Make sure appropriate testing is done on a timely basis.

- Communicate closely with insurer to maximize positive outcome for worker and minimize possible negative treatment of worker by insurer.
- Make sure initial benefits are paid on a timely basis by insurer.
- Communicate closely with worker to identify any potential problems with the way the insurer is handling the matter and let the worker know about your efforts to address any problems.
- Consider obtaining independent medical evaluation if needed.
- Work with insurer to develop return to work and/or light duty work that may be available and appropriate for injured worker.
- Review cause of injury with safety personnel (both in-house and from insurer) to learn from the occurrence and make changes as appropriate to reduce future exposures.
- After proper care is provided to an injured worker, it is important to have procedures in place to gather the information that will be important in making sure the claim is handled properly. Here is the kind of information that needs to be gathered:

## About the worker
- Name—including nicknames, maiden name if female, previous names
- address—current and previous (including how long at each address)
- phone number, both home and cell
- social security and driver's license numbers
- gender
- date of birth

- marital status
- dependents and immediate family contact
- non-relative contact
- date of hire (state hired, if applicable)
- job classification, if applicable (insurance class or company classification)
- vehicle information—make, model, year
- interests and hobbies (these might have a bearing on some injuries that might be claimed as work related but are really caused by leisure time activities.)
- how long residing in the state

## About the injury
- date and time of location, where at workplace injury took place
- date of death (if applicable)
- state of injury
- nature of injury (sprain, fracture, etc.)
- body part(s) affected; any previous injury to the affected body part(s)
- source of injury (machines, hand tools, buildings, etc.)
- type of injury (fall, struck by object or vehicle, overexertion, repetitive motion trauma)
- witness information
- work process involved (lifting, carrying, etc.)
- to whom was the injury reported
- who filled out the first report of injury report
- when was injury first reported

## About the claim
- date notification given to employer
- who was notified, by whom
- date insurance company notified
- date state agency notified
- state case number
- average weekly wage
- benefit rate

- health care givers providing services
- costs of medical care provided
- other benefits lost (Did the employer stop paying vacation, health benefits, etc.?)
- other benefits received
- offset for other benefits
- date disability started
- date of first payment
- projected return-to-work date
- date case closed
- date of maximum medical improvement
- impairment rating
- lost days
- total benefits paid
- reserves set by insurer
- vocational rehabilitation activity
- possibility of subrogation (Is some third party responsible?)
- second injury fund potential

### Oral statement from injured worker

- make sure all interviews with worker done in a non-confrontational, non-adversarial manner
- make sure interviewer demonstrates concern and empathy with worker
- allow the worker to talk and make sure to listen
- reenact the accident with worker
- check for any photos and/or video of the accident that may exist

### Written statement from injured worker

- note the location where the statement is taken
- let the employee write the statement himself, when possible
- statement should be written in ink
- record statement as soon as possible after injury occurs

- make sure to note the workers pre-injury and post-injury actions
- get signatures of worker and any witnesses on the statement, if possible
- make sure the employee initials any changes made on statement
- leave a copy of the statement with worker
- make sure statement contains date and time it was taken

### Oral statement from witness(es)

- note witness' location at the time of injury
- record witness' relationship to the injured worker
- interview witnesses individuall
- make sure the statement is unrehearsed

### Written statement from witness(es)

- make sure the witness statement is recorded in ink
- record the witness statement as soon as possible after injury
- make sure the witness statement describes witness actions before, during, and after the injury
- make sure the witness signs the statement and initials any changes
- make sure statement includes date and time it was created
- leave a copy of the statement with the witness

### If litigation occurs

- note the defense attorney and law firm used by insurer
- note claimant attorney and law firm retained by worker
- document carefully the history of dispute
- keep informed of any settlement discussions. Make sure insurer does not settle disputed claims too readily, to your deriment.

# Operating a Safe Workplace

MOST OF THE BOOK FOCUSES ON actions employers can take to reduce workers' compensation insurance costs by spotting common mistakes made by the insurance industry that inflate premiums. But keep in mind that workplace safety is also a necessary part of any program to control the cost of workers' compensation insurance. As you've seen earlier in this book, there are direct mechanisms that tie the cost of workers' compensation insurance for most employers to their own company's past losses. The experience modification factor is the most well known and obvious such mechanism, but there are others as well. The simple truth is that controlling workplace safety is a very effective way to control your company's workers' compensation cost.

In the long run, catching the typical insurance industry mistakes that inflate premiums is only half the battle. Here are some tried and true steps that employers can take to improve their workplace safety.

## Discuss Safety at Every Opportunity

Make workplace safety efforts an important part of every meeting. Don't just make it a part of your managers' meetings—make it a constant topic of meetings with workers. Make sure you communicate to them why safety is so vital, and how it affects the cost of workers' compensation coverage, and thus the bottom-line of the company. You might be amazed at the number of your workers who don't really understand how expensive workers' compensation coverage is for the company— or even that it's a cost for the company at all. Some employees think it's just some kind of government program that doesn't really translate back to direct costs for the company. So share information about the cost of the company's workers' compensation insurance and how the cost of claims drives up that cost. Post the company's safety goals, and how well the company is doing in regard to meeting those goals. Compare current injury information (without disclosing confidential information about injured workers) with information about recent past years.

## Examine Trends in Workplace Injuries

You can't rely solely on your insurance company to analyze this data and alert you to trends you need to address. Get all the information you can about what kinds of claims are occurring and at what part of your operations. Only by understanding what's causing your claims can you begin to address the causes. It's a terribly overworked cliché, but it's also very true: Safety is no accident. It takes planning, effort, and thought.

## Utilize Modern Resources

In this internet age, there is an ocean of information available at most people's fingertips. Don't be afraid to go surfing for information about what's working at other companies, safety advice from government agencies, insurance companies, insurance regulators, or even special interest groups on the internet. Do a Google search under "workers compensation safety programs," and you'll get over six million sites with information.

Some good sources of information:

- NIOSH, the National Institute for Occupational Safety and Health. You can find them online at: www.cdc.gov/niosh/homepage.html.

- OSHA, the Occupational Safety and Health Administration, at www.Osha.gov.

- An online Workplace Safety tool kit at: www.nonprofitrisk.org/ws/wsp.htm

- Online Office Safety information from Oklahoma State University at: www.pp.okstate.edu/ehs/links/office.htm

- The U.S. Department of Energy's Chemical Safety website at: www.eh.doe.gov/chem_safety

- Safety information from Saftek (an Australian based company) at: www.saftek.net/trainindex.html

- Model safety program from business owners tool kit at: www.toolkit.cch.com/tools/saferl_m.asp

- Workplace Safety weblinks compiled by BNA at: www.bna.com/webwatch/workplace-safety.htm

This is just a small sample of the wealth of information available over the internet that can help your company improve your workplace safety efforts.

# Captives and Rent-a-Captives

COMPANIES THAT PAY $500,000 OR more a year may have proposed to them some workers' compensation programs that involve use of a "captive" insurance company. Once captives were the exclusive province of very large corporations, but new developments in this field mean that much smaller-sized employers may also now be offered workers' compensation programs that utilize a captive.

Simply put, a captive insurance company is one that is owned by the insured. Captives are often established, or "domiciled" outside the United States. Some Caribbean jurisdictions have long specialized in these kinds of insurers, but some states such as Vermont have also passed regulatory systems that facilitate the establishment of captive insurers. According to the 2002 A.M. Best Captive Directory, the top five jurisdictions for domiciling captives were as follows:

| Domicile | Number of Captives | Net Written Premiums (In Billions) |
|---|---|---|
| Bermuda | 1,625 | $28.8 |
| Cayman Islands | 665 | 5.3 |
| Vermont | 674 | 3.5 |
| Guernsey | 408 | 3.6 |
| Luxemburg | 280 | 2.7 |

Setting up your own captive insurer is a fairly complex task, feasible only for larger employers. But recent years have seen significant growth in some versions of captives that are viable alternatives for many other companies that would not be in a position to consider a traditional single-owner captive.

Rather than one single employer establishing a captive insurer, an association of businesses may create a captive insurance program that is available to members of the association. Or a group of companies within the same industry may band together to form a captive.

Another variant is an "agency captive, where the captive is put together by an insurance agency or brokerage for their clients. And the most recent kind of captive program is the so-called "rent-a-captive." where a captive insurer is created by a sponsor and then participation in the captive is offered to multiple employers. These multiple employers typically would not find the creation and management of their own captive feasible, but by participating in such a multiple-participant captive they can obtain many of the historic benefits of a captive while avoiding the expense and difficulties associated with having a single-owner captive.

A subset of rent-a-captives is known as a protected cell company. A PCC is a rent-a-captive that segregates the capital and surplus of each employer from that of other renters.

Because states only allow approved insurance companies to write workers' compensation insurance, a captive normally would not be able to write a workers' comp policy. But modern insurance creativity has gotten around this with "fronting companies." A fronting company is a company that is approved by the states to write workers' compensation insurance. A captive insurance company can use a fronting company to get around the state's restrictions about which insurers can write workers' compensation. It works like this: the fronting company actually produces the workers' compensation policy for an employer, but then behind the scenes it enters into a reinsurance agreement with the captive so that the captive is really responsible for the claims that are covered by the policy. The fronting com-

pany receives a fee for this, and would be legally responsible for the claims if the reinsurance somehow didn't hold up, but in actual practice the fronting companies work hard to make sure that isn't very likely to happen.

By the use of fronting arrangements, captive insurers can get around the states' regulation that would otherwise prevent a captive from writing workers' compensation insurance.

## THE BENEFITS OF A CAPTIVE

The essential benefit of a captive is that is allows the employer to obtain many of the benefits that insurance companies themselves enjoy, such as access to reinsurance markets and investment income. A captive can also provide coverage that is difficult to find in the traditional insurance market for some employers, and avoid some of the large swings in cost that are a feature of the commercial insurance market. Plus, the owners of a captive get the benefit of the capital growth that can accrue to a well-run insurance company.

The issue of whether or not the premiums paid to a captive insurer are deductible by the insured has been a controversial one. Until a few years ago, the IRS had consistently insisted that premiums paid to a captive were not deductible unless the captive also insured a significant number of unrelated policyholders. But courts tended to not accept this doctrine when insureds challenged the IRS.

So in 2002 the IRS retreated from this position, agreeing that premiums paid to captives are usually deductible. However, the latest wrinkle in this area has just occurred as this book was going into print. In mid-June, 2005, the IRS returned to its position that an insured cannot deduct premiums paid to a captive if that insured is the only insured of the captive. The IRS further ruled that captive premiums would not be deductible if the captive insured a second policyholder if that second policyholder paid only 10% or less of the captive's premiums.

It seems clear that this issue of captive premium deductibility is going to be a contentious one for some time to come. For the moment, employers considering using a captive insurer will have to look long and hard at all the advantages and disadvantages of using a captive program, and they should look especially hard at whether or not the premiums for a particular captive program are likely to be deductible or not.

Captive insurers typically look most attractive when "hard" insurance markets are at their worst and become less attractive in the short run when insurance markets enter into prolonged "soft" market conditions. Still, the long run, well-structured and well-administered captive programs can offer price stability, increased availability of difficult coverage, and long-term financial benefits. But captive programs rely on the availability of reinsurance and, when it comes to using a cap-

tive for workers' compensation insurance, the availability of fronting carriers at reasonable cost.

At this writing (early summer of 2005) the availability of fronting carriers for captive programs is something of a worry for captive programs. Some insurers that provided significant fronting availability have gone out of business, and the remaining market is more cautious than it once was. Some in the insurance industry believe that the fronting activities of some recently defunct insurance companies contributed significantly to the demise of those insurers. Other analysts feel this view is overstated.

Whatever the truth of the matter, the perception among some in the industry is that fronting needs to be done more judiciously than in the recent past, and so the market for fronting carriers has tightened. This in turn affects the cost structures of captive insurance programs that write workers' compensation insurance.

Captive insurance programs can offer valuable alternatives to traditional insurance markets, but employers need to view such programs as long term approaches, not short term solutions to market fluctuations.

# Index

## S

## T

## U